TRANSFORMATION
MASSES MAN
HOPPLA, WE'RE ALIVE!

Alan Pearlman studied Philosophy, English and Comparative Literature at Princeton, Cambridge and Yale respectively, and Dramatic Art at the University of California Berkley. In the 60s he organised and directed theatre and living arts projects for the Civil Rights Movement in Mississippi. He has worked extensively as a freelance director in the USA and Europe and was Co-Artistic Director of the Open Space Theatre in London, where he directed the British première of David Mamet's *A Life in the Theatre.* He teaches Directing, Playwriting and Modern European Theatre at the University of Kent at Canterbury, where he established the nationally acclaimed Directing Programme.

Ernst Toller

PLAYS ONE

TRANSFORMATION
MASSES MAN
HOPPLA, WE'RE ALIVE!

edited and translated
with an introduction by

Alan Raphael Pearlman

OBERON BOOKS
LONDON

First published in this collection in 2000 by Oberon Books Ltd.
(incorporating Absolute Classics)
521 Caledonian Road, London N7 9RH
Tel: 020 7607 3637 / Fax: 020 7607 3629
e-mail: oberon.books@btinternet.com

A catalogue record for this book is available from the British Library.

ISBN: 1 84002 195 0

Cover photographs: AFD Köln

Cover design: Humphrey Gudgeon

Series design: Richard Doust

Printed in Great Britain by Antony Rowe Ltd, Reading.

For my wife Britta and my son Mischa
without whom it would not have been done.

And for
Walter Kaufmann, RP Blackmur and Raymond Williams
who all taught me a long time ago
among other things and in different ways
that translators need not be traitors.

Illustrations

(Numbered Plates)

Transformation

(Appendix iii, pages 122–124)

1. **First Picture**. Production photograph. Friedrich's Home.
2. **Fourth Picture**. Production photograph. *Between the Barbed Wire.*
3. **Seventh Picture**. Production photograph. Friedrich's Studio.
4. **Ninth Picture**. Production photograph. *Death and Resurrection.* Factory/Prison.

   Source: *Stiftung Archiv der Akademie der Künste.*

Masses Man

(Appendix v, pages 196–198)

Front cover. **Fifth Picture**. Colour design. The Hall. Attack.
Back cover. **Sixth Picture**. Colour design. Dream Picture. Prison Cage.

5. **Fourth Picture**. Design. Dream Picture. Prison Yard.
6. **Fifth Picture**. Design. The Hall.
7. **Fifth Picture**. Production photograph. The Hall
8. **Sixth Picture**. Design. Dream Picture. Prison Cage.
9. **Sixth Picture**. Production photograph. Dream Picture. Prison Cage.

   Sources: 7 and 9: *Stiftung Archiv der Akademie der Künste.*
   Others: *Theaterwissenschaftliche Sammlung Universität Köln.*

Hoppla, We're Alive!

(Appendix vi, pages 325–332)

10. Photographic collage of production.
11. The Scaffolding with screens and stairs.
12. **Prologue/Act V**. Design. The Prison.
13. **Prologue**. Production photograph. Attempted escape.
14. **Act I, scene** 2. Design. The Ministry.
15. **Act I, scene** 2. Production photograph. The Ministry.

Sources: 10–11, 17, 19, 24–25: *Stiftung Archiv der Akademie der Künste.* 12–16, 18, 20–23: *Nachlass Traugott Müller Institute Für Theaterwissenschaft der Freien Universität Berlin.*

Contents

Acknowledgements

I am very pleased, first and foremost, to acknowledge the kind and generous permission of Katharine Weber to publish these translations of Ernst Toller's plays and the ancillary material. All Toller material is now made available through her permission and I am grateful for her co-operation and support for this project.

Both Richard Dove and John Spalek supplied valuable help and advice at crucial moments, for which I am very thankful. I have, of course, benefited greatly from their pioneering work in Toller studies. I am also happily indebted to Dr Thorsten Unger for authenticating biographical information.

I would like to thank Dr Gerald Köhler of the *Theaterwissenschaftliche Sammlung* at *Universität Köln*, Dr Dagmar Walach and Jenny Schrödl of *Nachlass Traugott Müller* at the *Institute für Theaterwissenschaft der Freien Universität Berlin* and, above all, Dr Dagmar Wünsche at the *Stiftung Archiv der Akademie der Künste* for supplying the photographic material and the permission to publish it here in conjunction with the translations. Dr Wünsche fulfilled all my complicated research wishes with generosity and good nature, and I am particularly indebted to her for the photocopy of Piscator's promptbook for *Hoppla, We're Alive!*

At Oberon, I would like to express my full appreciation to my editor, Humphrey Gudgeon, for scanning and cutting and printing – for crafting and shaping – all this material together. And finally, I am deeply grateful to my publisher, James Hogan, for having the courage to take this project on and for his consequential encouragement to me.

Ernst Toller: A Chronological Portrait

1893 **1 December**: Ernst Toller born in Samotschin in Prussian Province of Posen which was historically Polish to a prosperous Jewish merchant family. Maternal great-grandfather first Jew permitted to live there. One older brother and an older sister. From early on he experiences the double dislocation of being Jewish in a privileged German community which dominated a Polish native population. Experiences of anti-Semitism from both sides. Strong sense of being an outsider and an early sense of social injustice and social barriers. Alienation from his own Jewish roots partly because of his material privilege, partly because of his sense of rejection by the dominant culture. Ill-health of both a physical and nervous nature. Early literary ambitions with rigid Prussian secondary education typical of the times for his class. Inspired by Hauptmann, Ibsen, Strindberg and Wedekind, all banned from the curriculum.

1911 **29 August**: Father dies of cancer. On his deathbed in his last words he tells Toller, who is 17: "You are guilty" – a decisive moment for the formation of his deep social conscience and sense of social responsibility. The question of guilt will echo throughout his work. (In a short autobiographical statement in 1923, Toller stated he was 16 at this time, but he remembered wrongly as the actual death certificate shows.)

1914 **February–July**: after passing his *Abitur*, he studies at the University of Grenoble in France.

August: as war is breaking out Toller returns to Munich via Geneva on one of the last trains to get across the border, with Germany declaring war on France on 3 August. Toller volunteers immediately and spends the next thirteen months at his own request on the Western Front.

1916 **January–April**: Independent Social Democratic Party (USPD) founded and breaks away from Social Democratic Party (SPD) as an anti-war party.

May: traumatised by the horrors of his war experience and having become a militant pacifist, Toller suffers a physical and mental breakdown and spends May to September recovering in hospital and sanatoriums. From end of the year studies at the University of Munich.

1917 **4 January**: declared unfit for active service and discharged.

Spring–Summer: contact with Frank Wedekind, Rilke and Thomas Mann who encourages his poetry writing. Identifies with Expressionism and its anti-war activism.

Summer–Autumn: writes first part of *Transformation*, probably up to Seventh Picture.

September: invited by the publisher Eugen Diederichs to attend Lauenstein Conference of artists and intellectuals to discuss the New Germany. Except for meeting Max Weber extremely disappointed by the endless talk and lack of practical action plan; goes to study in Heidelberg where Weber is.

November–December: beginning of political activities. Reads anti-war poems and scenes from *Transformation* to student groups to agitate for peace (Fifth and Sixth Pictures). Then founds Cultural and Political League of German Youth to campaign actively for peace. League disbanded by the authorities and Toller and other members expelled from Heidelberg. Just before he leaves for Berlin writes to GustavLandauer, the anarchist-socialist whose *Call to Socialism* decisively influenced him and whose political programme he will adopt for the end of *Transformation*. Makes contact with members of the Independent Socialists; is shocked to learn of Germany's responsibility for the war and makes his first political speech.

1918   **January**: meets militant pacifist Kurt Eisner who is head of Munich Independent Socialists in Berlin and follows him to Munich; participates in mass anti-war strike with him, handing out leaflets with scenes from *Transformation,* reading those scenes and speaking to gain support for it. Eisner arrested 31 January.

4 February: Toller arrested. In prison the final scenes of *Transformation* (8-13), so influenced by Landauer's utopian Socialism, come to him. He also reads the socialist classics and becomes a socialist by reasoned conviction instead of instinctive feeling. Held until May when he is released with charge of treason still pending and returned to a reserve battalion as his exemption from military service had expired.

August: At request of his mother who couldn't understand his political activism and wanted to blame it on nervous illness, he is examined by a psychiatrist, Professor Emil Kräpelin, on whom he will base Professor Lüdin in *Hoppla, We're Alive!*

September: Toller fully discharged from the army when it was decided he wouldn't be prosecuted for treason.

28–29 October: mutiny of Kiel sailors begins, which he will write about in *Rake Out the Fires (Feur aus den Kesseln)*.

3 November: mutiny reaches streets of Kiel; first day of the German Revolution which spreads to Munich and then Berlin. Strikes and demonstrations turn into revolutionary uprising and seizure of power.

7–8 November: Bavarian Republic declared and Eisner elected as Prime Minister. Revolutionary Councils or Soviets set up throughout Germany. Struggles between Independent Socialists who want them to wield power and Social Democrats who want a central parliamentary system of government.

9 November: Friedrich Ebert made Chancellor by the old regime, later to become President. Phillippe

Scheidemann declares a Republic in Berlin, largely to forestall Karl Liebknecht from declaring a Soviet Republic. Kaiser Wilhelm flees without a shot being fired. Ebert discovers secret telephone line to General Groener and promises him to fight against Bolshevism in exchange for protection from the Army.

11 November: Armistice signed.

Mid-November: Toller, who had been ill, joins Eisner in Munich and participates in the work of the Revolutionary Councils/Soviets, advocates a united socialist front.

December: German Communist Party (KPD) founded by Rosa Luxemburg and Karl Liebknecht from among the Spartacists.

1919   **6 January**: Spartacist uprising in Berlin begins, led by Rosa Luxemburg and Karl Liebknecht who are brutally murdered on 15 January after it is suppressed.

21 February: Eisner assassinated by right-wing nationalist Count Anton von Arco-Valley and Bavaria falls into political chaos.

March: Toller becomes Chairman of Bavarian Independent Social Democrats.

6–7 April: Soviet Republic declared in Bavaria and Toller becomes head of the revolutionary government and later, when it is taken over by the Communists (KPD) Eugene Leviné and Max Livien, Red Army Commander of troops at Dachau. Political and tactical conflicts between Toller and Communists. Toller refuses to shoot captives 20 April, some of whom return to fight against him, and on 30 April stops massacre of right-wing hostages, but not before eight are murdered.

2–3 May: Soviet Republic in Bavaria defeated and Munich taken over by government troops. Gustave Landauer murdered. Toller goes into hiding in disguise and a reward of 10,000 Marks offered for his arrest.

4 June: arrested after being informed on. Leviné executed the following day. Toller put in Leviné's cell.

14–16 July: trial for high treason. *Transformation* published shortly before it begins. Toller sentenced to five years fortress imprisonment under laws of the previous Imperial government which no longer existed. Prison conditions meant to be lenient for political prisoners, but as Germany leaned more and more to the right, the prison regime for left-wing prisoners became more and more stringent.

30 September: acclaimed première of *Transformation* in Berlin directed by Karlheinz Martin at the *Tribüne*.

October: begins work on *Masses Man*.

1920 **January**: writes *The Scorned Lover's Revenge*, which doesn't appear in book form until 1925. Early in 1920 Toller offered a pardon by the Bavarian Government on the hundredth performance of *Transformation*. Toller refuses because he doesn't want special treatment while others remain in prison.

13 March: Right-wing Kapp putsch. Lenient treatment for those involved.

15 November: private première of *Masses Man* for trade-unionists in Nürnberg.

1921 **June**: Toller elected as USPD delegate to Bavarian Assembly which he can't attend.

Summer: first book of poems published, *Prisoners' Poems* (*Gedichte der Gefangenen*).

29 September: landmark production of *Masses Man* directed by Jürgen Fehling at the *Volksbühne* in Berlin.

1922 **24 June**: Walter Rathenau, Foreign Minister, murdered.

30 June: première of *The Machine Breakers* (*Die Maschinenstürmer*) directed by Karlheinz Martin in *Grosses Schauspielhaus*, book published a little earlier.

3 November: Meyerhold directs *The Machine Breakers* in Moscow. Fifty-five performances.

1923 **31 January**: Meyerhold directs *Masses Man*. Fifty-eight performances.

19 September: première of *Hinkemann, the German* (*Der deutsche Hinkemann*) in Leipzig, published in the same year. *Wotan Unbound* (*Der entfesselte Wotan*) also published.

8–9 November: Beerhall putsch by Hitler in Munich. Lenient treatment.

1924 **17 January**: nationalist riot at performance of *Hinkemann* in Dresden. Further performances elsewhere also create commotion.

February: Toller resigns from Independent Social Democratic Party mainly because of factionalist in-fighting and dogmatism. Becomes for the rest of his life an independent left-wing socialist.

April: *The Swallow Book* (*Das Schwalbenbuch*), poems about swallows which nested in his cell and connected him with freedom, appears. Another collection of poems, *Before Morning* (*Vormorgen*) will appear later in the year.

15 July: Toller released a day early from prison so he could be escorted to the Bavarian border and expelled on the day of scheduled release.

18 July: sees a performance of *Hinkemann* in Berlin, the first time he sees one of his own plays.

3 August: attends performance in Leipzig of the mass spectacle *Awakening,* for which he wrote the scenario.

24 November: *Wotan Unbound* premièred in Russian in Moscow. Thirty performances.

1925 Toller lectures and reads from his works in Berlin and abroad.

26 April: Field Marshall Hindenburg elected President.

December: travels to England to speak to PEN clubs.

1926 **23 February**: *Wotan Unbound* directed by Jürgen Fehling for *Tribüne* in Berlin.

March–May: travels to Soviet Union.

December: begins campaign on behalf of Communist prisoner Max Hölz.

1927 **May**: *Justice: Experiences (Justiz. Erlebnisse)*, his reflections on the unjust treatment of left-wing political prisoners, published.

3 September: Toller/Piscator production of *Hoppla, We're Alive!*, another milestone in theatre history.

25 November: Toller co-directs a production of *Hinkemann* for the *Volksbühne*.

1929 **October–December**: travels in USA and Mexico on speaking tour.

1930 **31 August**: première of *Rake Out the Fires (Feuer aus den Kesseln)* in Berlin at the *Theater am Schiffbauerdamm* designed by Caspar Neher. Book published shortly before the production.

1931 **17 October**: première in Mannheim of *Wunder in Amerika (Miracle in America/Mary Baker Eddy)* which he wrote with Herman Kesten. Only a mimeographed acting version is published, signalling the difficulties Toller now has with publishing in Germany.

Late October: travels to Spain where he remains until March 1932.

1932 **31 October**: première of his play *The Blind Goddess (Die blinde Göttin)* in Vienna directed by Jürgen Fehling. This book was published in 1933 in Austria as Toller's books could not be published in Germany after 1933.

1933 **30 January**: Hitler made Chancellor of Germany.

27 February: Reichstag fire and Nazis begin to arrest left-wing figures. Storm-troopers break into Toller's flat to arrest him, but he had fortunately already left for Switzerland where he was to make a radio broadcast. Toller was never to return to Germany.

10 May: Nazis publicly burn 20,000 left-wing and Jewish books; Toller's works prominent among them.

23 August: Toller among the first to have his citizenship taken away; his possessions and papers are confiscated and destroyed.

November: in Amsterdam Querido publishes his autobiography, *Eine Jugend in Deutschland* (*Youth in Germany,* published in English as *I Was a German*) in which Toller repossesses his Jewish identity, albeit in a wide humanitarian context.

26 December: his mother dies in Germany.

1934 **February–July**: exile in London. Toller begins his many anti-fascist activities and campaigns.

Spring: The actress Christiane Grautoff, his 17 year-old girlfriend, joins Toller in London.

17–22 June: founds anti-Nazi German PEN Club in Exile.

August–October: takes part in the First Congress of Soviet Writers in Leningrad.

1935 **January–February**: Toller co-directs *Draw the Fires* (*Rake Out the Fires*) which opens on 10 February in Manchester.

16 May: marries Christiane in London.

Autumn: Querido publishes *Briefe aus dem Gefängis* (*Letters from Prison*) in German in Amsterdam.

1936 **March–April**: travels with Christiane throughout Spain and Portugal.

11 June: première of *No More Peace* in English at the Gate Theatre London. Christiane plays the female lead.

17–18 July: Spanish Civil War begins.

12 October: anti-fascist lecture tour in USA and Canada until February 1937.

1937 **February**: Toller lives in Santa Monica and works on film scripts (none produced) for MGM, collaborating with Sidney Kaufman, who will later hold the rights to his work.

September: *No More Peace* is published in English in London.

September–December: suffers from acute depression, particularly pessimistic about Nazi Germany, with feelings of his own lack of success.

1938 **10 February**: returns to New York and lives at the Mayflower Hotel; continues his anti-fascist activities, now harassed by Nazi agents and sympathisers. He is treated for depression. Works on *Pastor Hall*.

12 March: Nazi troops "annex" Austria unopposed.

July: Toller and Christiane separate. He cancels the contract with MGM, which will cause him financial problems. Travels to Spain and experiences the Civil War at first hand.

End September: in London addresses meetings to warn against appeasement and advocate force to stop Hitler.

29 September: Munich Treaty of appeasement signed.

September–December: sets up international relief project with his own money to aid civilian population of Spain (Spanish Relief) for which he travels and raises large sums of money and supplies; wins the support of prominent politicians, including President and Eleanor Roosevelt.

9–10 November: *Kristallnacht* (Crystal Night) in Germany when Jewish homes, businesses and synagogues vandalised and broken glass is everywhere. Thousands of Jews killed, 30,000 more imprisoned.

1939 **January**: reworks last scene of *Pastor Hall* which he is having difficulties in publishing; the English edition doesn't appear until after his death. Financial problems.

15 March: Hitler invades Czecholslavakia.

27 March: Republican Spain defeated by Franco; Madrid surrenders. Toller bitterly disillusioned.

1 April: USA, England and France recognise the Franco government. Toller's relief plan collapses and some of the supplies may well have fallen into the hands of fascist troops.

Early May: speaks in memory of victims of Nazi atrocities to PEN Congress. Worries about fate of his brother and sister who are later to die in concentration camps.

19 May: Franco holds huge victory parade in Madrid.

22 May: Ernst Toller hangs himself on the hook of the bathroom door in his room at the Mayflower Hotel.

Compiled by Alan Raphael Pearlman, 2000

PREFACE

Charles Wood

I first knew of Ernst Toller's play *Die Wandlung* here translated as *Transformation* in 1952 when as a young soldier I attended German lessons in Munster, Westphalia. I found a copy of the play on a windowsill in the room we used as a classroom and tried to translate it while waiting for the instructor to arrive. I didn't do very well, my German not good enough but I got a sense of its form and its mystery and I think, of its power though the only thing I knew for certain was that it was written by Ernst Toller. I was so taken by it that I considered stealing it. But as things go, as soon as I got the notion that I might slip it into my battledress jacket without anybody noticing, everybody seemed to be looking at me, in German, which is a very serious way of looking, so I funked it. The next time I turned up for German the book was gone.

I knew nothing at all about Ernst Toller then but, his name stayed with me and later in 1957 when I saw his autobiography, *I Was a German*, long before I became a playwright myself, I remembered the name, bought the book and was fascinated by what I read. Here was an amazing man, a pacifist of the best kind, one who'd come to it through soldiering, and a staunch but independent socialist. A Jew, born in Prussia, he'd fought in the trenches, a student volunteer, been broken by the experience mentally and physically, been imprisoned for treason, helped bring about the Socialist Republic of Bavaria and served as its Red Army Commander, all by the age of twenty six. His acquaintances and influences were such as Rilke, Wedekind, Thomas Mann, and Max Weber. He wrote anti-war poetry, plays and when his first play *Transformation* opened to great success in Berlin he was in prison for treason – on the occasion of its hundredth performance he was offered a pardon but, "I refused; to have accepted would have meant supporting the hypocrisy of the Government; besides, I stuck at the idea of going free while others remained behind in prison". Whilst in prison he wrote the second of the three plays here published, *Masses Man*.

When I came to write *Dingo*, my own play about attitudes to the Second World War, I can't say that I was directly influenced by *Transformation* because I didn't read it properly in English until a long time after, but I certainly remembered the boldness of its imagination, and staging and religious ferocity. I don't think for one moment that *Dingo* can compare artistically with *Transformation* but it shares the same youthful integrity and anger – I hope.

I hope also that these excellent translations by Alan Pearlman now published by Oberon Books will lead to Ernst Toller's work being staged more frequently in English.

Charles Wood
London, 2000

INTRODUCTION

Alan Raphael Pearlman

TRANSLATED TOLLER

The plays of Ernst Toller have suffered a wasteful and undeserved neglect in the English-speaking world, not least because of their inaccessibility. Such neglect has deprived both our theatre and theatre studies of a working knowledge and experience of plays which have made major contributions to the development of theatrical modernism on both textual and production levels and which still have a strong contemporary resonance. Of course, translation can only be more or less of an approximation, but at its best and when most sensitive to its mediation of times, languages and cultures, it can put us in close contact with the power of the original material and certainly in closer touch than can any secondary paraphrase, description, summary or interpretation. This is not to deny value to these, but for the English reader they must be grounded by – they must depend upon – the original in translation to be fully understood and evaluated. And besides, it is only the translated play that can be produced and performed – tested in the medium for which it was primarily intended.

That said, there have been five critical studies of Toller published in English over the last twenty years – since 1979. This indicates a significant shift, given that none at all appeared in the almost thirty-five years between the earliest critical study in English (1945) and the first of these. The most recent, *The Plays of Ernst Toller* by Cecil Davies, is voluminous and makes available a wealth of information on the plays and their productions; although at times it concentrates on the undoubted literary quality of the plays to the detriment of their theatricality. Toller's work also features prominently in a number of recent, more general studies of Expressionism and Weimar and German theatre. In addition, John Spalek published his massive *Ernst Toller and His Critics* in 1968 – perhaps the most comprehensive of all multilingual bibliographies and essential for any subsequent work on Toller. And Richard Dove published the first and only full biography of Toller in any language, *He was a German,* in 1990. (See the Further Reading List for all book references, p. 333.) All of this attests to a wide and ongoing interest in Toller, but one that is frustrated by lack of access to the original material for those without a knowledge of German.

In German, of course, the situation is different. The quantity of critical work is similar to that in English, but it is surprising that there isn't more and that the work in English is on the whole more recent; although new critical work is just now being published by the Ernst Toller Society. It is also surprising that so little of Toller's work was in print before 1978, although there are complicated historical and political reasons for this. That year saw the much heralded publication of the five-volume *Collected Works (Gesammelte Werke,* Hanser Verlag), a scholarly edition edited by John M Spalek and Wolfgang Früwald which contained most of Toller's plays, attempted for the first time to establish definitive and corrected texts and printed some alternative versions of the material. A further volume of commentary and documentary material – *Der Fall Toller* – followed in the next year, 1979. And in the early nineties the first five volumes were reprinted, signalling a continuing demand.

In English the track record of the plays has not been so good. In one sense Toller became a victim of his own early success. Such was the impact of his work, felt both across the Channel and across the Atlantic, that translations of most of his plays appeared within one or two years of their German publication, often in both English and American editions. In fact, reflecting this enthusiasm, there even seems to have been a bit of a race on to be the first to publish a work by Toller in English. Ashley Dukes, who as a producer, critic, translator, and playwright, was an early opponent of the lifelike realism that dominated English theatre, first introduced German Expressionism to the English stage with his version of Georg Kaiser's *From Morn to Midnight (Von Morgens bis Mitternacht,* 1916) in 1920 with the London Stage Society.

In the summer of 1922 he saw Karlheinz Martin's production of *The Machine-Wreckers* (*Die Maschinenstürmer*) at the *Grosses Schauspielhaus* in Berlin, which he wrongly attributed to Max Reinhardt. Liking this play about the English Luddites more than the production, he resolved to translate it, knowing that a translation of Toller's second play, *Masse Mensch,* was already being undertaken. He immediately went to visit Toller, who was then still imprisoned in Niederschönenfeld, and secured the requisite permission. (Dukes, pp. 70–76). And it was with an air of some satisfaction that he announced in the introduction to his translation published in 1923 how fitting it seemed "that *The Machine-Wreckers,* a drama of our own history, should be the first of Toller's plays to appear in England" (p. iv), thus preceding *Masses and Man* which, although begun earlier, did not appear until November of the same year in Vera Mendel's translation for the Nonesuch Press.

In 1935 in England and a year later in America, the volume *Seven Plays* appeared. For Toller, in his new introduction, it was a gesture of defiance towards the Nazi dictatorship which had just burned his books, blacklisted him, denounced him as a public enemy and stripped him of his citizenship. This book collected together the individually published translations, by then mostly out of print, and added three plays that had not yet appeared in English. It actually contained eight plays. I will list the main titles here in the order in which they are placed in that book, together with their German titles and dates of publication, for reference purposes, as in almost every case the titles of my translations are different. The asterisks indicate which plays appeared here for the first time, including, rather surprisingly given its reputation, Toller's first play.

The Machine-Wreckers	(*Die Maschinenstürmer*, 1922)
* *Transfiguration*	(*Die Wandlung*, 1919)
Masses and Man	(*Masse Mensch*, 1921)
Hinkemann (earlier called *Brokenbrow*)	
	(*Der deutsche Hinkeman*, 1923)
Hoppla! Such is Life! (earlier called *Hoppla!*)	
	(*Hoppla, wir leben!*, 1927)
The Blind Goddess	(*Die blinde Göttin*, 1933)

* *Draw the Fires*   (*Feuer aus den Kesseln,* 1930)
* *Mary Baker Eddy* (written with Hermann Kesten)
                              (*Wunder in Amerika,* 1931)

To complete the picture of the major plays, *Der entfesselte Wotan* (1923), his frighteningly prescient and biting satire on the rise of Hitlerism, has never been translated and will appear as *Wotan Unbound* in the second volume of these Toller translations. His puppet play based on a tale of Bandello, *Die Rache Des Verhöhnten Liebhabers* (1925) appeared as *The Scorned Lover's Revenge* in *8 New One Act Plays of 1935* (London: Lovat Dickson and Thompson, 1935). And the two of his plays written in exile, *No More Peace* (1937) and *Pastor Hall* (1939) were published in book form in English only, for obvious political reasons. At least at first, then, Toller was served reasonably well by translation, attesting to the importance and popularity of his works. To take a wider perspective for a moment, by 1934 his work had been translated into a remarkable twenty-seven languages.

With the single exception of *Hinkemann,* however, which appeared in a collection of Expressionist war plays called *Vision and Aftermath* (London: Calder and Boyars, 1969), no new English translations of Toller's plays have appeared since the publication of *Seven Plays.* In English, then, Toller has been frozen in time, or perhaps one should say frozen out of time, as all the existing translations have been out of print for so long. And as well, although the original translations served the important purpose of making Toller's innovative work known outside of Germany in the 20s and 30s, they tend now to sound stilted and old-fashioned in a way that makes performance and production very difficult. They are also often inaccurate, leaving scenes and speeches out, embellishing them, and even adding them in, without explanation or indication of source. The latter is particularly important for Toller, as many of his plays went through a great number of German editions which incorporated often substantial changes, not all of which were necessarily those of Toller himself.

The most recent major production of a Toller play in England – unfortunately a rare occurrence – is a case in point. The Royal National Theatre commendably rose to the worthwhile challenge of staging Toller with a production of *The Machine-Wreckers* in the Cottesloe Theatre. It was directed interestingly by Katie Mitchell and opened on 11 August 1995. The reviews confirm that Toller's play about the Luddites was gripping and thought to have contemporary relevance, not surprising for a market economy even now in the throes of privatisation and shifting emphasis from an industrial to a service/information base, with democratic principles and public interest bent to economic gain. Unfortunately, however, the production chose to make use of the original translation by Ashley Dukes referred to above, instead of commissioning a new one. Even for an historical play set in England, the language is stilted and not as powerful as the original. In addition, the Dukes' version is based upon the German second edition (fifth to tenth thousand published also in 1922), although this is not stated. As Cecil Davies has persuasively argued in an appendix to *The Plays of Ernst Toller* (pp. 627–636), the changes made for this edition probably came from the production rather than from Toller himself, and the first version is, therefore, probably the stronger and more authoritative one. It is also the version used for the German edition of *The Collected Works.*

For these reasons, in my view, the Cottesloe production did not achieve the full impact and did not receive the full acclaim that it might have done with a different version and translation, one more conducive to performance. At the very least, the new material ought to have been available to make use of, if so desired. I will return to the specific issue in the second volume in which the new translation of this play will appear. But it is one of the goals of this project to provide fresh versions of Toller's plays which draw on all the available material and thus provide a solid and more fertile base for interpretation and future production work.

Given the stature of Toller's work, its theatre historical importance and its theatrical vitality, it is astonishing that there have not been more recent translations. The reasons for this are not exactly clear. It is partly, I think, a question of a combination of the timidity and financial plight of publishers – two factors which often go hand in hand. It is almost impossible to get a play translation published in the present climate, unless it is attached to a recent, current or prospective production and can be sold and marketed on that basis. Publishers are very reluctant to speculate in this sense, even when there is a project of artistic worth to be undertaken. This, of course, creates its own vicious circle. Without the availability of a performable translation, the play will never find a production. And translators, too, want to see the results of their labours in actual publication and production. They don't want to work "on spec". "No publication without production; no production without publication," has almost become a stock response – a stock response that Toller, too, must have heard.

With deep irony, Toller found himself caught in the same kind of vicious circle towards the end of his life in exile. He had great difficulty in publishing his last play, *Pastor Hall,* in an English translation, the only option then available to him. There were some problems with the translation made by Stephen Spender, but in both England and America the fact that there was not the possibility of a forthcoming production – due mainly to the "controversial" nature of its concentration camp subject matter – was the major reason for not publishing it immediately. In America, it seems to have appeared shortly before his death by suicide, as the blurbs on the dust jacket are written as if he were still alive. In England it did not appear until after his suicide and this stalemate of a publishing situation was certainly one of the contributing factors. A more enlightened publisher might have helped to make a difference.

There also seems to have been a residual attachment to the older translations. In my own quest to publish these translations of the plays, I was asked by one potential editor to include some of the original ones. And one potential publisher advised me that it would be very difficult to secure all the rights. In fact, my own approaches were met with generosity and encouragement from Katharine Weber for the Toller Estate. For the permission to proceed with this long overdue project which will bring these vital works of the modern theatre back into circulation for the English-speaking world, I am very grateful.

TOLLER TRANSLATED

For the first volume of this new edition of Ernst Toller's plays in English, I have decided not to proceed strictly chronologically, but more dynamically. I shall begin with his first two plays, *Transformation* (*Die Wandlung*, 1919) and *Masses Man* (*Masse Mensch*, 1921), both published during his first two years in prison. Instead of progressing through the rest of the plays Toller wrote during his imprisonment, which will comprise the next volume, including *The Machine Breakers* (*Die Maschinenstürmer*, 1922), *Hinkemann, the German* (*Der deutsche Hinkeman*, 1923) and the heretofore untranslated *Wotan Unbound* (*Der entfesselte Wotan*, 1923), I will conclude with *Hoppla, We're Alive!* (*Hoppla, wir leben!*, 1927), the first play Toller wrote after his release from prison and a major contribution to the political and documentary theatre of the Weimar Republic.

The reason for this strategy is fourfold. First, in spite of their stylistic diversity, these three plays form an auto-biographical group within the work of Toller, although they are not, strictly speaking, autobiography. These are the plays which draw most directly on his own active participation in the major historical events of his time. Very few playwrights indeed have played a part in the history books to the degree that Toller has. In these plays he fictionalises, dramatises and universalises his own individual and political experience to such an intense degree that it is not merely vividly autobiographical, but becomes typical and exemplary. To paraphrase Francis Bacon, that great neo-Expressionist, on Picasso: Toller "sucked in the psyche of [his] times...and found a visual [and verbal] equivalent for the whole psychic side of one's sense of reality" (in unpublished conversation with David Sylvester quoted in *Life: The Observer Magazine*, 21 May 2000, p. 33). In that sense, these plays track the cataclysms of early twentieth century Germany – war, revolution, imprisonment and the politically charged atmosphere of the Weimar Republic – and their psychic ramifications.

Second, precisely because of their stylistic diversity, they serve as a strong introduction to the wide range of Toller's work. In these plays he connects with and extends some of the major artistic movements created in the revolutionary ferment of the Weimar period. In their divergent ways *Transformation* and *Masses Man* are formative works of German Expressionism. But Toller was not simply an Expressionist; his work is much more varied than many critics suggest. *Hoppla, We're Alive!* uses elements of the *Neue Sachlichkeit,* the New Objectivity, and multimedia production to create a challenging example of the political documentary theatre, which became so characteristic of the Weimar period. Toller's own comments on his reservations about the New Objectivity and how he extended its scope with a political frame are most illuminating (*Transformation,* Appendix ii, pp. 120–121).

Third, these plays all inspired productions which became landmarks in the development of modern theatre practice, extending in substantial ways the newly discovered expressiveness of the full panoply of theatrical language. For each of them there exists important pictorial material which indicates just how innovative they were. The full visual record, brought together here for the first time, should yield a vivid sense of the modern theatre in the making, as it significantly shifts from an emphasis on text to an emphasis on text in performance. The Weimar period became one of the most fertile cradles of theatrical innovation in the whole history of theatre – even surpassing that of revolutionary Russia. In fact, the great Soviet director Meyerhold drew much inspiration from Toller and directed two of his plays in Moscow in the early 20s. In many ways, the revolutionary spirit of the failed German uprising was kept alive in the struggles to create new forms of theatricality. Toller was at the very centre of this rich artistic turbulence, even from the cell of a prison, and it is this which creates such theatrical vitality for his plays.

Finally, these three plays seem to connect with the contemporary theatrical *Zeitgeist* in especially strong ways. Arthur Miller's production *Mr Peter's Connections,* recently on in London at the Almeida, drew deeply and emotionally on the Expressionist tradition. Among many other examples, the success of Mark-Anthony Turnage's opera version of Sean O'Casey's *The Silver Tassie* – a play that was directly influenced by Toller's *Masses Man* – showed that the Expressionist style, used so effectively in the second act, still has the power to shock and provoke and to take us into areas of experience that too often cannot otherwise find forceful expression. The early plays of Toller cry out for operatic versions, and perhaps the powerful example of Turnage here will lead to a repayment of the long-standing debt O'Casey owes to Toller. In any case, Expressionism continues to be an important element of contemporary and post-modern performance. And Toller created some of the most powerful images in that style of what has become the characteristic modern condition: the shattered consciousness in a shattered world. He has left a lasting legacy for theatricality in modern theatre and modern performance.

Toller has had a direct impact on the new British playwriting as well. Mark Ravenhill, cutting-edge author of *Shopping & Fucking*, based his second major play, *Some Explicit Polaroids*, on *Hoppla, We're Alive!*. He updated Toller's plot about a political activist who is arrested at a time of revolutionary uprising, incarcerated in a mental asylum and released eight years later into a world that is no longer revolutionary, which he struggles to understand and come to terms with. Ravenhill has his English activist arrested in 1984 and released into a world of former comrades and new friends who regard his political beliefs as out of touch with the current realities of a hedonistic, consumer capitalism. The parallels drawn reveal the abiding effectiveness of Toller's plot line for examining social change and the continuing relevance of his concern with political activism and consciousness in both his plays and his life. In discussions of Ravenhill's play, *Hoppla, We're Alive!* has been referred to as "obscure" and "little-known". I hope that the appearance of this translation will change that situation, as the play still has important contributions to make to the modern repertoire. A way in which this is particularly so is in its startlingly advanced use of multimedia production techniques. It achieved effects which contemporary mixed media and virtual reality performance work is only now beginning to grasp and grope towards.

That is the rationale for the contents of this first volume of Toller's plays. The rationale for my approach to translating them is, of course, the hope that they will be performed, as well as read; that these new translations will stimulate a vigorous return of Toller to the English-speaking stage. If there is one overarching principle at work, it is the new minimalism in translation which does not embellish by so-called elegant variation, does not create a false stylistic smoothness and does not attempt to "improve" upon the original by making it, on the one hand, more literary, or, on the other, more colloquial. I am reminded of the Yiddish joke about the Yiddish edition of Shakespeare which was *ibergezetst un farbesert* – "translated and improved" – by the translator!

What signals this most strongly for me is the shift that has taken place in the translation of Marcel Proust's *À la recherche du temps perdu*. The original title, *In Remembrance of Things Past* (C.H. Scott Mancrieff's version), has now been replaced by *In Search of Lost Time* (Kilmartin/Enright's version). The elevation of the allusion to Shakespeare's sonnet (30) is no longer present, but that was mostly irrelevant and certainly inaccurate anyway. The new minimalist title is accurate, closer to the wording of the French, and it sets up the thematics of "search", "lost" and "time" which echo linguistically and thematically throughout this labyrinthine masterpiece. The rest of the translation follows suit, deflating what is often precious and embellished English prose, so that the novel in English is now "closer" to the French and a more fulfilling read.

I have tried to do the same for Toller, guided by accuracy and concision, but also by the criterion of performability. In that sense, I have tried to translate not just as a linguist, but also with the sensibility of a director and a playwright.

On the one hand, I have tried to avoid variation for the sake of variation, although variation is something that many translators are taught as a matter of course – so as to make the text "more interesting". Wherever possible, particularly for key words, I have tried to use the same English word for the same German word as it appears in the original. There is much more to be gained thematically and linguistically from repetition than lost by it. Actual vocabulary is a most important constituent of the author's, of the play's and of the characters' worlds and helps to establish all of these.

And for the same reason I have not avoided "faithful friends" – words in English that look similar to the German words – when they fit, again an avoidance many translators are taught for the sake of a false notion of style. In the end, faithful friends work well – when they are faithful – and they can help to locate an author's or a character's style closer to that found in the original.

Similarly I have retained certain cultural markers where appropriate, such as forms of address (e.g. Herr So-and-so), so as to firmly establish the social and cultural surround of the plays. Even in the more abstract plays there is still cultural specificity. And for the very same reason I have tried to avoid what is called cultural transference – what I regard as one of the great sins of translation: that is, using an English cultural equivalent for something that is substantially different in German. A German bar or tavern is never like a British pub, unless it is an actual reconstruction of one on German soil. It is much more effective to find a culturally more neutral term, as nothing destroys the cultural atmosphere as completely as this kind of transference or false equivalence. The same is particularly true of money terms.

On the one hand, then, I have tried for close, minimalist translation; at times literal in the best sense of that word, but never the word-for-word or one-to-one kind that produces 'translationese'. On the other hand, I have tried to mould this method so as to fit and create appropriate speech patterns for the various characters, looking from within them from a playwright's point of view. And I have tried to do the same, while respecting the metre and rhythm of the German for the passages written in poetic free-verse form. Here I have tried to capture and reproduce the staccato rat-a-tat-tat of Expressionist momentum and other forms of poetic rhythm. As well, I have been particularly careful not to allow the subtext to leak into the top-text. That is another dangerous temptation for many translators as they try to spell everything out, for the sake of displaying their own understanding or over-clarifying things for the reader/spectator.

At the same time, I have paid particularly close attention to clarity in the stage directions – something which earlier translations often neglected to do – and other directorial matters, as these are essential elements of Toller's dramaturgy and often reflect and reinforce major themes on the visual level of production mechanics. In other words, blackouts can create a certain rhythm or momentum for the piece in performance. And stage structures and transformation from façade to façade or from façade to interior can create an attitude or point of view towards the world of the play – can establish meaning visually.

In all of these procedures it has been my hope to capture as faithfully as possible the full verbal intensity of Toller's writing and the vivid visual imagination of his words and dramaturgy, so as to provide stage-worthy versions of his plays in English which will inspire production.

Transformation: The Struggle of a Man (1919)

I have worked from and followed the first edition of this text, comparing it with later editions and the reprint of the first edition in *Gesammelte Werke 2*. The word "indicated" (*angedeutet*) was added to the stage directions six times in the fourth impression (1922) and six more times in the following second edition (1924). The stage directions for all the pictures including the Prologue, except for 10 (The Wanderer) and 11 (Public Meeting) now included this word, presumably emphasising the non-realistic nature of the scenes. I have inserted it here. This was in keeping with the original production (1919) by Karlheinz Martin which didn't distinguish between dream and reality in scenic terms (see plates 1–4) and probably reflects that same decision taken by Jürgen Fehling for his production of *Masses Man* (1921). Toller himself comments on this latter decision in his Foreword to that play. The fourth impression also tones down and condenses the third and fifth stanzas of the prefatory poem, *Shake-Up*, but I have kept the stronger, original version. Notice how echoes from this powerful poem, which foreshadows the dramatic action and its revolutionary theme, permeate and inform the play.

The play was published as an early volume in a series called *The Dramatic Will*, which, as it says on the dust jackets, printed all its plays as continuous prose with run-on lines and character names willy-nilly in the midst of those lines, so as to "make drama for the first time as readable as the novel." The free verse passages – mainly the Prologue and the dream pictures which are designated as taking place on the rear stage (2,4,5,8,9,10,12), but other sections as well – were printed continuously with stroke marks separating the lines. I have returned to the usual format for the prose passages, separating the speeches and the character names from the speeches for the sake of clarity. And I have used the free verse format with separate lines for the poetry passages. This, I feel, reveals the full power of the language much more effectively. As drama was becoming the defining literary form of the times, the series was attempting to give it the full immediacy and impact of the novel. This might have had a point then – particularly for the breathless outcry of the Expressionist style – but it certainly does not apply now. It would muddle the effect of the piece as a play to be read or a script to be performed.

Toller used different words to designate his scenes, and I have followed his purposeful choices as accurately as possible. In *Transformation* and *Masses Man* he chose *Bild*, which can also be employed for "Scene" in German. However, I have translated it as "Picture" because this reflects his intention more fully, emphasising the intense verbal visuality of his writing and the succession of essential and visionary images which structure these plays.

As further background I have included some of Toller's own remarks on the play, which capture its revolutionary force and spirit. As he says, before it was finished he handed out and read scenes (Fifth and Sixth Pictures – The Hospital and The Maimed) from it at strike meetings to further his anti-war activism. I personally can attest to the power of his example. In Berkeley in the 60s, I directed for a political theatre company. Inspired by Toller, we performed scenes from our own anti-Vietnam War play at draft boards and demonstrations, with some success in convincing potential conscripts to refuse the draft. As for Toller, theatre became an effective political weapon in the struggle against the war.

Some commentators regard the play as derivative and naïve. While there is some truth to this, I still think it is remarkably strong for a first play. It was written in the white heat of Toller's traumatising war experience after his discharge on health grounds and completed during his first imprisonment for his strike activities. On one level it is a quintessential rites-of-passage play and follows, through Friedrich, his own transformation from an enthusiastic soldier to a militant anti-war activist and revolutionary. Friedrich rejects his own Jewish origins in a false attempt to belong, through war heroics, to his Christian Fatherland which he then transcends through commitment to a revolutionary, secular and spiritual humanism. Animated by the fire of Toller's experience, the play consolidates and extends typical Expressionist structures and themes, bridging in an important way the gap between the usually separate modes of subjective Expressionism and social Expressionism.

The alternation between dream scenes and real scenes is more sophisticated and more effective than in the plays of his contemporaries in the way that it probes the psychic dimensions of reality and conveys the felt life of experience. His exploration of themes such as generational conflict and the transformation of the title, so central to Expressionism, is also deeper. Generational conflict is treated as a part of a larger social conflict, not as a substitute for it or a reduction of it. And transformation – that fundamental Expressionist experience – is treated as an active, developmental process with different stages, not an instantaneous event as in so many other contemporaneous plays. It is complicated and problematised as Friedrich even goes through what is demonstrated to be a false transformation. He attempts to belong to his Fatherland through identity with the empty Christian symbolism of the cross. He is shown to reject this conventional symbolism for his own actual passion and to become transformed only after he undergoes actual human experience, a twist on the Wandering Jew (Ahasuerus) motif that runs through the play. Toller thus reanimates and reclaims the symbolism of the passion and the cross for his own secular revolutionary ends.

That is a major reason for choosing to translate the play's title as *Transformation*, not *Transfiguration* which was used for the first English version and signals a more passive and a more traditionally religious occurrence. Throughout the play, individual transformation is not treated as a discrete event, but as the pathway to wider social transformation. The rhetoric of that social transformation and revolution may well be utopian and naïve, but it is powerful and effective nonetheless. It was the same kind of rhetoric that accomplished the bloodless first stage of the German Revolution as the war came to an end. That rhetoric could still be heard in the 60s and is even now heard in the burgeoning anti-globalisation and anti-corporatism movements of today. And its relevance is certainly enhanced by the more recent, formative importance that has been given to the notion of cultural hegemony in political theory and practice.

In fact, if the play is read closely, it is not merely empty rhetoric at all, but rhetoric that has practical implications. Whatever his disagreement with the Agitator in the Eleventh Picture, Friedrich too wants the People finally to march and smash the palaces. He wants them to take action, but only after they have been imbued with the spirit of humanity, so that theirs will be a revolution with a humanitarian face and force. The severe difficulty of this contradictory combination – but for Toller the necessity of continuing to act within it – will be explored in his next play, after he undergoes further political experiences of direct action.

All in all, the driving intensity of *Transformation*'s revolutionary humanism wins through and that certainly helped to make its first production by Karlheinz Martin, designed by Robert Neppach, into the first true breakthrough of Expressionism on to the German stage. This is vividly shown in the production photographs included here – images inspired by the play which have become icons of the Expressionist style – jagged fragments of distorted reality which cut to the core of psychic experience.

Masses Man (1921)

Here, too, I have worked directly from the first edition (1921), comparing it with later editions and the text as reprinted in *Gesammelte Werke 2* and incorporating some minor changes. The only major difference is Toller's Foreword in the second edition (1922) to Jürgen Fehling, the "creative middleman" who directed the first public production of the play at the *Volksbühne* in Berlin (29 September 1921) to such acclaim. I have included it here. Toller added the word "indicated" in the second edition (second impression) to all the odd-numbered pictures, presumably to emphasise the non-realistic nature of these scenes and make them closer in atmosphere to the even-numbered dream pictures which already contained this word, except for the Sixth Picture which is clearly in that style anyway. This reflects what is said in the Foreword to the second edition. Toller also added the word 'ardent' to 'arduous' in the next impression (p. 128) to play neatly on the similarity between *selige* and *müh-selige* in German.

All the editions after the first show the title with a hyphen: *Masse-Mensch*. In order to emphasise the unresolveable opposition within the title and within the play, I have chosen not to link the words with "and" as other translators have done. I will return to this later.

I have also included here Jürgen Fehling's illuminating note on his production (Appendix i, p. 189). It appeared as a postscript to the first edition of Vera Mendel's English translation (*Masses and Man*, London: The Nonesuch Press, 1923). There does not seem to be a published German version. Mendel's edition is an interesting one and deserves further comment. It contains a production photograph from the Sixth Picture and black-and-white designs by Hans Strohbach for the Forth, Fifth and Sixth Pictures, all of which are included here together with another production photograph of the Fifth Picture. (see plates 5–9). Mendel's edition is thus a forerunner of the model books later created by Brecht to document productions of his plays and points towards the very close interaction between text and performance that was being developed at this time. She even incorporates a few stage directions not in the text, but taken from the Berlin production.

In addition to the above, two spectacular colour versions of the Strohbach designs for the Fifth and Sixth Pictures are printed on the front and back covers of this book respectively. Because of the prevalence of black-and-white photographs it is often wrongly thought that the Expressionist theatre aesthetic was mainly one of black-and-white. These rarely seen colour designs, however, graphically reveal how colour and the chiaroscuro effect vividly interacted to produce heightened visual intensity for Expressionism in performance.

The stage direction, "The third, fifth and seventh pictures in the visionary beyond of a dream", needs some comment, particularly in relation to Fehling's production. There probably is a mistake here. Following *Transformation* which uses a similar expression – "in the inner beyond of a dream" – to characterise its dream pictures, this ought to apply to the even-numbered scenes (2,4,6) which are designated Dream Picture (*Traumbild*) as they occur in the text. However, this was never corrected in subsequent editions, and it just might have been Toller's way of showing that the odd-numbered scenes were not to be taken as full-blown Naturalism – in which case the first scene should be included as well. In any case, Fehling had the uncorrected text to work from and it might well have sparked off his production decision to give the "real pictures" as well as the Dream Pictures a visionary appearance, as commented upon in Toller's Foreword. This is another indication of the close intertwining of text and performance. Incidentally, Vera Mendel translates this stage direction as "…are visionary abstracts, of reality", a very useful phrase, if not a very accurate rendering of "…*in visionär Traumferne.*"

The two sets of pictures (odd and even) in *Masses Man* differ both from the ordinary conventions of Naturalism and also from each other in the degree of their abstract stylisation, their visionary intensity and their Expressionistic distortion. Jürgen Fehling's landmark production, underscored this by having closed black curtains as the scenic surround for the odd numbered scenes. These focus on the essential moments of the uprising, its defeat and aftermath in stylised, largely black and white group images lit by intersecting broad beams of light (see front cover and plates 6–7). Fehling became well known for his innovative directorial use of light. In the even-numbered scenes, which directly project the psychic effects of the events in contorted nightmare images, the black curtains at the back were raised at times to reveal a cyclorama lit with changing colours which eerily illuminated the stage and gave sharp relief to the distorted shapes and images of the set (see back cover and plates 5, 8–9).

There was only one exception to this alternating pattern. At the end of the Fifth Picture (see front cover and plates 6–7) which shows the defeat of the uprising, just after the workers were gunned down by the disembodied sound of machine-gun fire, the back curtains looped up to reveal the threatening figures of the soldiers and their rifles against the yellow background of the cyclorama in a distorting haze of smoke. Loud drumbeats were used for the rattle of guns, accentuating the eerie effect of this moment. The two levels of visionary experience established by the play crossed over and coalesced at this point of highest intensity, emphasising both the nightmare and the essential actuality of defeat. It was this kind of theatrical flair that made this play and production a highlight of both the Expressionist and political theatre of the 20s.

The American theatre writer, Kenneth Macgowan, and scene designer, Robert Edmund Jones, were so impressed by this play and production that they documented it fully, including Jones' artistic impressions of certain scenes, in *Continental Stagecraft* (1922). Through that decisively influential book and the later Theatre Guild production (1924), designed and directed by Lee Simonson who also saw the Karlheinz Martin production, Expressionism had an innovative and liberating impact on the American theatre and its design, influencing many of the leading playwrights of that time, such as Eugene O'Neill, Clifford Odets and Elmer Rice. The American edition of the play, translated by Louis Untermeyer as *Man and the Masses*, contains photographs from that production. Again this indicates the close relation between text and visual realisation which is such an important part of Toller's work and this new kind of theatre.

I have included some further reflections on the play by Toller which have a strong bearing on its central debate between revolutionary force and non-violence, the unresolvable contradiction of political action. Toller wrote the play in prison having just been sentenced for high treason for his participation in the Bavarian revolution as, for a time, Head of the new Bavarian Soviet Republic and later as a Red Army Commander.

He was given the minimum sentence of five years as the judges recognised his "honourable motives," a phrase that is also ironically applied to The Woman in the play.

The usual interpretation of this play identifies The Woman with Toller and argues that her self-sacrifice in refusing to escape wins out over The Nameless in the end. Although she is executed, the two Women Prisoners are redeemed because they put back the mirror and the scarf that belonged to her.

The revolutionary optimism of *Transformation* is certainly gone, wrenched out of Toller by the *Realpolitik* of his revolutionary activities. But the standard interpretation still sees hope in the actions of the Women Prisoners, inspired by the conduct of The Woman. I think a different reading is more appropriate in the light of Toller's own remarks. Toller is not one or the other of the two main figures, but both. And the play is then a kind of medieval psychomachia – a war in the soul – which is unresolvable – a tragic contradiction – as the issue was for Toller.

The arguments of The Nameless are not refuted. He is often identified with Eugene Leviné, Toller's militant Communist adversary in the political struggles over the Bavarian Soviet Republic. While the debate in the play certainly reflects the issues between them, the situation is certainly not black and white nor are the questions resolved. Toller, it seems, even had at least a grudging respect for Leviné's sense of commitment. He gives Leviné's famous line from his last speech before execution – "We Communists are all dead men on leave" – to Albert Kroll, one of the most positive political figures in *Hoppla, We're Alive!* Toller varies it in accordance with his more inclusive principles: "We revolutionaries are all dead mean on leave, as someone once said" (p. 208).

In any case, the Woman's self-sacrifice leads nowhere in relation to the political circumstances. And the two Woman Prisoners, in the writing and staging, certainly do not give the objects back because of her noble example. The Prisoners clearly react in terror to the gunshots, hardly an image of redemption or noble behaviour. Perhaps it is the law of private property reasserting itself through the threat of violence. In any case, the scarf and the mirror would have been better used by them than left behind. And they are certainly better off for not returning the bread. Toller may well be ironising and darkening the supposedly noble sacrifice of The Woman's personal martyrdom. And their final words – "Sister, why do we do these things?" (p. 188) – may well have a wider and more general reference to The Woman, to the shooting, to other elements of the play – than just to the theft they almost committed.

This kind of interpretation would fit the final, universalised images of fear and abjection more closely – and also Toller's own political activism. What Toller has done, with verbal and visual force and with the dimensions of classical tragedy, is dramatise the unresolvability of the contradiction inherent in any revolutionary action for social change – in fact, the unresolvable opposition and polarisation heralded in the title of the play, with the consciousness of which one must still be able to act.

Bertolt Brecht dealt with the same question in a different way a little bit later in *He Who Says Yes/No* and *The Measures Taken*. He resolved it, somewhat facilely, in favour of revolutionary force within the framework of Communist teaching. But, then, he didn't have the actual experience of revolutionary activism in the way that Toller did. In retrospect, Toller's position is probably the more complex and comprehensive. And the tragic dilemma of political action as Toller sees it is still with us today. Toller goes on to examine it from a different perspective in *Hoppla, We're Alive!*

Hoppla, We're Alive! (1927)

I have worked directly from the first edition of this play. This was the first of his plays to have only one edition, although in this case it was a large one of 10,000 copies. As conditions in the Weimar Republic worsened, Toller had greater difficulties with publishers and fewer editions were issued. There are, therefore, no textual changes to consider here. Rather there is a different kind of issue.

Toller worked very closely together with the director Erwin Piscator, who decided to open his new theatre with this play.

This was a collaboration full of creative friction, as is so often the case with director and playwright. The complex working relationship between Chekhov and Stanislavski is the classic example. Toller seems to have completed a first version which consisted of the prologue and four acts, ending with a scene similar to the Madhouse scene (IV, 4) in the published version, without a fifth act. The first version reached proof-stage. Piscator then persuaded Toller to add the fifth act which takes place in prison and in which Karl Thomas hangs himself. This then became the published first edition. Interestingly, the dust jacket to that edition states "a prologue and four acts", whereas the title page reads "a prologue and five acts". Obviously the jacket had already been made up for the first version, which shows the kind of time pressure under which the text evolved. Piscator used the actual sheets from the published first edition as the basis for his promptbook copy to which he, often without the agreement of Toller, made further changes and cuts.

I include here first the published edition, trying to indicate throughout in square brackets what the production added or subtracted, based on the promptbook copy. As neither the films nor the shooting scripts have survived, I have drawn on the reviews reprinted in Knellessen and Rühle to augment the information on the film sequences in the promptbook. Then I give the last part of the last act as it appears amended in Piscator's promptbook. I have taken this from the promptbook itself, checking it against the version printed in *Gesammelte Werke 3* and what Piscator wrote in *The Political Theatre*. And then I give the original version of the Madhouse scene (IV, 4) with which Toller ended the first version of his play, taken also from *Gesammelte Werke 3*. I have also included supplementary material from both Toller and Piscator which should give some idea of the difficulties and frictions of their working relationship. I have tried to supply as complete a picture as possible of the available material so that readers and directors can form their own opinions and construct their own composite versions, as they so wish.

As Toller tells us, *Hoppla, We're Alive!* was the first play he wrote after his release from prison in July 1924. It did not come easily. In his five prison years Toller wrote prolifically – five plays, scenarios for three mass spectacles, two choral works and *The Swallow Book* among other poems. But it was over three years after his release before *Hoppla, We're Alive!* was to appear. This partly reflects his coming to terms with his own dislocation in the post-revolutionary Weimar Republic, but also his other activities. Cyril Connelly counted intense political involvement and journalism as two of the greatest enemies of promise. Toller wouldn't have agreed with the negativity of this judgement, but his fervent commitment to both of these did impede his theatrical output, as it would throughout the rest of his life. *Hoppla, We're Alive!* is in part a "state of the nation" play in its severe critique of the hypocrisy of Weimar society and in part an attempt to examine and find a political way forward in a post-revolutionary situation. It is one of the most panoramic and powerful dramatisations of that era.

Among other shortcomings, the original English translation of the play by Herman Ould is timid at times and leaves out some crucial elements of the play. First, it waters down Eva's spirit, particularly her sexual independence, by leaving out certain lines, in an almost censorious way. I am happy to restore these because the transformation that takes place in Eva – from her innocence in the Prologue to her experience created under the pressures of the Weimar world – is an important theme of the play. She becomes an interesting example of the New Woman with strong political commitment and, as such, acts as a commentary on the ineffectual revolutionary romanticism of Karl Thomas, which he too will almost learn to abandon.

He also leaves out the short first section of Act III, scene 2, where Karl tells Mother Meller that he has had his face made up by a beautician to always look as if he is smiling in order to get a job. It is a small scene, but it reinforces on a personal level the thematics of unmasking the façade which echo through the play on both the level of content and the level of production mechanics. Throughout the rest of the play the façade of the Hotel will literally transform into the façade of the Madhouse and back, and to the Prison, enacting the metaphors of this madhouse, prison world. And throughout the play, projected façades physically open or become transparent by backlighting to reveal what is going on behind, so as to both situate the scenes in a sociopolitical world and to unmask the pretence – the ideology – behind which they are hidden.

Using the gauze and film in this way, scenes actually emerge from and return to their social context and/or the political-historical conditions which shape and determine them. And this same technique enables commentary, critique and connection to be made by the various transformations of visual images. For example, in the opening sequence of the play, the film of the historical events of the uprising, including characters from the play, visually dissolves into the façade of the Prison, out of which the Prologue with Karl's imprisonment and breakdown into madness literally emerges. The prison scene and its façade, in turn, dissolve into a filmic collage of Weimar life and the historical events of Karl's eight missing years and this, then, transforms into the façade of the Lunatic Asylum. In this way metaphors of the prison world and madhouse world are established visually. The Madhouse façade then transforms into a filmic collage of the hardships and changes which Karl must now confront, out of the midst of which the minister's office with the projection of the Kaiser – the locus of unchanged political power – literally emerges to dominate the stage and the conditions of the stage world. The transformations from film to projection to scene and back are particularly effective in establishing connections and meanings visually and theatrically. And the scaffold stage structure that makes these complex interactions possible is one of the most versatile ever created.

Although Ould doesn't make this same mistake, it is important to point out in this context that several writers on Toller and Piscator mistranslate the "Note to the Director" at the beginning of the play (p. 202). In Benson (p. 82), for example, we are told that Toller stated: "all scenes of the play can be played on a tiered scaffold which would make scene changes unnecessary." Of course, exactly the opposite is the case. The many scene changes, which can be effected dexterously and often in full view without having to rebuild the scaffolding at all, are an important part of the way in which the play creates theatrical meaning. The façade of the scaffolding with its screens and gauze can be changed easily with projections and film as the photographs show (see plates 10–25) and various compartments of it can open up or appear by backlighting and be established with back projections to reveal the 'inside' of things. The scaffolding itself can revolve and move forwards and backwards on tracks, thus creating the effect of different camera angles and close-ups for different scenes and also allowing a playing area in front for set pieces or stage wagons. This set is a dynamic, kinetic platform or instrument of performance which is responsive to the play and enables its wide-ranging vision of Weimar life to be realised in an eye-opening, theatrical way.

Finally, the Ould translation leaves out the "theme song" which was performed at the front of the stage at beginning of Act III as a cabaret act and repeated elsewhere, even on the radio. I am aware that Cecil Davies argues that this song should not be considered as part of Toller's play, but of Piscator's production. I think, however, that this is, particularly in this case, a false and unhelpful distinction. The play is certainly the poorer without it and its major themes are encapsulated by it. The song brilliantly captures the cabaret atmosphere of the times and with biting satire critiques the hypocrisy of Weimar life, warning , as the play does, that history has not turned, but will repeat.

Further, it very effectively and forcefully extends the metaphorical reach of the Grand Hotel, the set and the play as microcosmic cross sections of the sociopolitical world at large. And finally, it hints at the revolutionary undercurrents still alive, in many ways at the moral centre of play in the painstaking political work of Eva, Albert Kroll and Mother Meller – no matter which ending is chosen. It's juxtaposition with the secret right-wing conspiracy scene between Count Lande and the Student which follows, with its reprise at the beginning of the Hotel scene, is a theatrical masterstroke which embodies exactly the fluctuating temper of the times.

It is true that the song does not appear in the German published version of the text, but the song was written expressly for the play by Walter Mehring, who was a close friend of Toller. He used the same title as the play for it and it resonates with that title's irony and rhythm, which I hope my translation, *Hoppla, We're Alive!*, has captured. Using *Alive* also provided a set of rhymes which made it possible to follow the rhyme scheme of the original quite closely. In any case, Toller dedicated the published play to Walter Mehring as well as Erwin Piscator, and it is probable that the only reason it did not appear in the printed text is that the play had already gone to press before it was finished.

As for the ending, in my view the one from the prompt script with the last line as it appears in *The Political Theatre* is the strongest. And because it also includes the second Madhouse scene you get the best of both worlds with a stronger reinforcement of the political maturity that Toller wanted Karl Thomas to acquire: "At that moment he understands his old comrades who carry on with the idea in the tougher work of everyday life" (p. 320) The fifth act, with its knocking and projected captions is theatrically very effective, and Karl's comrades are shown to be carrying on with their revolutionary work more explicitly here than in the Madhouse scene. It also does create a certain symmetry with the Prison scene in the Prologue. Karl's suicide may be thought to be a sticking point, but it does make a political statement in the context, if by negative example, and it does articulate known aspects of Karl's character. In any case, I feel the implication that he goes crazy again at the end of the original Madhouse scene is a less compelling outcome and negates both what Toller wanted him to learn and any danger he may prove to be to the state.

This does not mean that Piscator was always right – witness his often unfortunate cuts. His production ideas do need to be treated with circumspection, and this Toller certainly tried to do. He is particularly wrong in suggesting in his letter to Toller (p. 322) that the scene in Police Headquarters should not have the telephone call, but a personal appearance by Lande. It is good that Toller seems to have won out here, because the staging of the telephone call is a most striking metaphorical image (see plate 24) for one of the major political scandals and betrayals of the Weimar Republic: the secret telephone line between Chancellor Ebert and General Groener – the secret connection between the head of the Social Democratic Government and the head of the Army which was to continue throughout the Weimar years. This complicity, for long unknown, led to the suppression of so much left-wing activity and the leniency for right-wing terrorism which were so instrumental in the collapse of the Republic. The play is brutal in its revelation of the seeds of this collapse.

Overall, then, in my view, however fraught the collaboration was, it still led to one of the most stirring and innovative productions in the Weimar years. It is far ahead of its time in its technical resources which derive from both Toller and Piscator, as well as from set designer Traugott Müller, John Heartfield and other collaborators. And these are technical resources, which amplify and vivify Toller's biting dissection of Weimar political and social life.

Without the mechanics of the stage machinery and the interaction between film and performance, Toller's unmasking of the reality behind the Weimar façade would simply not be as effective and forceful as it is. And without the substantive critique that Toller makes textually of the way in which the old power structure resurrected itself behind the façade of Weimar republicanism, the staging apparatus would have been empty and devoid of meaning. While it certainly wasn't the perfect marriage of production and text for both Piscator and Toller, the two, even so, interacted with enough creative friction to produce both a political and theatrical vitality seldom accomplished. The accompanying design and production photographs should convey a strong sense of this. Once again a Toller text – even with the attendant difficulties – inspired a landmark production which substantially advanced the new spirit in the theatre.

Here, too, I can bear personal witness to the ongoing influence of Toller. Again in Berkeley in the 60s – a time that had a particular affinity for Toller – I co-directed, with the Polish critic Jan Kott, a modernised, multimedia production of Euripides' *Orestes*. It drew directly on techniques used in *Hoppla, We're Alive!* The ancient Greek spectators would have recognised the parallel between the Trojan War in the play and the Peloponnesian War that then was raging around them. We worked with the parallels between the Vietnam War and the Trojan War and how military violence abroad generates civil violence and disorder at home for our anti-war production. And one of the most effective ways we put this across theatrically was through he interaction of live performance and film, inspired by the innovative ways in which it was employed in *Hoppla, We're Alive!*

For example, Menelaus' supposedly triumphant return from the Trojan War was staged as follows. As the chorus described the chaos that gripped the city after Orestes killed his mother and then announced the "magnificent" arrival of Menelaus, documentary film of American soldiers moving through the jungle over dead Viet Cong bodies was shown. Menelaus then entered, in an American General's uniform, through a split in the screen stepping over those same bodies. As with *Hoppla, We're Alive!*, film was used to bring the wider sociopolitical context to bear upon the play and the staging device both commented on the text and articulated its political subtext with meaningful images. This revelatory technique of multimedia staging is a legacy from Toller and Piscator that will continue to bear fruit in modern theatrical times.

HOPPLA, YOU'RE DEAD!

It may have been Piscator who was responsible for having Karl Thomas hang himself on the hook of the door to his prison cell, but it was Toller who tragically committed suicide by hanging on 22 May 1939, ironically on the hook of his bathroom door in his room at the Mayflower Hotel in New York. There was no suicide note, so we will never know the immediate reasons. There was even some suspicion of murder by Nazi agents who had been hounding him, but the position of the body behind the bathroom door seems to have precluded such a possibility. Even so, the Nazi's despicable reaction to Toller's suicide in his German obituary is a measure of just how great a threat his revolutionary humanism was to their regime and its twisted mentality: "Hoppla, you're dead, but Germany lives." (Quoted in Dove 1990, p. 264.)

It certainly was an over-determined suicide. Toller was beset by clinical depression and health problems, worries over finances and publication of his work, and by attendant doubts about his continuing creativity. He was also separated from his wife and extremely worried bout the fate of his brother and sister in Nazi Germany. They both were eventually killed in concentration camps. The collapse of Republican Spain, signalling the increasing threat of Nazi Germany, might well have been the last straw – throwing into great disarray and disappointment all his anti-fascist hopes and actions. Of all the tributes to him – bewildered, sad and angry – I find that of Dorothy Thompson the most moving. She was the wife of Sinclair Lewis, the first American writer to win the Nobel Prize for Literature, and an important anti-fascist journalist in her own right who befriended and supported Toller. Her tribute describes all those photos of him (see plate 10) with those searing, staring eyes so well, yet it does not seem to have been taken up in the literature on Toller:

> "He looked upon the world with torn-open, incredulous eyes. They remained to the end incredulous eyes. They looked eagerly for beauty, sincerity, dignity, justice, truth. What they saw appalled them. Toller was appalled to death."
>
> (In her *New York Herald Tribune* column,
> *On the Record*, May 24, 1939.)

The plays of this volume render into vivid theatrical form the enormity of what he saw with that appalled and shattered consciousness in those tortured days of war, revolution, imprisonment and the chaos of Weimar life. It is an achievement and a contribution to theatrical modernism for which Toller deserves continuing recognition. I hope that this volume will make a start on a millennial afterlife for his plays in English and re-establish for them their rightful place in the repertoire of theatrical modernism.

HOPPLA, YOU'RE ALIVE!

Alan Raphael Pearlman
Canterbury, 2000

TRANSFORMATION

THE STRUGGLE OF A MAN

The first draft of this work was written in 1917, the third year of the world bloodbath. It was completed in its final form in February and March 1918 during detention in military prison.

You are the Way.

SHAKE-UP

Smash the chalice of sparkling, dazzling crystal,
And wonders like pearly drops of dew will fall,
Like dusty pollen out of dark red tulips.

Striding through this twilight world of wonders,
Dream-struck we plucked off fairy tales with tender hands,
While faith with sunbeams fashioned tall cathedrals,
And gifts of roses fell from high-arched gates.

Suddenly murderous, loathsome beasts came creeping
Spewing flames upon the earth!

Dream-bound we raised our blinking eyes
And heard right next to us the screams of men!

We saw depravity orgy away,
Europe, naked, oozed with muck of the sties,
Every hole gushed forth a whirlpool of lies,
Smoke entwined corrosive spirals round our head,
Despair gurgled at our feet.

A man screamed out.

A brother who possessed surpassing knowledge
Of all grief and of all joy,
Of illusion and tormenting scorn,
A brother who possessed surpassing will,
Ecstatic to build a temple of highest joy
And open wide its gates to highest grief,
Ready for action.
He hurled this hard and blazing cry:
The Way!
The Way! –

Oh poet, show us.

Characters

FRIEDRICH

PEOPLE

FRIEDRICH'S SISTER

MOTHER

UNCLE

CHILDHOOD FRIEND

GABRIELE (FRIEND'S SISTER) *Friedrich's lover*

FIRST SOLDIER

SECOND SOLDIER

WOUNDED SOLDIER

MADMAN

CORPORAL

RED CROSS NURSE

DOCTOR

OFFICER

WAR INVALIDS (HUSBAND AND WIFE)

CHAIRMAN

OLD MAN WITH A DECORATION

UNIVERSITY PROFESSOR *Prof. Kräpelin?*

PRIEST

AGITATOR OF THE DAY

WORKER

MALE STUDENT

FEMALE STUDENT

MAN WITH TURNED-UP COLLAR

SICK MAN

LADY

DEATH AS ENEMY OF THE SPIRIT IN THE
FORM OF A SOLDIER, THE PROFESSOR,
THE JUDGE, THE NOCTURNAL VISITOR

SOLDIERS

THE MAIMED

NURSES

MEDICAL ORDERLIES

SKELETONS

PRISONERS

The pictures "Troop Trains", "Between the Barbed
Wire", "The Maimed", "The Night Lodger", "Death
and Resurrection", "The Wanderer", "The Mountain
Climbers", are shadows of reality, to be thought of as
taking place in the inner beyond of a dream.

The action takes place in Europe before the dawn of
rebirth.

BARRACKS OF THE DEAD

A Prologue, which can also*
be thought of as Epilogue

Characters of the Prologue: WAR-DEATH / PEACE-DEATH / SKELETONS.

Night. Indicated: Vast graveyard. Military graves arranged in companies. Each company has the same simple grey crosses of iron. Some crosses with a painted rose on the crosspieces, other crosses with a bleeding heart, others with a small wreath of wild flowers. On each cross there is nothing but the name and unit of the dead soldier. The officers' graves are situated at the side of each company. They are marked by larger, grander crosses decorated with flaming suns. In addition birth date and civilian status of the dead are given on the cross. PEACE-DEATH enters, top hat on his skull and a tartan handkerchief in his hand, and with him WAR-DEATH, steel helmet on his skull and a leg bone in his hand – his swagger stick. Many medals adorn his chest.

WAR-DEATH:
    We've just about arrived, Herr Comrade.
    Had I known you had such trouble breathing…
    On my honour, I am sincerely sorry…
    I hope that you have no regrets.
    Well then, here you are…
    The arrangement is very simple.
    They are buried in companies,
    The lower ranks are on the flank.
    Just like in life, simple numbers,
    Our courageous heroes.
    The names should have been superfluous…
    Indeed we did it out of piety,
    Numbers would have been enough.
    And there to the side the Officers rest…
    If you are interested in what they were
    As civilians… I most humbly beg you,
    If you want to take the trouble…

conflict: do War and death really serve as social/class levellers?

PEACE-DEATH:

Hm, hm, hm, hm!

Marvellous, my dear Herr Colleague.

Marvellous – all appreciation.

I'm almost overcome with envy.

WAR-DEATH:

Too much praise, Herr Comrade.

Your mistrust seemed inexplicable,

Indeed, I too have lived on civvy street.

I'd really love for you to be convinced.

With your permission, I'll get them to form up.

PEACE-DEATH:

Please do.

WAR-DEATH:

In company ranks, form up.

March!

(*The SOLDIER- and OFFICER-SKELETONS climb out of the graves, all wearing steel helmets. They stand at attention in front of their graves.*)

To arms!

(*Each SKELETON rushes to his cross, pulls it out of the ground and positions it next to himself. The OFFICERS handle their crosses like swords.*)

Attention!

The Officers should now

Take up their posts.

(*The OFFICERS rush to the right flanks and deploy themselves as company commanders.*)

Dress ranks!

Eyes front!

Parade march!

In place, mark time!

Forward march!

PEACE-DEATH:

My compliments! My compliments!

I think how sad and horrid it would be

If I attempted anything like this

With those women and children of mine –

With stooping veterans for officers perhaps...
Propped up on umbrellas.
Yes, my dear Herr Colleague.
I feel that I am beaten –
You are the very principle of order.
Chaos prevails with me.

WAR-DEATH:

Oh please, Herr Comrade,
I feel I'm being flattered –
With a little discipline and practice,
You too will be successful.
– And so, attention.
In groups, right wheel...
March!
Attention!
At ease.
Please, who is now
The senior officer?
(A COLONEL salutes and approaches with halting steps.)
Thank you, Herr Colonel.
Attention!
Order arms!
*(The OFFICERS and SOLDIERS put their crosses back in
the ground.)*
Attention!
Head rolls!
Independent drill...
Begin! –
Herr Colonel, please, you will
Take charge.
*(The SOLDIERS, with arms on hips, roll their skulls. The
COLONEL supervises the troops. The OFFICERS their
companies.)*

PEACE-DEATH:

Have you invented all of this, Herr Colleague?
Is it, so to speak, your own idea?

WAR-DEATH:

What do you mean, Herr Comrade?

PEACE-DEATH:

 I mean, was this whole plan
 Born afresh in your own cranial cavity?
 That's what I mean...

WAR-DEATH:

 Not completely I admit...
 But yet, how can I put it...
 – You understand me.

PEACE-DEATH:

 I almost think I understand you.
 But I need time to think it over.

WAR-DEATH:

 Halt!
 Attention!
 Whole regiment...about face!
 Into the grrraves!

>   (*SOLDIERS climb into their graves.*)

WAR-DEATH:

 My thanks, Herr Officers...
 Critique next time.

>   (*The OFFICERS climb into their graves.*
>   *Silence. After a few minutes PEACE-DEATH bursts into*
>   *pealing laughter, which dies off in spasmodic snorts.*)

 I am bewildered, Herr Comrade.
 Did any mistakes occur,
 Or were the men too slack?

>   (*PEACE-DEATH snorts with laughter and fans himself*
>   *with his handkerchief.*)

 Herr Comrade, mind what you are doing.
 My honour won't put up with laughter.

PEACE-DEATH:

 My honour won't put up with cant.
 My mistrust was justified –
 What a fool to let myself be duped.
 My realm – I called it chaos.
 I've run myself down by much too much.
 Before me all are equal.
 There are also differences of course –

Money, the vampire, is on the make and has no tact,
But your principle of order is not of our world –
You play the victor,
But you are beaten –
War has beaten you, dear sir.
And you are forced
To follow his system,
With ranks, grade and prejudice.
Just like running a barracks.
You ought to be a sergeant!
A Death that submits to the German war machine,
Whoever would have thought it!
I've caught you out, my friend!
I advise you, be on your guard.

WAR-DEATH:

Infamy, insult.
Useless to reply…

PEACE-DEATH:

I'd like to end this conversation
Quickly with a paradox.
You are a modern Death –
You conduct yourself like Life
Which slowly rots behind the circus tinsel.
You puny Death! You hypocritical show-off
Propped up by military phrases.
Convey my respects to your master, the War-System.
Ha, ha! Ha, ha! Ha, ha, ha, ha!

(PEACE-DEATH goes off snorting with laughter.
WAR-DEATH stands aghast: Rips a tuft of grass from the
ground, wipes the sweat from his bony face.)

WAR-DEATH:

God damn! I think I've lost the game.

The stage closes.

Peace-Death has won this argument.
Toller's pacifist tendencies are vindicated.

FIRST STATION

First Picture

Forestage. Indicated: Room of urban ugliness. Twilight blurs the shimmering shapes and colours. In the houses across the street, the candles on the Christmas trees are being lit up. FRIEDRICH leans on the window.

FRIEDRICH: They're lighting the candles over there. Candles of love. Mysteries are being revealed. A blaze of love... Outcast, I lurch from shore to shore. A stranger to them over there, distant from the other ones here. Disgusting half-breed. Wasn't there a touch of pity in the room when she said, "Come visit us"? Thank you, Fräulein – your humble servant – will be there punctually. Artificial smile on cue. A tragicomic extra. Tried and tested spectator...no...a tumbling clown toy always bouncing back... I won't lug this inner split around with me any more. What are they to me! What does it matter that their blood flows in me? I belong to them over there. A unified man, ready to prove himself. An end to all this fragmentation. No more proud protecting of what I despise. Courage!

(MOTHER enters.)

MOTHER: At last you've come back, Friedrich. Where were you all day?

FRIEDRICH: Wandering, Mother. Wandering... As always. Don't look at me like that, Mother... I told you, wandering. Like Him, Ahasuerus, whose shadow creeps through chained up streets, who hides in pestilential cellars and digs up rotten potatoes in freezing fields outside at night... Yes, I was searching for Him, my big brother, Him, the eternal homeless one...

MOTHER: You sin against yourself, Friedrich. Are you homeless?

FRIEDRICH: Where's my home then, Mother. Over there they have a home where they have roots. Over there they are at one with themselves and their native ground...free from that inner split which corrodes thought and feeling like a festering sore... They can laugh and act with a glad heart. They have their own land where they have roots...for which they can sacrifice themselves...

MOTHER: You're feverish, Friedrich.

FRIEDRICH: Yes, I am feverish, Mother! Wouldn't you like to give me a tranquilliser? I wish you were as feverish as I! Now you are sad, Mother. You are grieving because I am not a good son...who always smiles lovingly...like the sons of all your friends. Oh, how moving they look, these well-composed family portraits from civilized homes!

MOTHER: I'm not listening to your words, Friedrich. You are morose and indulge in foolish thoughts, because...because you don't have a profession. I don't want to stand in your way, become a sculptor. But first provide a foundation for yourself, take up a good bourgeois bread-and-butter profession. Your Uncle Richard gives the same advice.

FRIEDRICH: So, my uncle gives the same advice?! Didn't he tell me the story of Strindberg as an example, how he "went to seed" in his last ten years? Didn't he sprinkle it with a few drops of regret that he...missed his chance to become immortal through Strindberg...? "A figure in literary history," as he so beautifully puts it. Yes, if he had only given him money when Strindberg approached him! If he had only done it, this noble bourgeois! But if he came upon a second Strindberg, he'd point out his dilettantish decadence, leave him to starve and tranquilise his own agitated feelings with the rising share prices. This good businessman!

MOTHER: Your father was a good businessman too.

FRIEDRICH: I know, Mother. Oh yes, he was good and generous. He left you to work...and meanwhile turned his life into a succession of glamorous shooting parties... A good father. He spoke to me about a respectable life and proper behaviour… And when I wanted to go away…get out…he forced me to stay here… He stunted my youth!

MOTHER: Quiet, Friedrich… I won't allow you to talk about your father like that – Friedrich, I know you hurt nobody but yourself with your words… I don't want to torment you today… I'll speak with you later when you are calmer. Now… Friedrich, I have a favour to ask you, a tiny favour… Do it for your old mother. Friedrich, go to Services. People would…

FRIEDRICH: People! Oh, why not call it Services for people instead of Services for God, whom you've turned into a fossilized, narrow-minded judge who wrote the one and only code of law by which he judges men. Always with the same dead statutes, which the narrow-minded serve. They disgust me, your people Services which I cannot call divine. Are you freer when you leave the House of God? No – no. – And the narrowness of your spacious Halls of God – it suffocates me.

MOTHER: When your father died, we were left in a bad way. I scraped and saved to provide for you, to send you to school so you could have it easier than we did. To lighten your material existence in every conceivable way. You must understand how worried I was as your mother. I gave everything to my children. I never allowed myself anything.

FRIEDRICH: Oh, Mother, I do know that. I could cry when I think about it. Am I an ungrateful, wayward son? No, Mother, no. You took care of me with money, you wanted to pave the way for me to earn money…yes, my material existence was secured. But what did you do for my *soul*? You taught me to hate strangers to our faith. *Why*?

MOTHER: They only tolerate us. They despise us.

FRIEDRICH: No they don't. Gentleness and kindness and love grow within them, all-embracing love. Do you see the candles over there? They radiate gracious embraces. – I called you Mother because you gave birth to me.

Can I still call you Mother now, when you abandon my soul like those foolish mothers who abandoned their naked babies to die.

(*MOTHER goes out silently.*)

FRIEDRICH: Now something has snapped... Or was it smashed long ago... It had to be smashed... Mother!... (*Silence.*) No, I'm not going after her...now they're passing out the gifts. The children are singing. When did I ever sing here as a child, really sing?

(*FRIEND enters.*)

FRIEND: Good evening, Friedrich. Gabriele sent me and besides I wanted...

FRIEDRICH: Tell her I cannot come. I'm ill, high fever.

FRIEND: I don't like to leave you alone.

FRIEDRICH: No? Many thanks, most kind, not leaving me alone is easy. Please take a seat, over there. Shall we do a swap for something? A good pocket knife for a drawing kit? The compass is damaged, I admit. But you won't easily notice it because I've arranged it so you can't notice it.

FRIEND: Friedrich! Why are you tormenting both of us? (*FRIEDRICH embraces his FRIEND and sobs convulsively.*) Poor friend!

FRIEDRICH: I am not poor, I don't want your pity. I object to your pity, I don't need it. And not your sister's either, tell her that. I release her from the embarrassment of being seen with me in the street. I have enough women over there in the narrow streets...my pocket money will cover that. I don't want you. I'm strong enough by myself, completely by myself. I don't need anyone, not her and not you.

FRIEND: In that case I'd better go, Friedrich, but you can always call on me.

FRIEDRICH: Call on you? Perhaps call on you for help? Never...

FRIEND: Well, I didn't mean it like that. But before I go – what I really came for... There've been special editions this evening. The fight against the savages has begun, over there in the colonies. Posters are up: Volunteers can sign up. How much I'd like to, but my parents won't allow it.

FRIEDRICH: (*As if he has awakened.*) Won't allow it? – And you're satisfied with that? You really can't be serious... They need volunteers over there... Forgive me, dear friend, for being hard on you, forgive me all the angry words. They need volunteers over there. Now there's liberation from the stifling, tormenting narrowness. Oh, the fight will unite us all... In these great times, all of us will be born to greatness... The spirit will be resurrected, it will destroy all pettiness, demolish all ridiculous, artificial limits...once more the spirit will be revealed in all its infinite beauty... And me – this moment gives me a very special gift... They need volunteers over there. You bring me this news on a Christmas Eve of love, you dear friend. They need volunteers over there. Why did I get in a funk? I feel so strong! Now I can do my duty. Now I can prove that I belong to them. – Tell me, where can you sign up? At the town hall?

(*FRIEND nods.*)

Dear friend, I am so glad, so glad. Give my apologies to Gabriele. Now the Fatherland gives me a gift. Tell her I've been given a Christmas gift, even I, on this Christmas Eve of love. Do you see the Christmas trees? There's one beaming in every corner. Tell Gabriele I send my best wishes and my thanks. She will understand me, why I'm not coming, and be glad. (*Rushing out.*) *Now I can prove myself, prove myself* !

Blackout.

Second Picture
Troop Trains

Rear stage. Indicated: Barred wooden compartment of a travelling train. An oil lamp dribbles flickering light. Sleeping SOLDIERS huddle packed together. One MUTE SOLDIER (face of FRIEDRICH). A SECOND MUTE SOLDIER with a death's-head skull. Both shadows of reality.

FIRST SOLDIER:

> How long the train's been rattling on.
> Forever on the grinding pounding
> Of an engine whipped full throttle.

SECOND SOLDIER:

> We roam through never-ending spaces.
> Days, weeks – I can't keep count.
> Wish I slept in my mother's womb.

THIRD SOLDIER:

> Wish the house came crashing down
> When my father took my mother.

FOURTH SOLDIER:

> Wish that fiery daggers shot
> Down from heaven to kill the stranger
> Who had my mother in the woods.

FIFTH SOLDIER:

> Useless words. Too long a time
> We're trapped inside this loathsome coffin.
> Too long a time we're putrefying.
> Stinking, rotting human flesh…

SIXTH SOLDIER:

> Aimlessly we roam, frightened children
> At the mercy of blind and wilful force.
> We murder, starve, commit atrocities.
> But frightened children we remain
> Terrorised by blackest night.

SEVENTH SOLDIER:

> If I could only pray.
> All the sweet, caressing words
> My mother gently promised me
> Crack up in crazed and broken stammering.

FIRST SOLDIER:

> Forever on we travel.

SECOND SOLDIER:

> Forever on the engine pounds.

THIRD SOLDIER:

> Forever on men copulate.
> And curse does grow forever on from greedy lust.

FOURTH SOLDIER:

Forever on the primeval womb gives birth to stars.
Forever on the holy womb is ravaged.

FIFTH SOLDIER:

Forever on we rot.

SIXTH SOLDIER:

Forever on as children frightened by the father.

SEVENTH SOLDIER:

And sacrificed by mothers
To freezing need.

ALL:

Forever on we travel
Forever on...

The stage closes.

SECOND STATION

Third Picture

Forestage. An hour after sunset. Indicated: A water hole in the desert.

FIRST SOLDIER: Evening falls, but the heat settles like smouldering crust – Is the Lieutenant sleeping?

SECOND SOLDIER: Why shouldn't he sleep? Tent's pitched – mosquito net stretched – he just stood there like a master, hands in his pockets – and then he went to sleep.

FIRST SOLDIER: Master officers who like to bellow hymns, I'm fed up.

WOUNDED SOLDIER: Water!

FIRST SOLDIER: Give it to him!

(*FRIEDRICH gives him water.*)

WOUNDED SOLDIER: Take the dead away. My foot's always kicking the dead. – Think they'll saw my legs off? Hurt me. – But I wanted to be a dancing teacher, one, two, three…one, two, three, waltz should go one, two, three.

FRIEDRICH: Sleep, brother!

WOUNDED SOLDIER: But take the dead away. I don't want to teach them to dance…they…are tormenting… me…maybe I'd better do it… Won't anyone start to play… (*Sings.*) one….two, three, waltz should go one… two, three…

FRIEDRICH: Sleep, brother, give me your hand. Won't hurt you. Want to wet your forehead with cold towels. Dreams will ask you to dance…dreams decked with flowers… Dance with you over the heather, past your own home.

WOUNDED SOLDIER: (*Sings.*) One…two, three…one… two, three…

FRIEDRICH: Oh God!

FIRST SOLDIER: What's He for? For the masters. To bring true religion to the savages? With murder and burning. I am the Saviour, hurrah! Get your skull smashed up and salvation awaits you.

FRIEDRICH: It must be, it must be!

SECOND SOLDIER: What must be? Murder and burning? Madhouse and sick wards?

FRIEDRICH: For the sake of the Fatherland!

FIRST SOLDIER: Fatherland! Don't know Fatherland. Know masters who gorge and guzzle and workers who slave.

FRIEDRICH: But how can you live without Fatherland? I'd go crazy with all the horror…if I didn't grit my teeth for the sake of the Fatherland.

SECOND SOLDIER: *You* say that?

FRIEDRICH: Just as you too ought to say it.

FIRST SOLDIER: Ha, ha, and you a stranger?

FRIEDRICH: Am not a stranger, belong to you.

SECOND SOLDIER: And even if you fight a thousand times on our side you will still be a stranger.

FIRST SOLDIER: (*Without any emphasis.*) There's a curse on you, you man without Fatherland.

WOUNDED SOLDIER: Man…with…out…Fa…ther…land… one…two, three…waltz…should go…one…two, three…

FRIEDRICH: You dare spatter my head with the foul muck of those words and I'll go out of control. Haven't I proved myself in battle after battle on patrol and on guard duty? – Did I ever run away like a coward? Did I ever sneak into foxholes to hide?

SECOND SOLDIER: But you are still a man without Fatherland.

FRIEDRICH: So then I will fight for my Fatherland in spite of you. No one out of envy can snatch that away from me because I carry it deep inside myself.

FIRST SOLDIER: (*Good naturedly.*) You must get used to it. In the end we are all without Fatherland. Like whores.

(*Both soldiers lie down and go to sleep.*)

FRIEDRICH: Is the churned up earth shaking under me? Trees are withering – the desert advances – where shall I go? I walked into a house and they burned it down on me (*Bursting with laughter.*) hey, how the rafters crackled and fell through the air.

(*Meanwhile the MADMAN has crept up.*)

MADMAN: Little brother…

FRIEDRICH: Who's there?

MADMAN: Little brother…

FRIEDRICH: What do you want?

MADMAN: Don't need to be afraid.

FRIEDRICH: Where did you come from?

MADMAN: The desert sandstorm drove me here.

FRIEDRICH: Do you live over there?

MADMAN: Live? I died over there…ugh, lots die over there and are driven. –

FRIEDRICH: By the desert sandstorm?

MADMAN: I'm thirsty!

FRIEDRICH: Here, drink some water.

MADMAN: Swig my own blood, don't need yours… simpleton…fool…bleating camel…little brother…

FRIEDRICH: You're bleeding!

MADMAN: Don't worry, I'll swig it up.

SECOND SOLDIER: What's all the noise?

FRIEDRICH: I think –
      (*SECOND SOLDIER notices the MADMAN.*)

SECOND SOLDIER: He's sick, he is!
      (*MADMAN starts to stammer.*)

FIRST SOLDIER: A crazy man. Must have run away from the other company.

MADMAN: (*Starts to cry.*) Home…home…

SECOND SOLDIER: Take him to the Red Cross man.

FRIEDRICH: My God!

FIRST SOLDIER: I am the Saviour, hurrah. I'm going to the Red Cross now. Red means that the blood should be washed away.

FRIEDRICH: No, it must be, for the sake of the Fatherland.
      (*The CORPORAL enters.*)

CORPORAL: We're one man short. We must reconnoitre how far the enemy reserves have pushed out over the enemy front line. One must return, therefore five must go. Who from among you will volunteer?

FRIEDRICH: I. *I will, in spite of you.*

Blackout.

71

Fourth Picture
Between the Barbed Wire

Rear stage. Dark clouds sweep across the moon. On the right and left, barbed wire on which lime-spattered SKELETONS hang. Indicated: Earth of the no-man's-land between the barbed wire churned up by shell craters.

FIRST SKELETON:

> I am all alone.
> All the others sleep.
> Still…not freezing anymore,
> Like I was when I had to die between friend and foe.
> The quicklime burned, the shreds
> Of bloody flesh quickly shrivelled up.
> Ha, ha, now I can rattle my hands.
>> (*SECOND SKELETON on the barbed wire to the right straightens up.*)

SECOND SKELETON:

> The scum over there starts up again!
> And so I'll have to keep on ducking.
> Still…not starving now –
> Who's grabbing me? A cold and bony hand…
> Let go, let go. I tell you.
> Let go of me.
> Or else… I'm out of control… –
> It's my own right hand
> Coldly clenching my left.

FIRST SKELETON:

> Get on with your act, old friend,
> With my loose joints, I'll rattle out
> An exquisite nigger dance to accompany you.
> Now we are no more friend and foe.
> Now we are no more white and black.
> Now we are all the same.
> Worms ate my coloured shreds of flesh.
> And now we are all the same.
> My dear sir… We shall dance.

(*The SKELETONS between the barbed wire shake the
earth off their bones.*)

SKELETONS:

>And now we are all the same.

>My dear sir... We shall dance.

FIRST SKELETON:

>Our coloured ribbons rotted long ago.

>Our names stare out from newspaper notices.

>Completely fenced in by borders of black.

>Ha, ha – we shall dance.

SECOND SKELETON:

>You over there, you without legs,

>Pick them up! And rattle them!

>Rattle them for our dance!

ALL SKELETONS: (*Laugh.*)

>You over there, you without legs,

>Pick them up! And rattle them!

>Rattle them for our dance!

>(*Those without legs pick up the leg bones and rattle them.
The others dance.*)

FIRST SKELETON:

>Ha, ha, what's going on?

>You over there, why don't you dance?

ALL:

>My dear sir...we shall dance!

SKELETON: (*Partly hidden.*)

>I'm so ashamed!

SECOND SKELETON:

>So ashamed?

>Gentlemen... Shame.

>>(*Covers his sexual organs with his hands.*)

>I think it once existed.

>>(*All cover themselves at once.*)

FIRST SKELETON:

>The desert has driven shame to hell.

>Who can now still be ashamed?

>Stupid fools!

>All of us are fully naked!

And behind our naked bones
Yawns an empty swamp.

SKELETON: (*Partly hidden.*)

No, not a swamp.

FIRST SKELETON:

Who's that?

SKELETON: (*Partly hidden.*)

The Virgin Mary lives...

ALL:

Hi, hi! Ho, ho!

Hi, hi! Ho, ho!

FIRST SKELETON:

My dear sir, you are not very well.

My dear sir. We shall dance!

ALL:

Shall dance. Shall dance!

SKELETON (*Partly hidden.*)

I'm not a man!

SECOND SKELETON: What are you then?

SKELETON: (*Partly hidden.*)

A...girl...

FIRST SKELETON:

What?

SKELETON: (*Partly hidden.*)

A...girl...

FIRST SKELETON:

Gentlemen! We must cover up our nakedness!

SKELETON: (*Partly hidden.*)

I am only thirteen years old.

But... Why are you all staring at me like that?

SECOND SKELETON:

Fräulein, you are under my protection.

SKELETON: (*Partly hidden.*)

Then I don't need to be afraid?

You see there were so many of them then.

FIRST SKELETON: When?

SKELETON: (*Partly hidden.*)

On that night.

Even now I don't know why they did it.
Dear sir, did it really have to be?
Hardly had one finished with me
When the next one leapt into my bed.

SECOND SKELETON:

And then?

SKELETON: (*Partly hidden.*)

Then... I died from it.

FIRST SKELETON:

She died from it!
A beautiful phrase! An elegant phrase!
She died from it!
Gentlemen! You are dumbstruck
And have your hands upon...ho, ho...
And still you have your hands upon...
   (*All drop their hands.*)
Fräulein, do away with shame!
What's the good?... Do you see a difference?
I think you've never really seen one!
Yes, today...upon my lime-bespattered honour,
Yes, today, we are all the same.
Therefore, Fräulein, into the middle,
If I may be so bold!
You have been raped...
God, we too have been raped.
It means so little
It's hardly worth a mention.
Quite right! You are so smart!
Take your place in there.
   (*ALL form a circle around the SKELETON and*
    frenziedly dance ring-a-ring-o' roses.)

The stage closes.

THIRD STATION

Fifth Picture

Forestage. Dawn. In a military hospital. Indicated: Simple, white-washed hospital room. Over the bed a crucified Christ.

DOCTOR: He's still sleeping.

NURSE: Been tossing and turning and groaning for the last three nights. Fancies he's wandering desert roads. Craves for water. Screams he must reach the mountains, the rocky peaks, but the desert expands and doesn't let him get up there.

DOCTOR: Quinine, double dose of quinine. Nervous shock one might think. Think! Think! The new Grippelin School could diagnose it. Not right, not right, it's something completely different. What? Chronic debility of the bowels – three spoonfuls of castor oil and every evening and morning two aspirin tablets – uninteresting little case, very uninteresting. Where's the new patient? Did he take his castor oil on admission? No, didn't? Nurse, I'm angry. I cannot bear neglect of duty. On principle! On principle!

NURSE: When he awakens and asks, should I let him know?

DOCTOR: Naturally. Naturally. A little excitation. Stimulates muscle activity in the rectum.

(Both go out.)

FRIEDRICH: *(In a fever.)* Where are you others...oh desert sandstorm...grainy fog...don't stop...go on...further... don't know you...who are you... Ahasuerus... Wretched man...sneak back...to your nightmare-gasping towns, here you'll find no cellars... I will not wander with you...no *(Screams.)* no. *(Awakens.)* Thirsty!

(RED CROSS NURSE enters.)

NURSE: Here, drink this.

FRIEDRICH: Are you the Mother of God?

NURSE: You must lie completely still.

FRIEDRICH: You bear the cross... The cross hangs on you... Red cross...my God, is this where the blood is washed away?

NURSE: We want you to convalesce here.

FRIEDRICH: Yes, convalesce... Your hands are stroking me so gently and soothingly. Let me see. How callous and hard.

NURSE: Work has roughened them and deepened the crevices.

FRIEDRICH: You are the bearer of the cross and herald of love... Your love doesn't flow from ties of blood, it bathes the ill and heals.

NURSE: All who lie here, you and the savages both.

FRIEDRICH: That's all? Too few, nurse. Why not those outside...all of them...

NURSE: They fight against our Fatherland.

FRIEDRICH: Yes, I know, it must be... How long have I been here?

NURSE: For three days. You are a courageous young hero!

FRIEDRICH: Was I captured?

NURSE: They found you bound to a tree. The sole survivor.

FRIEDRICH: Not to a cross... The sole survivor...

NURSE: Do you feel well enough? An officer wants to give you a reward!

(*FRIEDRICH is silent.*)

OFFICER: I congratulate you, young friend. Bravely you risked your life in battle, regardless of the greatest torture. The Fatherland esteems your service most highly. Through me it presents you with the Cross. You were a stranger to our people, but now you have earned your civil rights.

FRIEDRICH: The Cross? Do I belong to you now?

OFFICER: You belong...

(*Noise outside.*)

What's going on?

NURSE: (*Joyfully.*) With God's help we have beaten the enemy – ten thousand dead!

OFFICER: Yes, young friend... Victory sweeps our country, and you belong to the victors.

(FRIEDRICH alone.)

FRIEDRICH: What jubilation dances in their faces. Ten
thousand dead! Because of ten thousand dead I belong to
them. Why don't I burst into laughter? Is this liberation?
Are these great times? Are these great men? *(Eyes stare
straight ahead.) Now I belong to them.*

Blackout. acceptance brought about only by murder of thousands

Sixth Picture
The Maimed

*Rear stage. Indicated: A vast hall extending out of sight with a low
roof which is heavily oppressive. Beds in rows in which THE MAIMED
lie dressed in grey shirts. MEDICAL ORDERLIES appear from
somewhere.*

MEDICAL ORDERLIES:
The beds are placed in perfect rows –
Straight as a die
Not a single one is out of line
We have done our duty.
Be sure – the doctor can come in.
The visit may begin.
*(The PROFESSOR in a large, open coat, through which an
elegant, black frock coat can be seen, enters with his
STUDENTS. There's a death's-head skull on his neck –
his eye sockets glow through gold-rimmed spectacles.)*
PROFESSOR:
Yes, gentlemen.
We are armed against all horrors here.
We could call ourselves the positive branch,
The armaments industry is the negative one.
In other words: we are agents of synthesis,
The armaments industry proceeds by analysis –
All its chemists and engineers
Are calmly willing to forge new weapons
And manufacture unheard-of gases
And we keep up.
Their service to war will be credited to them

But we, gentlemen, are satisfied,
And modestly so, with this:
The work of salvation is the doctor's job.
But before we make our patient rounds,
I want to show you the achievements,
I say it not without some pride,
My labours have accomplished.
If you please, place
The seven model specimens
In front of this white screen.

> (*The MEDICAL ORDERLIES set up a square white
> screen. A MEDICAL ORDERLY gives a signal. Naked,
> seven of THE MAIMED step forward from somewhere like
> clockwork robots. Their bodies are stumps. Arms and legs
> are missing. In their place there are black artificial arms
> and legs which move in mechanical jerks. In rank and file
> they march in front of the screen.*)

MEDICAL ORDERLY: (*Commands.*)

Halt!

(*All seven stand still which causes a loud clicking to be heard.*)

Left – turn!

> (*The seven complete the left turn. At that moment a
> spotlight flashes on, throwing a dazzling white beam on the
> seven whose faces all have the same stereotyped expression.*)

PROFESSOR:

So, gentlemen, if I may be so bold.
This is the perfect place.
Where they can be inspected best.
These men, through our scientific work,
Have been raised from the dead to a brand-new life –
They were stumps of flesh,
Now they once again are men.
Did you see with how much joy
And exactitude
The seven followed orders?!
Yes, gentlemen, now once again
They can serve our state
And all mankind as well!
Valuable members of a useful community!

And now I want to tell you
What else I have succeeded in doing.
Special mechanisms were constructed
So these men can once again fulfil their highest duty.
A method, most ingenious, was created –
I have restored their powers of procreation
And the pleasures of the marriage bed await these men.
(*A STUDENT (face of FRIEDRICH) faints. MEDICAL
ORDERLIES give him water.*)

PROFESSOR: (*Courteously, but smiling indulgently.*)
Fainting, young man, from the work of love!
How would you be outside on the field of battle?
(*The STUDENT covers his face with both hands and goes
off. Involuntarily his feet move just as mechanically as the
artificial ones of THE MAIMED.
The electric spotlight goes out. The PROFESSOR, the
STUDENTS, THE MAIMED and the MEDICAL
ORDERLIES fade out.
A blind and maimed SOLDIER gets out of bed.*)

BLIND SOLDIER:
Tell me, brothers, is it evening…
Is it night…
The night is soothing for me.
The night has soft, cool hands
Which stroke the empty sockets of my eyes
With tender, cleansing touch…
The day is cruel. The sunlight stabs.
I feel it's like a sea of brimstone.
Scalding me with searing steam…

ARMLESS SOLDIER:
No one hears me…
I'm crying out for help,
I'm begging you, dear comrades.
Just a little help to relieve myself.
Who will help me? Quick, I beg you…
It's so awful to lie in your own shit.

SOLDIER WOUNDED IN THE SPINE:
What's a little shit to you –
With me it's become a habit.

I don't know if I'm still a man
Or a living shit latrine.
My bowels are paralysed...
And only my heart is beating...
Does no one here possess the power
To paralyse my heart.
I'm stuck in my own shit –
I pollute myself and you beyond disgust.
I curse my heart –
My soul has died from disgust –
And only my heart receives no pity –
When I awakened, the doctor said to me:
The bullet grazed your spinal cord,
But we have saved your life –
If that doctor knew
What happened to me –
Then he mocked me,
Or else he should have given me
The means to croak.
And if he did not know,
They should shut him in a madhouse.

WOUNDED SOLDIER: (*Whose body is racked continuously by
terrible spasms.*)
In a madhouse – yes, shut him
In a madhouse.
No, you know...
I know another way.
Shut him in a dugout,
And shoot the dugout all to pieces.
Bam! – the shell exploded...
I looked around...no way out.
With my nails I scratched
On splintered planks –
With my mouth I ate the earth,
Eating out a hole for air.
Oh what a great amount of earth I ate –
I never knew that earth could taste so good.
Then I slept –
Awakening, I lay here.

Is it the earth, the earth I ate,
Which causes me such spasms?
Did I want to turn to earth too soon
And do I have to pay for it now?
Or is it that I escaped from earth
Whose vengeance pursues me now?
Whatever I hold in my hands I spill –
I even spill my blood –

SOLDIER POISONED BY GAS:

My breathing is a sparrow
Always going pip…
My lungs are a sparrow's nest…
Can you tell me?
There also must be sparrows
Who fly away to the South
When our winter comes.
Pip…pip…

ALL:

So each one knows his own true song.
We ought to sing a joint refrain.

(*PRIEST (face of FRIEDRICH) enters from somewhere.
His raised hands clasp a crucifix, which he holds out
towards THE MAIMED.*)

PRIEST:

I bring you Christ, the Saviour,
You poor afflicted ones.
He knows your suffering and your trouble –
Oh come to Him, you deeply dejected ones,
He gives you healing, gives you love.

THE MAIMED:

If He is so all-powerful,
Why does He allow all this?!
And if He is deemed all-good,
This great big "Wherefore-Ask-Me-Not",
Why must we stay alive?
You say He knows our pain,
Then He is evil if He redeems us not.

PRIEST:

You blaspheme.

THE MAIMED:

> You dare call us blasphemers!
> He blasphemes against us,
> If He wants to make us believe
> He knows about our pain!
> Just dare call us blasphemers,
> You'd better look at us first.
> Don't you dread your ministry?
> Just look at us.
>> (*THE MAIMED rise up in their beds.*
>> *The PRIEST raises his head slowly… His eyes*
>> *widen…and freeze.*
>> *His raised hands slowly break the cross to pieces. He falls*
>> *to his knees.*)

PRIEST:

> How could I dare to think myself a priest –
> We are called – what a foolish fantasy.
> I'm filled with dread for those who solemnly called us.
> Now I see the abyss which the priest conjures forth
> And want to shout: Free yourselves from uncalled priests.
> – Oh Jesus, your sacred teachings are corrupted –
> Why else would they so weakly crumble away?
> There is no salvation…
> I see no way of light to lead us out of this dark night,
> Nowhere do I see a hand of light.
> Prepare to redeem yourselves…
> How could I, in need of consolation, give you consolation
> Which I crave more fervently than you?
> All feeble veils of pity have fallen from your eyes,
> How could anyone attempt to deceive you now
> With such devout and pious words –
> I cannot.
> I will go ahead of you…
>> (*PRIEST fades out.*)

THE MAIMED:

> Good luck!
> We envy you!
>> (*THE NURSES enter in a long line.*)

THE NURSES:

> We bring you medicine…
> You poor afflicted ones…
> Potions to quench your thirst…
> We bring you cooling cloths
> To ease your pain…
> We bring you soothing pills
> To give you calming sleep.

THE MAIMED:

> What use to us is sleep, you nurses…
> Tomorrow's just another groaning day…
> Oh please, just bring us medicines
> To make a long, long night. We never want to awaken.
> We never want to awaken!

THE NURSES:

> You ask too much, you poor afflicted ones.
> Our duty is to heal,
> We are not allowed to kill.

THE MAIMED:

> Too late, you nurses –
> What a mess of patching and botching you practise here.
> Why didn't you resist in peacetime!
> *Why be patching and botching now*
> *When you could be dancing*
> *With happy and healthy men?!*

THE NURSES:

> You do us wrong.

THE MAIMED:

> Just look at us
> And dare to say again
> We do you wrong.
> You know not who you are, dear nurses.
> Put on mourning, wear black veils –
> *Do not call your actions charity,*
> *Call your actions shabby, shoddy botchwork.*
> *(THE NURSES raise their heads. Their lips unleash a*
> *shattering cry. They collapse and fade out.)*

Blackout.

(The spotlight flares up.
The seven MAIMED stand in front of the screen again. In
front of them the PROFESSOR, STUDENTS, MEDICAL
ORDERLIES.)

PROFESSOR:

What exceptional luck it is –
To have such cases here together.
Tomorrow we'll look at other patients.
Let me repeat what I said at the start!
We are armed against all horrors here.
We could call ourselves the positive branch,
The armaments industry is the negative one.
In other words: we are agents of synthesis.
The armaments industry proceeds by analysis.

The stage closes.

FOURTH STATION

Seventh Picture

Early morning. Indicated: A studio. FRIEDRICH is working on a larger than life-size statue, a naked man, very muscular with clenched fists raised. In a pose which has a brutal effect.

FRIEDRICH: (*Working.*) The stone still resists. My hand grips the chisel, alone it can't make it glow. The chisel chips marble...dead marble. Am I too weak to fill the stone with blood? Then I'll have to stop... I don't want to make a memorial stone!... Glowing waves of life must stream from it... Shaking up men... So they never forget to defend their Fatherland... So they stand tall and show defiance... Show...defiance...against whom? Against the enemy. But who determines that someone is an enemy... Is there some spiritual power which forces us to fight?... Or is it arbitrarily determined who the enemy is?... There's a gaping contradiction there – Why can't I seem to succeed... The task is always just as big... Am I too small to give it artistic form?... Can't I pierce the iron armour? Is the armour all too hard?...
(*The FRIEND comes.*)
FRIEND: Worry made me come. But you are working. Foolish thoughts crept into my head. But I will go now.
FRIEDRICH: My good friend, stay. You are not disturbing me.
FRIEND: The finishing touches will soon crown your work. Your labour has lasted a long time.
FRIEDRICH: One year. But what's a year to create a symbol for the victorious Fatherland, our Fatherland.
FRIEND: Do you still have doubts?
FRIEDRICH: That we share *one* Fatherland, no – only...
FRIEND: Only?
FRIEDRICH: Whether there's not something higher. But I don't really want to know. Because if I knew there was, I couldn't escape my fate any longer – I'd become Ahasuerus!

FRIEND: And Gabriele? Would she let you wander? Wouldn't you find fulfilment in her?

FRIEDRICH: The struggle goes beyond women. Perhaps beyond our own selves as well.

FRIEND: Gabriele would be brokenhearted.

FRIEDRICH: Gabriele is strong.

FRIEND: Yes, she is strong.

FRIEDRICH: We come to each other in proud joy.

FRIEND: How strong you both are!

FRIEDRICH: We are strong!

FRIEND: Farewell!

(FRIEND goes out.
FRIEDRICH works. Bell rings, FRIEDRICH opens the door.)

FRIEDRICH: You! My love!

(GABRIELE enters, she tries to smile.)

Are you sad, my love? I wish I could ask the good fairy to turn these coarse hands into butterflies so I could brush away the sadness which shadows your white brow, like dark pollen. I want to frolic with you outside in the sand dunes where children play and climb the high mountains with you where we'll wander together over the peaks. To stride with you at night through dream-towns and catch you in poppy fields to kiss you joyfully. – But you are silent, my love. You are not even smiling.

GABRIELE: Tears are trying to burst out of me…but they cannot.

(FRIEDRICH silently sits down beside her and takes her hands.)

I am going to leave you.

FRIEDRICH: *(Repeats, as if he had known it.)* You are going to leave me, *(Then just as if he were awakening with a cry.)* you…are going…to leave…me?…

GABRIELE: It must be.

FRIEDRICH: On account of me?

GABRIELE: Also on account of you.

FRIEDRICH: Do you still love me?

GABRIELE: I love you like a woman loves a man whom she wants to flow into her like a roaring storm, whom she wants to father her child…

FRIEDRICH: And yet?…

GABRIELE: When my father told me he would renounce me if I married you, I felt like I was in a snowstorm and the snowflakes froze me and burnt me at the same time. I came to you smiling. But my father keeps possession of my native soil. From which he wants to expel me. I could never enter it again, never see it again. The native soil I cling to with all my childhood dreams, that I'm rooted in with all my lifeblood. I struggled over it for many days and nights. And today I found clarity. I cannot give it up.

FRIEDRICH: But you are strong!

GABRIELE: Perhaps because I am strong!

FRIEDRICH: But I am left… No, I too have put down roots, I too have a native soil in which I'm rooted with all my lifeblood. Native soil which has been coloured red by it. My native soil is our Fatherland. The whole great Fatherland. You are small, Gabriele, you are small.

GABRIELE: Perhaps… Farewell!

(*GABRIELE goes out.*)

FRIEDRICH: Farewell, my strong one! Now the twilight has descended upon me, eternal twilight. Golden day slips into the distant sea. Night dreams in chasms where black butterflies play and will rise no more. Gabriele! If only you had left me brokenhearted. If only you had taken away my belief in you! But instead you shake my belief in myself.

(*Sunbeams fall on the statue.*)

Do you urge me on?

The Victory of the Fatherland,

I believe in it,

And I want to believe in it.

I want to give it artistic form,

With my lifeblood I want to give it artistic form.

(*FRIEDRICH works, a hurdy-gurdy twangs in the courtyard. FRIEDRICH goes over to the window, returns to work. Bell rings. FRIEDRICH opens the door. A WOMAN WAR INVALID enters, wretched and in tatters.*)

WOMAN WAR INVALID: Money for war invalids.
    (*FRIEDRICH starts to given her a coin, stops and thinks.*)
FRIEDRICH: Are you too a war invalid?
    (*WOMAN cries.*)
WOMAN: Do I have to tell you about it?
    (*Shows him her hands covered with running sores.*)
FRIEDRICH: Poor woman.
WOMAN: They crept around me like jackals, both our own
    men and theirs… How could they help it? They were
    herded into pens like beasts. What do beasts know about
    your good morals? And what do beasts want to know? It
    happened to me there – someone – diseased and poxed
    infected me. How do I know if he was evil? You call
    them heroes. You call them all heroes, your poor beasts
    for slaughter.
FRIEDRICH: Poor woman, we had to do it for our Fatherland.
WOMAN: For your Fatherland! For the rich few who gorge
    and guzzle, gorge and guzzle and suck us dry, who
    gamble fast and loose with the profits of our labour. Oh
    how I hate them, these henchmen. I know them well;
    I was even one of them once. God rewards you for what
    you do, they say. What kind of a God is it who lets us rot
    in misery? Who mocks us by saying: Blessed are the
    poor for theirs is the kingdom of heaven. The God of
    love and pity and charity fêtes. When I sneak past the
    brightly lit banqueting-halls, I think I see their God at
    the conductor's podium throwing confetti all around. We
    are beasts…just beasts… We are always beasts.
    (*WOMAN collapses on a chair, sobbing.*)
FRIEDRICH: (*After a pause.*) Was your husband out there?
WOMAN: Over there in the colonies. My handsome
    husband.
FRIEDRICH: Wouldn't you like to bring him in?
WOMAN: Should I? I'll frighten you. You will not be able
    to work any more. He doesn't look very pretty, my
    husband. The disease keeps on eating away, year by year.
    Sir, if you really want to see him. He was the one who
    infected me.

89

> (*WOMAN goes out.*
> *WOMAN brings in her HUSBAND who carries the*
> *hurdy-gurdy. His face is covered with running sores.*)

You must say good day, Husband.

HUSBAND: (*Stammering.*) Jesus…be…with you.

> (*FRIEDRICH looks at him for a moment, then starts*
> *trembling.*)

FRIEDRICH: Is it really you, Comrade? My poor Comrade!

HUSBAND: (*Afraid.*) Jesus…be…with…you.

FRIEDRICH: No, don't be afraid, my poor Comrade. Look, it's me, Friedrich, who was in the same company with you, who marched with you through the burning desert, who suffered from hunger and thirst along with you. Do you remember, when they asked, who volunteered to reconnoitre the strength of the enemy? The two of us. They only needed one. We drew lots. It fell to me. Now do you remember, dear Comrade?

> (*HUSBAND begins to cry miserably.*)

WOMAN: Sir, there's no point in talking to him. He doesn't remember anything any more. He cries because he thinks he must cry. He can think just that much. But otherwise… The doctor says I will have to get rid of him soon. Well, have you had your little drama, sir? Can we go away now?

> (*WOMAN takes her HUSBAND, who continues to cry*
> *miserably, and walks him out.*)

FRIEDRICH: It's driving me crazy. Where to go? Where are you, Ahasuerus, so I can follow you? I will follow you gladly. Let's get out of here. Millions of arm stumps are stretching out towards me. The roaring pain of millions of mothers rages in the room. Where to go, where to go? There the whimpering of unborn children, here the weeping of the mad. Oh holy weeping! Deformed speech! Deformed men!… For the sake of the Fatherland… God…can a Fatherland demand so much? Or has the Fatherland sold itself out to the State? And the State speculates with it in dirty business deals? Is the State a pimp and the Fatherland a trampled whore who sells herself to every brutal lust? Invested with the blessing of the procuress Church? Can a Fatherland which demands so much be holy? Worth the sacrifice of a single soul? No, a thousand times no. I'd rather wander, restlessly wander, with you, Ahasuerus!

(Attacks the statue.)

FRIEDRICH: *I'll smash you up, Victory of the Fatherland!*
(He grabs a hammer and smashes the statue.
He collapses, after a while he straightens up.)

Now I must wander through the wilderness, restlessly and forever on... I cannot do it, disgust for myself clutches me. Gabriele leaves her man for the sake of her native soil... I betray my Fatherland, in which I believed, for which I risked my life, for which I wanted to create my life's work...for the sake of a pair of married beggars. No, certainly not for a pair of married beggars... Certainly not betrayal... I don't want to take that way. It runs through nights of rain, through plague-ridden streets, and ends up in the wilderness. Farewell, Gabriele!

(Goes to the desk, takes a revolver out of it.
His SISTER enters through the door which has remained
open, sees the smashed statue and FRIEDRICH.)

You come too late.

SISTER:

I come at the right time.

FRIEDRICH:

My way is blocked.

SISTER:

Your way leads upwards.

FRIEDRICH:

Back to mother?

SISTER:

Higher, but also to mother.

FRIEDRICH:

Back to Fatherland?

SISTER:

Higher, but also to your land.

FRIEDRICH:

I cannot see it, I am dazzled.

SISTER:

> Let me shield your eyes and you will see. Your way leads
> you to God.

FRIEDRICH:

> Ha, ha, God at the conductor's podium throwing confetti
> to the rich.

SISTER:

> To God who is spirit and love and strength,
> To God who dwells in mankind.
> Your way leads you to humanity.

FRIEDRICH:

> To humanity…
> I am not worthy of it.

SISTER:

> Much of what you think is worthiness now
> You will soon cast off like a mask from your face.
> Who knows where you first will find your truest worthiness.
> Whoever would go to humanity
> Must first find humanity in himself.
> The way I bid you go
> Leads through all the depths and heights.
> You must clear your way through dark and murky
> undergrowth,
> Undergrowth called criminal by fools,
> But you yourself are the accused and you yourself the judge.
> (*FRIEDRICH buries his face in his hands. Then he stands
> up, staggers and reaches out.*)

FRIEDRICH:

> Sunlight surrounds me,
> Freedom streams through me,
> My eyes see the way.
> I will wander on it, Sister,
> Alone, and yet with you,
> Alone, and yet with all.
> In knowledge of humanity.
> (*Strides ecstatically out of the door.
> SISTER leans on the window, eyes closed.*)

The stage closes.

FIFTH STATION

Eighth Picture
The Night Lodger

Rear stage. Indicated: Dark and murky bedroom of an urban, barracks-like tenement. In the two beds: WOMAN, CHILDREN, NIGHT LODGER (face of FRIEDRICH).

NIGHT LODGER: (*To Daughter.*)
>To have to sleep with groaning like this,
>I cannot bear it.
>Come here, I want to slip you on
>Like a soft and woolly cap.

DAUGHTER:
>Stay here... I won't leave you.
>Since the news first came
>That the big hammer crushed him to death,
>She groans through every night.
>She carried then her eleventh child,
>She aborted – a stillbirth.
>Great luck for me.
>I would have had to wash the nappies all myself.
>No one wants her as a cleaning lady now
>Because in the middle of her work
>She'll start to sing and dance
>And then burst out in holy hymns...
>She never puts the bottle down.
>Who's to care for the kids...
>Only me.
>And got to work at the factory too –
>Just stay here, I'll do whatever you want –

NIGHT LODGER:
>Yes, I'll stay.
>I think she keeps me here
>With all her groans and shrieks –
>Does she mind you playing the whore?

DAUGHTER:

    She would nod her head

    When the lodger before you beat me...

    Are you angry with me for that?...

NIGHT LODGER:

    How stupid to be angry –

    What could you do about it,

    If he forced you...

    Only, you know, I always feel hounded

    When I hold you in my arms

    And suddenly she shrieks or groans. –

DAUGHTER:

    I could almost envy the children,

    They sleep all day from hunger

    And all night from dirt and exhaustion –

    They'd be better off raised

    In an orphanage.

NIGHT LODGER:

    That's not so...

DAUGHTER:

    No, you're right. Only a thought.

NIGHT LODGER:

    She nods when a scoundrel beats her daughter

    And she shrieks and she groans

    When her daughter embraces me.

    What did you say...in an orphanage...

        (*The room sinks into darkness. Dreaming.*)

    In an orphanage...in an orphanage...

        (*Silence. Dreaming.*)

    Now she will shriek no more, groan no more...

    Are you content...

    Now they are in an orphanage...

    In an orphanage...

    (*THE NOCTURNAL VISITOR enters, a thick shawl tied
        around his death's-head skull.*)

THE NOCTURNAL VISITOR:

    Arise, Night Lodger.

    It's time for work.

NIGHT LODGER:

Yes, I am coming now.

THE NOCTURNAL VISITOR:

Hurry up...

NIGHT LODGER:

Will you lead me?

THE NOCTURNAL VISITOR:

Just come.

With me you are in good hands.

*(Bursts of phosphorescence flicker around THE
NOCTURNAL VISITOR and the NIGHT LODGER who
stands in front in his work-clothes. THE NOCTURNAL
VISITOR hooks his arm.)*

Do you see the building...

NIGHT LODGER:

Over there, it's beginning to glow –

How strange – are you leading me the right way –

THE NOCTURNAL VISITOR:

I'm leading you the right way –

The crooked way! The right way!

NIGHT LODGER:

No, that is not the factory.

THE NOCTURNAL VISITOR:

Strain your eyes.

What is it then?

NIGHT LODGER:

It seems to be a prison...

How brightly the roof is shining!

I think it's inlaid with coins of gold.

THE NOCTURNAL VISITOR:

True! True!

What else do you see?

NIGHT LODGER:

High walls that are topped with iron spikes

And holes that are covered with grates.

THE NOCTURNAL VISITOR:

True, true.

NIGHT LODGER:
> No, that is not the factory –
> A prison shoots up here –
> Let go – I want to go to work –

NOCTURNAL VISITOR: (*Grips him tightly.*)
> I am leading you to your work –
> The work that you and your kind must do.
> Take off your everyday spectacles
> And learn to see:
> They've put the building in ballet dress
> Because it can't take the risk of shaming itself –
> At first glance you imagined with joy
> Oho – that a prison blossomed here –
> Strain your eyes!
> We have already arrived!
> Do you see the sign?
> You're trembling – let me read –
> I won't deceive you:
> *The Great Factory!*

Darkness.

(*For a few moments the roaring of hammering pistons, the screeching of whirling wheels, the hissing of molten metal…*)

Ninth Picture
Death and Resurrection

Rear stage. Indicated: Ground floor of a prison. (The Great Factory.) Triple-bolted cell doors in the gangways. The spiral staircases leading to the upper floors have a rectangular stairwell to allow overall surveillance. On the cement floor at the bottom of the stairwell a PRISONER (face of FRIEDRICH) lies, his head bent back, arms outstretched as if he were crucified. Officious JUDGES in black cloaks with death's-head skulls hurry by.

THE JUDGES: (*Threateningly.*)
> The facts of the case!
> The facts of the case!

(*PRISONER hisses…shrill sounds…groans. A WARDER
comes down the staircase with the HEAD WARDER.*)

WARDER:

Wasn't my fault –
I was trying to take him down,
Like you told me to,
To his wife who had visiting permission.

(*WARDER and HEAD WARDER rush over to the man,
try to help him, raise his head.*)

HEAD WARDER:

He's still breathing.

WARDER:

I knew he was a godless man.
He wished an old woman who gave him trouble dead.
In that dream he murdered her.
And now he's murdered himself.
He's sinned two times against
The Church's Christian commandment.

HEAD WARDER:

Those who want to jump
Should be pushed.

(*The officious JUDGES hurry by.*)

THE JUDGES: (*Scornfully.*)

The facts of the case!
The facts of the case!

(*PRISONER moans and wails…*)

WARDER:

God be with me…
For a man to scream like that!

HEAD WARDER:

It's the devil screaming!

(*PRISONER screams out accusations. They pierce through
the cell doors, break them open.
All the cell doors fly open…
The PRISONERS stand in the gangways with slack,
dangling arms. Their eyes stare upwards ecstatically.*)

PRISONER: (*Begins to speak softly, then louder and louder.*)

Horror lurks in these cell walls –
Wherever I look – shoreless swamps –

Only grey swamps – always grey swamps.
In the lengthy twilight hours
Maggots wriggled out of iron bars.
I fought them off – but then – what could I do…
Grey and gruesome maggots tore at my flesh.

THE PRISONERS: (*At their cell doors.*)

Hear us! We are united in suffering.
Horror lurks in these cell walls –
Shoreless swamps –

PRISONER:

Once I saw red flowers
I grabbed for them –
And they became my heart –
And as I held it mutely in my hands
Grey maggots ate it up.
I ate it too.

THE PRISONERS:

Hear…
United are we in suffering.
Once we saw red flowers
How sweet they seemed – these red flowers,
They became our heart –
And as we held it mutely in our hands
Grey maggots ate it up –
We ate it too.

PRISONER:

I looked down the stairwell –
There I saw the bottom –
There I saw the shore – .

HEAD WARDER:

And there inside your wife is waiting –

PRISONER:

My wife is waiting…

WARDER:

You trespassed against the Christian commandment.
Repent, before you die.

PRISONER:

What do you know about it, brother…
It lies so far beyond all good and evil

Beyond all duty and commandment...
Beyond repentance and heavenly reward.
I heard a voice pronounce:
You learned delusion.
Romans didn't nail him to the cross.
He crucified Himself.

THE PRISONERS:

We know that...
We knew it long ago...
He crucified Himself...

HEAD WARDER:

Think about your wife!
It's me who has to tell her...
I don't look forward to that!
What's my job after all?
Keeper of my brother men!

PRISONER:

I'm thinking about my wife,
I'm also thinking about my child
Which she carries towards the light
In her body racked by pain,
My very own child...
This is the only guilt
Forever renewing itself:
We go through all the painful stations
And send out little children
To their own crucifixion...

(A pregnant WOMAN rushes in through a door in the
background, screams...throws herself on her husband...)

WOMAN:

Oh, why did you do it?
I was waiting for you...

PRISONER:

That is a very great sorrow.
Our people are waiting for us –
But we burn the last remaining bridges
And run into night on every path
That would kindly lead us to them.
We wander on...

We know that they are waiting
And wander on...
Yes, mockingly we wander on...
Even when we are waiting for ourselves.

WOMAN:

The child...
Did he matter so little, your child?

PRISONER:

He mattered so much...
But my guilt for my child
Hurled me into the scorched abyss,
Scorched ever since that time when men
Staggered to their feet
And murdered each other in hate.
We are least of all
A saviour for the child...
Helpless we watch his passion take its course...

WARDER:

He blasphemes...
Holy Mother of God, forgive him.

PRISONER:

She too is helpless.
Her quivering forgiveness is a lie.
She will bewail her Son forever,
And only because she does so
Is she pure and immaculate.

WOMAN:

What is life to me now...
I'll kill myself...and the child...
What's the use?
What for?

PRISONER:

What for:
Come closer and I'll tell you,
Maybe crucified the child can free himself,
From his wounds shining strengths will grow.
Maybe crucified the child can redeem himself,
Resurrected to a higher freedom.

THE PRISONERS:

Brother, your words herald new ways.

Crucified we want to free ourselves.

Crucified we want to redeem ourselves,

Resurrected to a higher freedom.

PRISONER:

Wife… Mother…

(PRISONER dies.)

HEAD WARDER:

Come. He is redeemed.

WARDER:

He was burdened with sins.

THE PRISONERS:

He has freed himself from sins.

Too weak to redeem himself. –

WOMAN: *(Screams.)*

Husband…

(WOMAN writhes with pain.)

HEAD WARDER:

Come.

WOMAN:

I cannot…

The child…

The child…

(Silence…

A soft tolling of bells…

The PRISONERS leave their cells – form a half circle

around the WOMAN, illuminated by sunlight.)

A WOMAN PRISONER:

A child.

How long it's been…

Since we heard the laughter of children.

How long it's been…

Since we played with children.

(The PRISONERS look at the WOMAN full of awe. She

holds the child out to them, her face distorted by pain but

sparkling with joyous lights.

The roof arches out to endless sky.)

Blackout.

Tenth Picture
The Wanderer

*Rear stage. Thick mist. A country road can be seen. THE WANDERER
(face of FRIEDRICH) rises out of a ditch.*

THE WANDERER:
    I feel as if today
    I am awakening for the first time,
    As if I rolled away a heavy tombstone
    And I am resurrected.
    The earthbound vessel smashes.
    The judge is now the accused,
    The accused is now the judge,
    And both, forgiving, shake their bloodstained hands.
    And both take off their worthiness – their shame –
    Like a crown of thorns.
    The morning dawns,
    The mist now parts.
    I know the way to the workplace,
    Now I know it.

Blackout.

Eleventh Picture

*Forestage. Evening. Public Meeting. Hall decorated in the style of a
veterans' club with deceitful war pictures and colourful paper flowers.*

CHAIRMAN: The old gentleman wearing the decoration
    may have the floor.
    (*The OLD GENTLEMAN mounts the speaker's platform.*)
OLD GENTLEMAN: Yes, those were the days, when our
    victorious brothers stamped from victory to victory,
    when the savages ran from us like cowardly dogs, when a
    fervent cry ran through the land: Down with the rabble!
    (*FRIEDRICH enters the hall.*)
    (*Continuing.*) Those were the great and glorious times.
    But today you whine for bread. What's the point of a little

bit of bread. If you want to work, you find work and whether you eat potatoes or roast is finally all the same.
(*PEOPLE grumble.*)
Have you already forgotten the deeds done for our Fatherland and the blood of our heroes?
A CRY: Are we less than heroes because we are still alive?
(*The OLD GENTLEMAN leaves the speaker's platform.*)
CHAIRMAN: The University Professor may have the floor.
(*The UNIVERSITY PROFESSOR mounts the speaker's platform.*)
UNIVERSITY PROFESSOR: Indeed, I, as the chosen representative of that science which a high Church once called *ancilla ecclesiae*, handmaiden of the Church, and which today is proud to be the handmaiden of our State which is the final truth and the ultimate knowledge, because it finds in the State its concrete and abstract reward. Now I, as the chosen handmaiden of that science, would like to affiliate myself with the honourable speaker who preceded me. It is not bread which is necessary for us, but science, education. Go, learn to comprehend what we call causal connections, the associations of different appearances!... The science which I commend to you is full of holy seriousness. It serves the preservation of the State; it is an *apologia* for that most complete of all ethical systems.
(*Loud grumbling among the PEOPLE. The UNIVERSITY PROFESSOR leaves the speaker's platform*).
CHAIRMAN: The Reverend Priest may have the floor.
(*PRIEST mounts the speaker's platform.*)
PRIEST: Brothers in Christ. Let me speak to you as Christians. Because our Saviour once said: "I am not come to bring you peace, but a sword," I also wish to say: I am not come to bring you half-hearted words, but the *iron* truth. When you fought against the savages, I preached to you: Hit the enemy with all your weapons, with poison gases and flame throwers, with submarines and forced starvation...and you are pleasing to God because the Lord of Hosts was among our weapons and sent an angel to stride ahead with bloody scythes and mow down

row upon row of the enemy. Think of those glorious
days and forget your petty cares. Think of Him who died
on the cross.

PEOPLE:

Down with the dog collar!

Out with the rich!

We are starving, we are starving.

CHAIRMAN: (*Rings a bell.*) Herr Doctor may have the floor.
(*AGITATOR OF THE DAY mounts the speaker's platform.*)

AGITATOR: You are right, brothers! What good are the old
vets? What good are the university professors? What
good are the dog collars? Jesus has become the family
God of the rich. We don't need him any more. What we
need is bread. What we need is money. We must fight
against stupidity. In its place we must put common sense,
which means you, the Masses. First of all we need to
dissect what the expert said: "*State*" is a new term for
Fatherland. That is a lie. It is a concept which has only
a few thousand square kilometres as its base. A few
languages of which only one is permitted and the
others suppressed. And many signs that say: Forbidden.
I should say: Permitted to the rich, forbidden to the poor.
And taxes which I should call: Reduced for the rich and
unlimited for the poor. If the rich don't have enough
palaces and want fancier holiday villas, they say: "Damn
it. We'll have a war." They sit down and telephone a few
lies around the world, cause war to be declared. Set up
societies to care for the poor wounded – a few more or
less doesn't matter – and at the same time a memorial
for the dead is erected. "Give generously, Herr Privy
Councillors." That's what a State is. Number Two:
"*Science*". That's a bit easier to sort out. In the year such
and such this happened, in the year such and such that
happened, etcetera. A few rhetorical expressions and
because of that you have a set rule. Another example:
the technique of mystifying the simple – a certain
vocabulary is necessary for that, which you have to learn
by heart. A vocabulary of a few thousand foreign words
– mixed into phrases they make what is simple, natural

and right into something complicated and the healthy
human common sense which you have is deceived.
That's what it comes down to: hand-maiden of the State.
Of the State which I just depicted for you. I described
the handmaiden and I described the State – a mixture of
both gives you number two, "Science". Number three is
left, "Church and Dog Collars". Shall I dissect them too?

PEOPLE:

Down with the dog collars!

AGITATOR: I thought as much. So what is left? To put
healthy human common sense as represented by the
Masses on the throne. That's how you will get bread and
prosperity and work and rights. What must we do? Push
stupidity off the throne and therefore I preach: smash the
palaces! Oh I can see you now – all your pent up energy
let free, glorious images of struggle. Men waving the flag
of freedom! Women hugging you in hot embraces! The
Masses surge! Shots resound! I will write verses and
pamphlets for you which are bloody deeds. My writings
will go with you like blaring trumpet blasts. Blood flows!
Blood of freedom! I call on you to *march, march*!

PEOPLE:

Yes, we want to march!

We are starving, we are starving.

We want to march!

Bread! Bread! Bread!

CHAIRMAN: (*Rings the bell furiously.*) The man called
Friedrich has the floor.

> (*FRIEDRICH pushes through the PEOPLE onto the
> speaker's platform.*)

FRIEDRICH: Stop, brothers! I know you need bread.
I know that poverty eats away at your flesh. I know
your misery, know your wretched, stinking rooms.
Know your oppression and the look of the rejected.
I also know your hate. – But in spite of all that I call on
you to stop, because I love you.

PEOPLE:

Stay, listen to him.

He is right.

He loves us.

FRIEDRICH: Your deep disgust for the priests who desecrate
the divine, I understand it. But I want to warn you against
the words of the man who called on you to march. Warn
you against the half-truths glittering in his words. He
pretended to expose the middlemen and the philosophers,
yet he only exposed these who have spoken here. But they
were organ-grinders who sold their professions like pimps.
Don't you know his type? Yesterday he cried: Separation
from the People! Today he shouts: the People are God!
And tomorrow he will proclaim: God is a machine.
Therefore the People are a machine. And nevertheless he
will be delighted by the swinging levers, whirling wheels
and hammering pistons. But for him the People are
masses. Because he knows nothing about the People. Do
not believe in him, because he has no belief in himself and
no belief in humanity. But I want you to have belief in
humanity, before you march. I want you to suffer your
need so you will not be possessed by it.

PEOPLE:

He wants us to suffer need!

Down with him!

Down!

We will march!

We are hungry!

Listen to him first!

Listen to him first!

FRIEDRICH: I'm not speaking about physical need,
brothers. You should not have to suffer hunger any
longer. But you should know that it is not enough to eat
your fill. I want you to eat your fill, but I also want
spiritual need for you. – For the sake of love that unites
us all. I don't want you to be starving creatures who
satisfy your hunger greedily and wantonly. I want you to
be rich and abundant, full with life. I want to struggle
with you against poverty and misery, but tomorrow…just
wait one day, *wait until noon*. Come to the market place,
I will speak to you there.

(*Excited turmoil among the PEOPLE.*)

WORKER: I think that we've starved for so long we can just as well starve until tomorrow.

PEOPLE:

> Yes, let's wait!
> No, don't wait!
> We are hungry!
> We are hungry!
> Let's wait!
> Wait!
> We will wait!

(The PEOPLE go out.
Some young men remain behind. A STUDENT approaches
FRIEDRICH.)

STUDENT: What good is education for us when the spirit is martyred? What good is our common sense, when we suffer for it? You must be our leader.

FRIEDRICH: We will stride forward together!

(GIRL STUDENT approaches FRIEDRICH.)

GIRL STUDENT: For the sake of love, be our leader. Love must flow through humanity once again. We will bear no more children until love embraces us with radiant hands. You must be our leader!

FRIEDRICH:

> The high-arched gate of the Cathedral of Mankind,
> Born from the womb of the world, now opens wide.
> Aflame the youth of every People stride
> To the sparkling crystal shrine divined by night.
> With awesome force I'm struck by radiant visions.
> Misery no more, no war, no hate.
> Mothers crown their shining boys with wreaths
> For joyful play and sacred fertility dance.
> Stride on, dear youth, forever being fertile,
> Forever overthrowing all that's sterile,
> Creating life that's glowing full with spirit.

(The young men join hands and in twos or threes leave the
hall which is now half-dark.
When FRIEDRICH starts to go, the GIRL STUDENT
appears from a corner.)

GIRL STUDENT: You, my lips throb with desire. My heart beats with glowing passion… You… I want to serve you… Leave the others, you can only force them…even if you force them for the good… I want to serve you.

FRIEDRICH: Serve the spirit, serve your God.

GIRL STUDENT: I'm terrified by Him. He radiates coldness.

FRIEDRICH: *Seas of flames!*

GIRL STUDENT: They scorch me. But you – I love you… I want to give myself to you, embrace me. Touch…my hot breasts… My womb moans… I ache for your embraces… Give me your child…

FRIEDRICH: I don't want your embrace. Did I give away every right to my body?

(*The GIRL STUDENT goes out slowly with bowed head.*)

Poor woman! Unredeemed.

(*A MAN with a turned-up coat collar rushes in hurriedly.*)

MAN: I hate you!

FRIEDRICH: But I call you brother.

MAN: I hate you. I know who you are. Don't think I don't recognise you. I see you. It's you I spotted in my room on lonely nights. Why don't you become a monk? Leave humanity in peace. Why do you go to the mob? You desecrate God.

FRIEDRICH: I sanctify Him.

(*MAN rushes out.*)

MAN: I hate you!

FRIEDRICH: *Brother, you deceive yourself.*

The stage closes.

SIXTH STATION

Twelfth Picture
The Mountain Climbers

Rear stage. Steep rock face leading to a narrow ridge. Two men are climbing on the rock face.

SECOND MOUNTAIN CLIMBER: (*Face of FRIEND.*)
　　Stop, I'm dizzy.
FIRST MOUNTAIN CLIMBER: (*Face of FRIEDRICH.*)
　　Be brave, soon we'll reach the top.
SECOND MOUNTAIN CLIMBER:
　　The ridge is narrow.
　　We'll plunge back into the abyss.
FIRST MOUNTAIN CLIMBER:
　　We might, but even if into the depths
　　What does it matter! The new ridge
　　To which we'll climb
　　Will be even higher, more radiant with light.
SECOND MOUNTAIN CLIMBER:
　　I beg you, my friend, please stop,
　　It's blowing icy cold up there.
FIRST MOUNTAIN CLIMBER:
　　That's why glacier light is dancing around us.
SECOND MOUNTAIN CLIMBER:
　　The silence up there tolls a mournful note.
FIRST MOUNTAIN CLIMBER:
　　You hear ghosts.
　　Take your rope and tie them up.
SECOND MOUNTAIN CLIMBER:
　　Should I thank you
　　For freeing me from this rocky cleft
　　When you lead me on to terrors new.
FIRST MOUNTAIN CLIMBER:
　　Not everyone who is freed
　　Is therefore free.

SECOND MOUNTAIN CLIMBER:
They will not hear you way up there.
FIRST MOUNTAIN CLIMBER:
Don't you worry –
The rocky walls adore strong voices
And joyfully echo them on.
SECOND MOUNTAIN CLIMBER:
I won't go on –
FIRST MOUNTAIN CLIMBER:
But I'll go on.
SECOND MOUNTAIN CLIMBER:
You'll leave me behind,
Me, your old companion?
FIRST MOUNTAIN CLIMBER:
You leave yourself behind.
SECOND MOUNTAIN CLIMBER:
For the sake of our friendship
Stay!
FIRST MOUNTAIN CLIMBER:
For the sake of our friendship (*Climbs higher.*)
I go on.
SECOND MOUNTAIN CLIMBER:
Can you still hear my voice?
Think of our youth!
FIRST MOUNTAIN CLIMBER:
Your voice becomes a landslide rubble
Which can't be stopped and hurtles down. –
Youth is wandering ahead of me here,
Hey, how nimbly it climbs!
SECOND MOUNTAIN CLIMBER:
Now you've gone too far.
Think of yourself –
I fear for you.
FIRST MOUNTAIN CLIMBER:
Because I will not leave myself (*Almost at the top.*)
I must leave you...
Farewell!...

Blackout.

Thirteenth Picture

Forestage. Noon. Indicated: Square in front of the Church. FRIEDRICH enters, leans on the portal of the Church.

FRIEDRICH: Sun shines on the roofs, strokes the dazzled windows of narrow attics. My breast swells.
  (*His MOTHER crosses the square dressed in mourning.*)
  Mother!

MOTHER: (*Hardly looking up.*) You haven't known me for years and I began to think that I was pregnant with you again like before.

FRIEDRICH: I bring you all my love, I want to embrace you tenderly, kiss your tired wrinkles.

MOTHER: You are not alive any more! You left your family and are estranged from your people.

FRIEDRICH: I am nearer to them now than when I was at home.

MOTHER: You belong to strangers.

FRIEDRICH: To strangers, but also to you.

MOTHER: Whoever sides with strangers, does not belong to our people. Our people are a proud people.

FRIEDRICH: Mother! Don't you feel how the earth is in ferment? That the earth is one almighty womb throbbing in the throes of birth? Think of the agony when you gave birth to me: the whole earth is convulsed like that today…a ripped, bleeding womb giving new birth to humanity.

MOTHER: I am too old, my life-force has gone out. I don't understand you.

FRIEDRICH: (*Buries his head in his hands.*) Mother!
                    (*MOTHER goes off.*
                    His UNCLE enters.)

FRIEDRICH: Dear Uncle!

UNCLE: What does that mean? Don't you have any more money? Don't count on me. I don't know you any more.

FRIEDRICH: I don't need your money, Uncle, but I want you to know me.

UNCLE: Stop it. What for? Tell me, have you earned so much you can take care of yourself? No, your suit is shabby.

FRIEDRICH: Uncle, you're lying to yourself.

UNCLE: Lying? If I have to lie, you are forcing me to. You almost ruined my business. "Your nephew is an enemy of the State", they said. You brought misfortune on your family.

FRIEDRICH: If I did, then I surely had to.

UNCLE: You're pestering me. You have no sense of distance.

FRIEDRICH: Uncle, I'm struggling against you because I must. But I'm not really struggling against you, I'm struggling against the walls of arrogance and barriers you've erected around yourself.

UNCLE: I saw it coming, you traitor. Shamelessly you attack your own flesh and blood.

FRIEDRICH: I've been attacking it for a long time, Uncle.

UNCLE: You'll find I'm armed.

(*Goes on.*
DOCTOR enters.)

FRIEDRICH: Good day, Herr Doctor. Do you still remember me?

DOCTOR: Ah... You...aha, yes, that uninteresting little case from long ago. Relaxation of the rectum muscles. How is it now? Everything in order... Bowels regular?

FRIEDRICH: Herr Doctor, do you believe in humanity?

DOCTOR: Stupid question. A very simple-minded question. I believe that most of humanity has good bowels. Those who have bad bowels should be given castor oil, a tablespoon for adults, a teaspoon for children. Stupid question. A very simple-minded question. I must examine a man who asks such a question thoroughly. – Stand still. – Say aah – Close your eyes – Psychosis, highly developed.

FRIEDRICH: Your medicine won't cure man. Freed from the sewers of plague-ridden cities, he will stride upright through a redeemed world.

DOCTOR: Sign up with me. Today. I've bought a clinic. Perhaps a water cure might still work. But don't expect

anything. Typical, completely ordinary case. This afternoon come to Room 17 and sign up with the nurse.
(*Goes away hurriedly.*
A SICK MAN with a restless glance shuffles on.)

SICK MAN: Yes, you really seem to believe in it!

FRIEDRICH: In what?

SICK MAN: In yourself and in humanity in general. –

FRIEDRICH: I believe in it!

SICK MAN: Ha, ha, ha – and in love.

FRIEDRICH: I want to live it.

SICK MAN: And all that...

FRIEDRICH: In order to free humanity.

SICK MAN: So not just in order to build hygienic toilets. But why else then? I want to let you in on something, dear sir. – For a long time I too tried love. I will tell you why in a minute. – In order to set up hygienic toilets. The toilets which show our greatness are still too dark and secret. You'll want to know my ultimate goal. To teach mankind that the only true cure for itself is universal suicide. But I have come to realise that I won't achieve that through love. Love only obscures things. Now I try hygienic toilets.

FRIEDRICH: Didn't you ever want to make your proposal to the doctor?

SICK MAN: I went to him a few times. He didn't need my plans, he said, because he had already implemented them. Otherwise I was completely healthy and had the best bowels.

FRIEDRICH: Do you really want all men to kill themselves?

SICK MAN: Absolutely!

FRIEDRICH: Why don't you preach war then?

SICK MAN: No, not that. They must not kill themselves like that. They must do it voluntarily. So, what about it? I advise you to think it over once again. The building of hygienic toilets for the purpose of self-extermination.

FRIEDRICH: Poor man!

SICK MAN: You pity me! You...pity...me...

FRIEDRICH: You are sick. Inside you are full of dead holes.

SICK MAN: (*As if he is awakening, screaming.*) I cannot believe in love, always only whores...always only whores... No one has ever loved me.

   (*Runs off shaking his head continuously.*)

FRIEDRICH: I will have to hunt for him later today – I will ask my mother to take care of him...no...that girl student.

   (*LADY, who entered during the last scene, approaches FRIEDRICH, swaying her hips provocatively.*)

LADY: Man, what are you doing... Can't you really see that love pulsing with sweat is separated from goodness by a gaping abyss, that love lasciviously licking its lips like a red hound of Hell crouches ready to spring... That love and goodness glare at each other like deadly enemies... ha, ha... You are defeated now. Don't answer me. I reject your answer. I reject your goodness... Love whips bodies. Let my teeth bite your breast until blood flows, let me kiss your thighs... Your goodness...hah... You are a fool. A tormented fool. I could choke on your goodness.

FRIEDRICH: And you?

LADY: Woman!

   (*LADY goes off.*
   Silently FRIEDRICH leans on the portal of the Church.
   His SISTER enters.)

SISTER: Your eyes were shining, Friedrich.

FRIEDRICH: Dear friend.

SISTER: Will you now give artistic form to the Victory of Mankind, Friedrich?

FRIEDRICH: What need is there for special symbols? What need is there for proof? Men have seen it in themselves. Men should be able to see it in all my works.

SISTER: Are you staying here?

FRIEDRICH: I am staying here and I will still wander further on my way. Through plague-ridden streets and over poppy fields, on sunlit, snowy mountain tops and through deserts, knowing that I am not uprooted, that I am rooted in myself.

SISTER: So you must kill yourself and give birth to yourself to find your roots.

FRIEDRICH: That knowledge is only a beginning.

SISTER: And where does it show you to go?

FRIEDRICH: To humanity!

SISTER: And further!

FRIEDRICH: Further?... I don't care about that. It feels as if I am deeply rooted in an endless sea. It is so beautiful to know that one can have roots and still press on.

SISTER: Farewell, Friedrich, I will watch over your way.

(SISTER goes off.

PEOPLE stream out of the Church and in from the streets.)

THE PEOPLE: There he is, the one who will speak to us.

He said we should wait until noon.

Now he must speak.

We have waited.

FRIEDRICH: My brothers and sisters: I don't know any single one of you and yet I know you all.

You, child, you go to school and fear grips you on the way. The schoolroom looks like a rainy day with the sun shining in. The teacher sits at his desk like the evil spirit in one of those fairy tales you read in secret. He eyes you angrily and scolds you because you can't remember the lesson. And still your heart is so full of strange experiences. You'd like to ask him about them so much, but he snaps at you and claims you have not learned your Religious History and are not a good Christian.

And I know you, young maiden, delicately boned and tender as March... A few weeks ago you left school full of joy because you believed youth and freedom called with heavenly bells... But you work in the factory now. Day in and day out pulling a lever back and forth over and over again. Over and over again the very same lever. And you gasp for breath in the stifling air and your eyes brim with tears as you divine through dust-covered windows the daylight, and freedom and flowers and youth.

And I know you, wife, careworn and worked to the bone. You live in a cramped room with your starving and freezing children and every evening you open the door for your husband with a gloomy soul and tired hands.

And I know about you too, husband. How you dread to go home to that room with its foul smell and wretched poverty and festering disease. I know about your hate for those who can eat their fill and laugh at you for going to the bar and drinking yourself senseless, senseless so you don't have to think any more and see any more. –

And I know about you, young maiden, and your nights of hot desire.

And I know about you, young man, and your search for God.

And about you, rich man, and how you amass your money and despise everyone, all the others and yourself.

I know you, woman, fruit-bearing tree whom no one helps to support, and how you then break and whither away because of your own abundance.

And you, soldier, trussed up in an artificial uniform, who make all joy of life sterile. I know about your astonished look when you saw the figure of striding youth created by an artist –

How could he give him such artistic form?
Because he exists, truly does exist!

So all of you are distorted images of true humanity!
You are immured, entombed, choked and gasping for breath, joyless and embittered
Because you have buried the spirit alive...
Mighty machines are thundering day and night,
And thousands of spades are eternally in motion
To shovel more and more muck on the spirit.

Your own hearts are stretched on the cobbler's last.
The hearts of your fellow men are bell-pulls on which you can tug as you choose. You throw glittering pieces of gold at one another and convince yourselves that they are birds of spring flying jubilantly through the air.

You pave your way with pieces of gold and convince yourselves that you are passing across meadows overgrown with wild flowers.

Your lips babble out sterile laws, rust-eaten prisons of iron.

Your hands build up walls around you and you say there are savages on the other side.

You plant hate in your children because you no longer know love.

You carved Jesus Christ in wood and nailed Him to a wooden cross, because you yourselves would not go the way of the cross which led to His redemption...

You build fortresses and enthrone tyrants who serve neither God nor mankind, but rather a phantom, an evil phantom.

And what do you know of the temples divined in dreams?

For those who bear children and the children themselves you build ingenious pillories, – because you understand the mechanics of torture.

You women who bear children and from indifference or from false pride and vain lies sacrifice them to fake images – you are no longer mothers.

All of you are no longer human, you are distorted images of your true selves.

And yet you could be human, if only you had belief in yourselves and in humanity, if only you were full with spirit. –

You could stride upright through the streets yet today you creep along all bent. –

Your eyes could be alight with joy yet today they are half-blind.

You could fly on winged feet yet today you drag your ball and chain behind. –

O if only you were humanity, – unlimited, free humanity.

(During the speech the PEOPLE have been seized by an ever increasing commotion.
Some have knelt down. Others, crying, have buried their heads in their hands. Some have broken down and lie on the ground.
– They rise up joyfully. Others spread their hands to heaven.
A YOUTH rushes forward.)

YOUTH:

How could we forget! We are humanity!

A FEW WOMEN AND GIRLS: (*In an undertone.*)

We are humanity!

ALL: (*Screaming.*)

We are humanity!

(*Softly, as if smiling.*)

We are humanity!

(*Silence.*)

FRIEDRICH: Now, brothers, I call on you to march! March in the light of day! Now go to your rulers and proclaim in booming organ tones that their power is only illusion. Go to the soldiers and bid them beat their swords into ploughshares. Go to the rich and show them their hearts which have become muckheaps. Yet be kind to them, because they too are poor and misguided. But smash the castles; laughing, smash the false castles, built out of nothing but slag, sterile slag. March – march in the light of day.

Brothers, raise on high your tortured hand,
Sound a joyous end to persecution!
Let revolution stride through our free land,
Revolution! Revolution!

(*They all stand upright, hands raised high.
Then they join hands and stride off.*)

ALL:

Brothers, raise on high your tortured hand,
Sound a joyous end to persecution!
Let revolution stride through our free land,
Revolution! Revolution!

The stage closes.

A wee bit unrealistic/ too optomistic maybe?

The End.

Appendix i

Remarks On My Drama *Transformation*

"The first draft of this work was written in 1917, in the third year of the world bloodbath. It was completed in its final form in February and March 1918 during detention in military prison." –

Somewhere I read: "After Munich this piece seems like an explanation, like a justification, and that's upsetting."

"Upsetting" to the pimps of war, so a lot has already been won!

If a political leaflet means a guidebook, born from the pangs of external reality, from the pangs of conscience, from the fullness of inner strength, then I'm glad for *Transformation* to be considered a "political leaflet."

For me in 1917 this drama was a leaflet. I read out scenes from it to a circle of young people in Heidelberg, and wanted to *churn* them up (to "agitate" against the war!); and after expulsion from Heidelberg, I went to Berlin and there read the piece again. Always with this intention: to shake up the apathetic, to get the reluctant moving, to show the way to these groping about…and to win them all over to the practical, painstaking spadework of revolution. At Eisner's meetings before the January strike of 1918, I handed out flyers which had certain scenes of *Transformation* printed on them; at strike rallies I read out bits of it during my speeches.

Thesis drama, then? Thesis drama lies in the area of bourgeois Reformism (Motto: Be charitable and don't despise whores: they too are human beings!)

A political drama? Perhaps a broken step towards it.

The political drama is born from the absolute of the revolutionary *Must* (synthesis of psychic impulse and force of reason), political drama which does not consciously *want* to plough up and rebuild, but which *will* plough up and rebuild, which *will* destroy rotten forms and renew the spiritual content of human community life.

Precondition for the political writer: a man who feels responsible for himself and for every brother of the common human community. Once again: who feels responsible.

Fortress Prison Eichstät, October 1919

From: *Der Freihafen. Blätter der Hamburger Kammerspiele 2.* 1919, p. 145 f. (*Gesammelte Werke 2*, pp. 360–1)

Appendix ii

From *Works*

I wrote *Transformation* in the middle of the war. I mimeographed scenes in the military hospital and handed them out to women during the strike at the beginning of 1918. At that time only one thing about my writing mattered to me: to work for peace.

They call this piece Expressionist. Scenes of realism and dream scenes alternate with each other. Today many smile at Expressionism, but at that time it was a necessary artistic form. It opposed that trend in art which was satisfied with stringing impressions together without asking questions about essence, about responsibility, about ideas. The Expressionist wanted to photograph more than appearances; from the recognition that the environment, so to speak, sinks deeply into the artist and cuts many facets into his psychic mirror, he wanted to shape this environment from within its very essence in new ways. Because it was the intention of Expressionism to have an effect upon this environment, it wanted to change it, to give it a more just, a brighter face. Reality was to be caught by the beam of ideas.

Every event was resolved into an outer and inner event, both of which were equally important and equally strong as motive forces. In style, Expressionism – I am speaking of it only at its best – was tersely pregnant with meaning, almost telegraphic, avoiding the peripheral and always plunging into the centre of things. Man in Expressionist drama was not an accidental private individual. He was a type. Posited for many by the omission of surface characteristics. We scraped the skin off man and believed we found his soul under his skin.

The fullness of actuality at that time was so diverse and so powerful that no one could overcome it. One could only become master of it by abstraction, by the highlighting of those broad lines which determined the foundation of things.

The epoch of Expressionism was replaced by the New Objectivity and that art form they called Reportage. I believe that the New Objectivity was a modern form of 'Biedermeirism'; the artist of the New Objectivity was not close to men and things, but merely to the photography of them.

Today, when we have won some distance from individual events, when the important ones are separated out from the unimportant ones, when thousands of individual details are forgotten, we have come to a style which is saturated with reality and which all the same has ideas as foundation. Experience and distance are bound together again.

Whether Expressionism has created works which will outlast its time, we won't know for fifty years. But we must not forget that, born from its time, it wanted to have an effect on its time. Never since Schiller's *The Robbers*, since *Love and Intrigue*, has the theatre again been such a platform for contemporary events, so surging with the strife and counterstrife of public opinion. Passionate concern on one side, fierce accusations from a one-sided tendency on the other.

Every author wants to squeeze into his first work everything he knows, everything he has ever experienced. I did that too. And thus it is not astonishing that the private, the lyrical, squeezes out of this work more powerfully than dramatic architechtonics should allow it to do.

(*Gesammelte Werke 1*, pp. 137–139. Originally published in *Quer Durch*, Berlin, 1930)

Appendix iii: Plates

Transformation

Directed by Karlheinz Martin and designed by Robert Neppach
with music by Werner R. Hagemann (Die Tribüne, 30 Sept 1919)

1. **First Picture.** Friedrich (Fritz Kortner) at home with his Mother. A jagged,
brightly coloured flat with the distorted shape of a window, against a dark
curtain, which emphasised the fragmented nature of reality being presented:
as if fragmented pieces were broken out of reality. Note the relief effect. These
black-and-white photographs do not indicate how splashes of colour were
also used to heighten the searing visual effect: dreamscapes in black-and-
white and colour as if revealed by flashes of lightening.

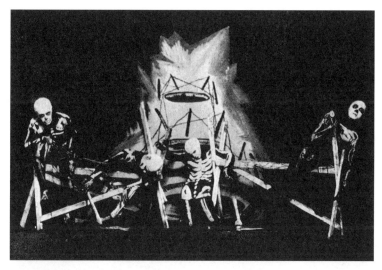

2. **Fourth Picture.** Skeletons hanging on barbed wire in front of jaggedly painted coloured flames in the middle of which the barbed wire motif was repeated with shell craters. Vivid background for an eerie dance of death.

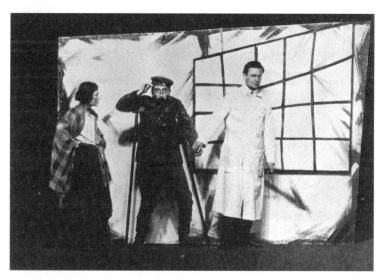

3. **Seventh Picture.** Friedrich in his Studio with the War Invalids just before he smashes the statue and begins his new transformation. The exaggerated, pock-marked make-up of the syphilitic Invalids was horrifying.

4. **Ninth Picture.** In the Factory/Prison just before the Woman gives birth. In the actual production Friedrich did not die, but broke free from his chains as the baby was born. This was placed as the final scene, thus somewhat de-politicising the play. Note the stylised gestures and facial expressions which were characteristic of the production.

MASSES MAN

A PIECE
FROM THE SOCIAL REVOLUTION
OF THE TWENTIETH CENTURY

World Revolution.
Womb giving birth to new pulsing force.
Womb giving birth to new social orders.
Red the century blazes.
Bloody fires of guilt.
The earth nails its flesh to the cross.

TO THE PROLETARIANS

*The first draft was written in October 1919,
in the first year of the German revolution.
Fortress Prison Niederschönenfeld.*

Foreword to the Second Edition

Letter to a Creative Middleman

There are critics who complain that, although the dream pictures had the appearance of a dream, you gave the "real pictures" a visionary appearance and thus weakened the boundaries between reality and dream. I would like to tell you expressly that you have acted according to my intention. These "real pictures" are not naturalistic "scenes of milieu", the figures (except for the figure of Sonia) are not individually stressed. *What can be real in a drama like "Masses Man"? Only the psychic, the spiritual breath of life.*

As a political person I act as if human beings as units, as groups, as functions, as power equations, as economic equations – as if any such material relations – were real, objective facts. As an artist I view these real, objective facts as highly questionable. ("Whether we have a personal existence is another question.")

I see convicts in the prison yard sawing wood in a monotonous rhythm. Human beings, I think emotionally. One might be a worker, another a farmer, another perhaps a notary's clerk… I see the room in which the worker lived, see his little peculiarities, the distinctive gestures with which he might throw away a match, embrace a woman, pass through the factory gate at night. I see the broad-shouldered farmer there and the small, narrow-chested notary's clerk just as clearly. Then…all of a sudden…they are no longer human beings X, Y and Z, but gruesome puppets controlled by the dimly sensed, ominous force of fate.

Two women once passed in front of the window of my cell while I was gripping the iron bars. Seemingly two old maids. Both had short, white hair; both wore dresses exactly the same in shape, colour and cut; both carried a grey umbrella with white dots and both moved with their heads waggling.

Not even for one instant did I see "real human beings" in a "real Neuberg" going for a walk in a narrow courthouse lane. A dance of death by two old maids, one old maid and the mirror image of her dead, stared me in the face.

❖

The drama *Masses Man* in its totality is a vision, which literally
"burst" out of me in two and a half days. The two nights which
I had to spend in "bed" in a dark cell by force of imprisonment
were abysses of torture; like I was being whipped by faces, by
demonic faces, by faces somersaulting over each other in
grotesque leaps. Each morning, shivering from an inner fever,
I sat at my table and didn't stop writing until my fingers,
numb and shaking, failed me. No one was allowed in my cell,
I refused to have it cleaned; with uncontrollable anger I turned
on comrades who wanted to ask me something or help me in
some kind of way.

The arduous (and ardent) work of reshaping its form and
polishing lasted one year. –

Today I take a critical view of the drama *Masses Man*. I have
recognised the limitation of its form which originates from (in
spite of everything!) an inner constraint of those days, from a
very human shame, which shied away from giving artistic form
to personal experience, to naked confession, and which could
not summon the will to pure artistic objectivity. The atrocities
of the days of revolution had not yet become a psychic *image*
of the days of revolution; they were somehow still painful,
agonizing, psychic *fragments*, psychic *chaos*.

I am astonished at the lack of understanding in the criticism.
The cause may be (and this is most probable) a defect in the
structuring. But perhaps there is also an additional cause in
the fact that what is merely "journalese" and "editorial jargon"
etc. for the bourgeois critics is for those of us who live close to
the proletariat and know its spiritual and psychic world, *who
create out of the psychic and spiritual world of the proletariat*, an
expression of the most moving and stirring idealistic struggles,
embracing the whole of mankind.

This is the case: in social life and its artistic image what
seems to be a quarrel about mere words to the bourgeois is to
the proletarian tragic schism, grievous assault. What appears
to the bourgeois as "deep" and "meaningful" knowledge, as
an expression of the most emotional spiritual struggles, leaves
the proletarian completely "untouched".

I don't need to stress that proletarian art must also lead to what is human, that it must, in its depths, be all-embracing – like life and like death. A proletarian art exists only insofar as the full diversity of proletarian psychic life is for the creative artist a pathway to giving form to what is eternally human.

Ernst Toller
Fortress Niederschönenfeld, October 1921

Players

MEN WORKERS

WOMEN WORKERS

THE NAMELESS

GIRL PRISONERS

OFFICER

PRIEST

HUSBAND (THE STATE OFFICIAL)

SONIA IRENE L., A WOMAN

Figures of the Dream Pictures

SONIA IRENE L., A WOMAN

THE COMPANION

BANKERS

THE STATE OFFICIAL

GUARDS (MEN AND WOMEN)

PRISONERS

SHADOWS

The third, fifth and seventh pictures in the visionary
beyond of a dream.

FIRST PICTURE

Indicated:
Backroom of a workers' tavern.
On whitewashed walls pictures of veterans' clubs
and portraits of heroes of the Masses.
In the middle a large and clumsy table around which
THE WOMAN and THE WORKERS sit.

FIRST WORKER:

Leaflets are handed out,

Meeting in the Great Hall. –

The factories will close early tomorrow.

The Masses are seething.

Tomorrow will decide.

Comrade, are you ready?

THE WOMAN:

I am.

My strength is growing with every breath –

How I burn for this hour,

When lifeblood turns to word and word to action.

Too often I've been paralysed – I clutched

My hands in rage and shame and pain.

When loathsome headlines bawl out "Victory"

A million fists grab hold of me...

And shriek: *You* are guilty of our death!

Yes, every horse with shaking, foaming flanks

Mutely accuses me – accuses me. –

If I tomorrow blast the Doomsday trumpet

When my conscience surges through the hall –

Am *I* the only one proclaiming "Strike"?

Man calls Strike and nature calls Strike!

It even seems my dog barks Strike,

Leaping to greet me when I come home...

And even the river gushes Strike!

My knowledge is so strong. The Masses,

Resurrected, free from the red tape chains

Of flabby boardroom bureaucrats,
As armies of humanity, will raise with heaving might
The factory works of peace to heaven's invisible dome.
Oh red flag,...flag of bright, new dawn,
Who will carry the vanguard flag?

SECOND WORKER:

You. They follow you.

(*Silence flickers.*)

THE WOMAN:

Our agents must not talk!
Do you think the police don't know?
And what if the army chains up the hall?

FIRST WORKER:

The police don't know. And even if they did,
They cannot know our true intent. –
Once the Masses surround the hall
They'll be a mighty flood which no police force
Can channel into peaceful fountains splashing in the park.
Besides: the police won't take the risk of such high stakes,
Subversion sobers up those drunk with power.
The regiments are with us now –
Soldiers' Councils everywhere!
Comrade, tomorrow will decide.

(*There's a knock.*)

Betrayed!

SECOND WORKER:

They must not capture you.

FIRST WORKER:

Only one door.

SECOND WORKER:

Through the window!

FIRST WORKER:

The window plunges down a light shaft.

THE WOMAN:

So near the struggle...

(*There's a louder knock. The door opens. THE
HUSBAND, with the collar of his coat turned up high,
comes in, quickly looks around, tips his bowler hat.*)

134

THE WOMAN:

    A...friend and nothing to fear...

    You come to me,

    You find me.

THE HUSBAND:

    I bid you good evening.

                      (Softly.)

    Please don't introduce me.

    Can I speak with you?

THE WOMAN:

    Comrades...

THE WORKERS:

    Good night.

    Till tomorrow.

THE WOMAN:

    Good night, till tomorrow.

THE HUSBAND:

    It must be clear,

    I don't come here as helper.

THE WOMAN:

    Forgive the blooming of a sudden dream.

THE HUSBAND:

    My threatened honour forced me here.

THE WOMAN:

    Am I the cause? How strange.

    Is it honour of the bourgeois class?

    Was it voted on? And does the majority

    Threaten to expel you from its ranks?

THE HUSBAND:

    I beg you, stop the joking.

    Respect, though strange to you, is law to me.

    For me the strict, objective code of honour holds...

THE WOMAN:

    And stamps you to a formula.

THE HUSBAND:

    Demands subordination, self-restraint...

    You have no sympathy for my words.

THE WOMAN:

    I see your eyes.

THE HUSBAND:
Don't confuse me.
THE WOMAN:
You…you…
THE HUSBAND:
To be brief,
I'm putting an end to your work.
THE WOMAN:
You…
THE HUSBAND:
The urge you feel for social service
Can find satisfaction in our circle too.
Namely: a home for children born out of wedlock.
This is a sensible field of work,
And testimony for the culture mocked by you.
Even your so-called worker-comrades
Despise unmarried mothers.
THE WOMAN:
Go on…go on…
THE HUSBAND:
You are not free in your actions.
THE WOMAN:
I am free…
THE HUSBAND:
I might assume a certain degree of respect,
If not from your sense, at least from your tact.
THE WOMAN:
I only have respect for the work,
The work I serve, the work, now hear, I must serve.
THE HUSBAND:
Let's analyse that:
A wish for public service determines your conduct –
A wish that's born from various motives.
Now far be it from my thoughts
To think these wishes base in nature.
THE WOMAN:
How much you hurt with every single word…
You know the pictures of Madonnas
Which hang in peasant huts?

Pierced by swords, their hearts are bleeding with dark tears.
Those prints so ugly, yet so movingly devout...
So simple-minded and so great...
You...you...
You spoke of wishes?
I know...a chasm is opening up between us...
It's not a wish that's changed my fate,
It was need...need from being human,
Need from deepest depths of me.
It's need that changes, hear me, need that changes me!
Not mood, not whim of idleness,
But need from being human changes me.

THE HUSBAND:

Need? Have you any right
To speak of need?

THE WOMAN:

Husband...you...let me be...
Now I hold your head...
Now I kiss your eyes...
You...
Speak no more...

THE HUSBAND:

Far be it from me to torment you...
This place... Can't we be overheard?

THE WOMAN:

So what if a comrade heard us,
They have tact and even without a code of honour.
If you could only understand them, only feel the breath
   of their need.
Need...which is...which must be...our own!
You degraded them...
Degrading thus your own dishonoured self,
You became your own true hangman...
Spare me the pity in your eyes!
I am not neurotic,
Not even sentimental.
And because I'm not, I belong to them.
Oh, the pitiful hours you devote to social service,
Appeasement caused by all that's vain and weak in you.

Plenty of comrades feel ashamed of you,
When they are not...laughing out loud at you...
See, like I am laughing now.

THE HUSBAND:

Then you should know the whole of the truth.
They know...the authorities know about you.
Wife... I swore allegiance to the State.
Staff security had to be informed,
Or else career advancement would be dead.

THE WOMAN:

And so...?

THE HUSBAND:

I tell you very bluntly,
I'll take the necessary steps,
And this, I assure you,
Will affect my feelings deeply...
Especially since, besides your husband's career,
You harm the welfare of the State...
You support the enemy within.
And thus you give me grounds for divorce.

THE WOMAN:

Then willingly...if I harm you,
If I stand obstructively in your way...

THE HUSBAND:

There is still time.

THE WOMAN:

Then willingly...
Then... I am ready...
I bear the blame...
Have no fear, the proceedings will not harm you.
You...
You...my arms are opening wide for you
In my great need.
You, my blood is in full bloom for you...
See, without you I become a withered leaf.
You are the dew unfolding me.
You are the mighty wind of March
Hurling torches in my thirsty veins...

What nights there were, and cries of thrusting boys
Rearing up in the ripeness of their blood...
Carry me off to fields and parks and woodland paths,
Meekly I shall kiss your eyes...
I think I shall be weak
Without you...boundlessly weak...
Forgive me, no, I've just been weak.
I see the matter clearly now, your conduct is justified.
Because, you see, tomorrow I shall stand before the Masses –
Tomorrow I shall speak to them.
Tomorrow, from off the State you swore allegiance to,
I shall tear the mask which hides the murderer's grimace.

THE HUSBAND:

Your conduct is treason to the State!

THE WOMAN:

Your State makes war,
Your State betrays the people!
Your State exploits, represses, oppresses,
Robs the people of their rights.

THE HUSBAND:

The State is sacred... War secures its life.
Peace is but a phantom of neurotics.
War is nothing but a broken truce of arms;
The State, so threatened by enemies without
And enemies within, perpetually lives by war.

THE WOMAN:

How can a body live devoured by plague and fire?
Have you seen the naked body of the State?
Have you seen the worms that gnaw upon its flesh?
Have you seen the Stock Exchanges getting fat
On human corpses?
You have not seen... I know you swore allegiance to
the State,
Do your duty and your conscience is clear.

THE HUSBAND:

Is this decision your last word?

THE WOMAN:

My last word.

THE HUSBAND:
Good night!
THE WOMAN:
Good night.
(*As THE HUSBAND starts to go.*)
May I go with you?
Now for one last time...
Or am I being shameless?
Or am I being shameless...
Shameless in my blood...
(*THE WOMAN follows THE HUSBAND.*)

The stage darkens.

SECOND PICTURE

(Dream Picture)

Indicated: Hall of the Stock Exchange. CLERK at the desk, around him BANKERS and BROKERS. CLERK: face of THE HUSBAND.

CLERK:
   I record.
FIRST BANKER:
   Weapon Works
   350.
SECOND BANKER:
   I raise the bid
   400.
THIRD BANKER:
   400
   I will sell.
   (*The FOURTH BANKER drags the THIRD BANKER forward. In the background a murmur of bidders and sellers.*)
FOURTH BANKER: (*To THIRD BANKER.*)
   Heard?
   Retreat
   Necessary.
   Great offensive
   Is going to fail.
THIRD BANKER:
   Reserves?
FOURTH BANKER:
   Manpower
   Is going bad.
THIRD BANKER:
   Nutrition not sufficient?
FOURTH BANKER:
   That too.
   Although
   Professor Ude

Thinks
That rye,
Ground pure
At 95 per cent,
Is a glutton's feast.
THIRD BANKER:
And leadership?
FOURTH BANKER:
Excellent.
THIRD BANKER:
Not enough alcohol?
FOURTH BANKER:
Distilleries
Are brewing
At full speed.
THIRD BANKER:
What is missing?
FOURTH BANKER:
The General
Has summoned 93 professors
To Headquarters.
And also our mastermind,
Councillor Gluber.
Results are rumoured.
THIRD BANKER:
Which are?
FOURTH BANKER:
To be covered up
In bourgeois spheres.
THIRD BANKER:
Does love between men
Weaken the soldiers?
FOURTH BANKER:
Strangely no.
Man hates man.
Something is missing.
THIRD BANKER:
Something is missing?...

FOURTH BANKER:
  The mechanism
  Of all life
  Has been revealed.
THIRD BANKER:
  Something is missing?
FOURTH BANKER:
  The Masses need lust.
THIRD BANKER:
  Something is missing?...
FOURTH BANKER:
  Sex.
THIRD BANKER:
  That is enough!
  And so the war,
  Our instrument,
  Our mighty, powerful instrument,
  Which causes Kings and States,
  Ministers and Parliaments,
  The Press and Church,
  Causes them to dance,
  Dance all over the globe,
  Dance all over the seas,
  That war is lost?
  Do you say it: lost?
  Is that the net result?
FOURTH BANKER:
  Your calculation is wrong.
  The source of error is found.
  And we shall make it good!
THIRD BANKER:
  By what?
FOURTH BANKER:
  In an international way.
THIRD BANKER:
  Will that be known?
FOURTH BANKER:
  Quite the reverse.
  It'll be dressed up as truly patriotic

And independent
Of foreign currency.
THIRD BANKER:
Well underwritten?
FOURTH BANKER:
A consortium of the biggest banks
Heads the enterprise
THIRD BANKER:
The profits?
The dividends?
FOURTH BANKER:
Regular distribution.
THIRD BANKER:
The form of the enterprise is sound.
But what about its content?
FOURTH BANKER:
The mask is Convalescent Home
For Strengthening the Will to Victory.
The content is:
Government Brothel.
THIRD BANKER:
Magnificent!
I subscribe for 100,000.
Another question,
Who will organise dynamics?
FOURTH BANKER:
Experienced generals,
The best authorities
On proven regulations.
THIRD BANKER:
Is a plan
Drawn up?
FOURTH BANKER:
As I just said,
According to regulations.
Three prices.
Three categories.
Brothel for officers:
Stay the night.

Brothel for N.C.O.'s:
Up to one hour.
Brothel for rank and file:
15 minutes.
THIRD BANKER:
My thanks.
When does trading begin?
FOURTH BANKER:
Any moment now.
(*Noise in the background.*
THIRD and FOURTH BANKER move to the back.)
CLERK:
Newly authorised:
National shares
Military Convalescent Home,
Limited.
FIRST BANKER:
I have no commission to buy.
SECOND BANKER:
The dividends don't attract me at all.
THIRD BANKER:
I subscribe for 100,000
At par.
CLERK:
I record.
FOURTH BANKER:
The same amount.
FIRST BANKER: (*To SECOND BANKER.*)
"Herr Cool" subscribes...
What do you think?...
SECOND BANKER:
Just now a telegram:
The battle on the Western Front
Is lost...
FIRST BANKER:
Gentlemen!
The battle on the Western Front is lost!
(*Cries, screams, shrieks.*)

VOICES:
Lost!
VOICE:
Weapon Works
On offer
At 150.
VOICE:
Flamethrower Trust
On offer.
VOICE:
War Prayer Books, Limited
On offer.
VOICE:
Poison Gas Works
On offer.
VOICE:
War Loans
On offer.
THIRD BANKER:
I subscribe for another
100,000.
VOICE:
Oh ho...
In such a slump?...
VOICE:
Who said the battle's lost?
VOICE:
Is it true, the news?
Or to rig the market?
"Herr Cool"
Subscribes for twice one hundred thousand.
SECOND BANKER:
Bear market!
I'll buy.
150.
VOICE:
I'll raise the bid.
200.

VOICE:

I'll buy.

300.

VOICE:

Who will offer?

400.

I'll buy.

CLERK:

I record.

FOURTH BANKER: (*To THIRD BANKER.*)

The sly fox guesses...

THIRD BANKER:

Forgive the question.

Our strongest instrument,

Is it saved?

FOURTH BANKER:

How can you have any doubts.

The mechanism of all life

Is very simple –

There was a leak...

Now it's discovered

And quickly plugged.

The slump

Or boom today

Is accidental.

This is the essential:

The mechanistic law is stable.

And this the consequence:

The system is saved.

CLERK:

I record.

(*THE COMPANION enters. His face, which bears a magic
resemblance to the face of THE WOMAN, is interwoven
with lines of death and lines of intensest life.
He leads THE WOMAN.*)

THE COMPANION:

Gentlemen,

You record too hastily.

Blood and system!

Man and system!

The proposition's flawed.

One kick

And the mechanism

Is a broken

Children's toy.

Take care!

(*To THE WOMAN.*)

You, speak!

THE WOMAN: (*Softly.*)

Gentlemen:

Human beings.

I repeat:

Human beings.

(*THE COMPANION and THE WOMAN fade out. Sudden*
silence.)

THIRD BANKER:

Did you hear?

A mine disaster,

It seems.

Human beings in need.

FOURTH BANKER:

I suggest:

A charity ball.

Dance

Around the Stock Exchange desk.

Dance

Against their need.

Proceeds

To the poor.

Gentlemen,

If you please,

A little dance.

I'll donate:

One share

In Military Convalescent Home,

Limited.

VOICE:

What about some girls?

FOURTH BANKER:

As many

As you like.

Let's order

From the porter:

Five hundred

Fancy girlies

Here!

Meanwhile…

THE BANKERS:

We will donate!

We will dance!

Proceeds

To the poor!

(*Music of clinking gold coins. THE BANKERS in top hats
dance a fox trot around the Stock Exchange desk.*)

The stage darkens.

THIRD PICTURE

The stage remains dark.

CHORUSES OF THE MASSES: (*As from afar.*)
> We, forever wedged
> In chasms of towering blocks.
> We, sacrificed
> To the mechanism of mocking systems.
> We, faceless in the night of tears.
> We, forever severed from our mothers,
> From the depths of the factories we cry out:
> When shall we live by love?
> When shall we do productive work?
> When will salvation come?
>> (*The stage brightens.*
>> *Indicated: The Great Hall.*
> *On the platform a long narrow table. THE WOMAN sits left.*
> *MEN and WOMEN WORKERS tightly packed in the hall.*)

GROUP OF YOUNG WOMEN WORKERS:
> No more toying with the bosses,
> No more wavering, no more feeble pacts.
> Orders for a band of comrades:
> Dynamite inside the machines.
> And tomorrow the factories are blown to pieces.
> Machines, they cram us together like slaughterhouse beasts,
> Machines, they crush us to death in their vices,
> Machines, they beat out our bodies daily
> Into rivets...and screws...
> Three millimetre screws...five millimetre screws,
> They dry up our eyes, they cause our hands to decay
> On our living bodies...
> Down with factories, down with machines!

SCATTERED CRIES IN THE HALL:
> Down with factories, down with machines!
>> (*At the table on the platform THE WOMAN rises.*)

THE WOMAN:
> I, too, once blind and assaulted
> By the torturing pistons of blood-sucking machines,

Desperately screamed that very cry.
It is a dream, which clouds your vision,
A dream of children terrified of night.
For see: We live in the twentieth-century.
The verdict is:
The factory cannot be destroyed.
Spread all the earth with dynamite,
And let one night of action blow up all the factories,
By next spring they will have risen up again,
Even more inhuman than before.
The factories must no longer be the bosses,
And human beings only the means.
Let the factories be the servants of a worthy life!
Let the soul of Man subdue the factories!

GROUP OF YOUNG MEN WORKERS:
Then both the factories and ourselves shall perish.
See, our words now whip themselves to rage and vengeance.
The bosses build their palaces,
While our brothers rot in trenches.
And dance springs up and meadows, merry games,
At night we read about such things and weep!
A yearning for knowledge lives in us...
They took our highest aim
And it turned evil.
Yet sometimes in the theatre it leaps out to us
So tender...and so beautiful...it mocks our plight.
They destroyed our youth in schools,
In schools they broke our souls.
Pure and simple need is what we cry...
Need that reeks corrosive fumes!
What are we now?
We *will* not wait!

A GROUP OF FARM WORKERS:
They dispossessed us of our mother earth,
Rich bosses buy the land like buying whores,
Philandering with our gracious mother earth
And forcing our rough arms to work in munition factories.
Uprooted from our soil, we sicken to death,

As joyless cities break our strength.
We want the land!
Land for all!
MASSES IN THE HALL:
Land for all!
THE WOMAN:
I went throughout the tenements.
Grey rain was dripping through the shingle roofs,
And fungus sprouted on the damp of shabby walls.
I found a room where an invalid sat
And stuttered: "Outside was almost better...
Here we live in sties like pigs...
Isn't it true...in sties like pigs?"
And a smile so shameful slipped from his eyes
That I too felt ashamed along with him.
Brothers, do you want to know the one way out?
There is one way out for us, the weak,
For us who hate all guns.
Strike! No handstroke more.
Our action is strike!
We, the weak, will be rocks of strength,
We will break our chains non-violently,
No weapon made can conquer us.
Call our mute battalions!
I call Strike!
Hear me:
I call Strike!
For six long years now Moloch gorges on our flesh,
Pregnant women are collapsing in the streets,
So hungry they no longer have the strength
To bear the burden of their unborn.
In your hovels need stares you down,
And raging diseases, madness, hunger, gnawing hunger.
But there, look over there:
The Stock Exchange is spewing up wild orgies,
Hard-won victories are drowned in champagne,
And the itch of lust performs its dance
Around the golden altars. And at the front?

Do you see the sallow faces of your brothers?
Do you feel their bodies
Clammy in the evening's
Damp and freezing frost?
Do you smell their breath's decay?
Do you hear the screams? I ask.
Do you hear the cry?
"Now your turn has come!
We who are chained to the barrels of guns,
We who are powerless,
We cry out to you:
You! Be our helper!
You: be our bridge!"
Hear me! I call Strike!
Whoever keeps feeding the munition plant
Betrays his brother. Did I say: betrays?
He murders his own brother.
And you, you women!
Do you know the legend of those wives
Forever stricken barren
For forging weapons of war?
Think of your men at the front!
I call Strike!

MASSES IN THE HALL:

We call Strike!
We call
Strike!

> (*From the midst of the MASSES IN THE HALL,*
> *THE NAMELESS hurries*
> *to the platform, stands to the right of the table.*)

THE NAMELESS:

Whoever wants to build a bridge,
Must first take care of the piers.
A strike today is bridgework with no piers.
We need much more than a strike.
Suppose the best result:
With a strike you force a peace,
A *one-time* peace.

You only make a pause. No more.
War must end
For all eternity!
But first a final, ruthless struggle!
What use is it to end the war?
When the peace you make
Will leave your lot unchanged.
Either a mask of peace and a lot that's old!
Or struggle and a lot that's new!
You fools, smash the foundations,
Smash the foundations! I call.
Then let the deluge come
And wash away the rotten house
Which only gold chains protect from collapse.
We will build a more liveable system.
The factories belong to the workers
And not to Master Capital.
Gone is the time when he climbed our bent backs
And greedily searched for faraway treasure,
When he plotted wars to enslave foreign peoples
And got dirty journalist liars to screech
"For the Fatherland! For the Fatherland!"
Although the true refrain could always be heard:
"For me! For me!"
Gone is the time!
The Masses of all lands have only one cry:
The factories belong to the workers!
Power belongs to the workers!
All is for all!
I call much more than a strike!
I call: War!
I call: Revolution!
Our enemy on high
Won't listen to pretty speeches.
Power against power!
Violence against violence!
A VOICE:
Weapons!

THE NAMELESS:

    Yes, weapons are all you need!

    Storm the town hall and take them yourselves!

    Our battle cry is victory!

THE WOMAN:

    Hear me!

    I will not...

THE NAMELESS:

    Be silent, comrade!

    Handshakes, prayers and passionate pleas

    Will not beget any children.

    Consumptives are not cured with watery soup,

    It takes an axe to cut down trees.

THE WOMAN:

    Hear me...

    I will not have fresh murder.

THE NAMELESS:

    Be silent, comrade.

    What do you know?

    You feel our need, I grant you that.

    But have you worked in the mines for ten hours long,

    Leaving your children like waifs in windowless rooms?

    Ten hours long in the mines, all night long in those rooms,

    Such is the daily lot of the Masses.

    You are not Masses!

    I am Masses!

    Masses are fate!

MASSES IN THE HALL:

    Are fate...

THE WOMAN:

    Just think for a moment,

    Masses are powerless.

    Masses are weak.

THE NAMELESS:

    How far you are from the truth!

    Masses are leader!

    Masses are strength!

MASSES IN THE HALL:

    Are strength.

THE WOMAN:

    Feeling urges me darkly,

    But my conscience cries out: No!

THE NAMELESS:

    Be silent, comrade!

    For the cause.

    What does the individual count?

    His feeling,

    His conscience?

    The Masses count.

    Reflect: a single bloody struggle,

    Then eternal peace.

    No fancy mask of peace, as in the past,

    With war beneath the shell,

    War of the strong against the weak,

    War of exploitation, war of greed.

    Reflect: Misery shall cease!

    Reflect: Crimes shall turn to fairy tales,

    And freedom shine on all the peoples come the dawn!

    You think I give unsound advice?

    War is necessity for us.

    Your words will bring dissension,

    For the sake of the cause

    Be silent.

THE WOMAN:

    You…are… Masses

    You…are…right.

THE NAMELESS:

    Comrades, the piers for the bridge are laid!

    If anyone stands in our way, he shall be trampled down!

    Masses are action!

MASSES IN THE HALL: (*Storming out.*)

    Action!!!

The stage darkens.

FOURTH PICTURE

(Dream Picture)

Indicated: Prison yard surrounded by high walls. Night.
In the middle of the prison yard on the ground, a lantern which
weeps a faint light.
From the corners of the courtyard WORKER-GUARDS appear.

FIRST GUARD: *(Sings.)*
> My old mum,
> She bore me
> In a dirty trench.
> Lalala la
> Hm, Hm,

SECOND GUARD:
> My old dad,
> He lost me
> In a drunken clench.
> Lalala la
> Hm, Hm,

THIRD GUARD:
> Three long years,
> I'm locked up
> In the prison stench.
> Lalala la
> Hm, Hm,

> *(From somewhere, THE NAMELESS approaches with ghostly,*
> *noiseless steps.*
> *Stands beside the lantern.)*

FIRST GUARD:
> My old dad,
> He forgot
> To give us maintenance pay.

ALL THE GUARDS:
> Lalala la
> Hm, Hm,

SECOND GUARD:

    My old mum,

    She's in pain,

    She's on the game they say.

ALL THE GUARDS:

    Lalala la.

    Hm, Hm,

THIRD GUARD:

    And me, I rattled

    The bourgeoisie

    On the king's election day.

ALL THE GUARDS:

    Lalala, la

    Hm, Hm.

THE NAMELESS:

    Begin the dance!

    I'll start to play!

THE GUARDS:

    Halt!

    Who are you?

THE NAMELESS:

    Did I ask you

    For your names,

    You, the nameless?

THE GUARD:

    Password?

THE NAMELESS:

    Masses are nameless!

THE GUARDS:

    Are nameless.

    He's one of us.

THE NAMELESS:

    I'll start to play.

    I, the herald

    Of decision.

        (*THE NAMELESS begins to play a concertina.*

    In rousing rhythms, at times sensuously swaying, at times

                stormily passionate.

*THE CONDEMNED MAN, with a rope around his neck,
steps out of the darkness.)*

THE CONDEMNED MAN:

In the name
Of those condemned
To death:
We beg a final
Favour:
Invite us to dance.
Dance is the core
Of things.
Life,
Born from dance,
Compels
To dance,
The dance of desire,
The dance of death
Of time.

THE GUARDS:

The final request
Of those condemned
Must always
Be fulfilled:
You are invited.

THE NAMELESS:

Come here!
Allegiance
Makes no difference.

THE CONDEMNED MAN: (*Calls into the darkness.*)

All those condemned
To death
Line up!
For the final dance!
Leave your ready
Coffins behind.

(*The CONDEMNED, with ropes around their necks,
appear out of the darkness.
GUARDS and CONDEMNED dance around THE
NAMELESS.*)

THE GUARDS: (*Singing.*)
>She bore me
>In a dirty trench.
>>(*They go on dancing. After a short pause.*)
>He lost me
>In a drunken clench.
>>(*They go on dancing. After a short pause.*)
>I'm locked up
>In the prison stench.
>>(*They go on dancing.*
>>*THE NAMELESS suddenly stops. The WHORES and*
>>*THE CONDEMNED TO DEATH*
>>*run into a corner of the prison yard. Night swallows them.*
>>*The GUARDS take up their posts.*
>>*Silence gathers around THE NAMELESS.*
>>*THE COMPANION in the figure of a GUARD, has*
>>*stepped through the wall.*
>>*He holds a woman (face of THE WOMAN) tightly.*)

THE COMPANION:
>Long and hard
>The journey.
>This effect
>Rewards the toil.
>Look over there:
>Just now
>The play's beginning.
>If the melodrama tempts you,
>Take a part.
>>(*A GUARD brings in THE PRISONER (face of THE*
>>*HUSBAND)*
>>*and leads him to THE NAMELESS.*)

THE NAMELESS:
>Condemned
>By the tribunal?

A GUARD:
>Sentenced himself
>To death.
>He shot at us.

THE PRISONER:
>Death?

THE NAMELESS:

Are you afraid?

Listen:

Guard! Answer me!

Who taught us

The death sentence?

Who gave us weapons?

Uttered "hero" and "good deed"?

Who sanctified the violence?

THE GUARD:

Schools.

Barracks.

War.

Always.

THE NAMELESS:

Violence... Violence.

Why did you shoot?

THE PRISONER:

I swore

Allegiance to the State.

THE NAMELESS:

You die

For your cause.

THE GUARDS:

Up against the wall!

THE NAMELESS:

Rifles loaded?

THE GUARDS:

Loaded...

THE PRISONER: (*At the wall.*)

Life!

Life!

(*THE WOMAN tears herself free from THE COMPANION.*)

THE WOMAN:

Do not shoot!

He is my husband!

Forgive him,

As I forgive him humbly.

Forgiving is so strong
And beyond all struggle.

THE NAMELESS:

Do they
Forgive us?

THE WOMAN:

Do they struggle
For the people?
Do they struggle
For mankind?

THE NAMELESS:

Only the Masses count.

THE GUARDS:

Up against the wall!

A GUARD:

Forgiving is cowardice.
I escaped just yesterday
From our enemies over there.
They stood me up against the wall.
Whipped my body raw.
Next to me the man
Who was meant
To shoot me down.
I had to dig
My own grave
With my own hands.
In front of us
A photographer,
Greedy
To brand his plates
With murder.
I shit
On the revolution,
If we let
Mocking murderers
Make monkeys
Out of us.
I shit
On the revolution!

THE GUARDS:

Up against the wall!

(*The face of THE PRISONER changes into that of a GUARD.
THE WOMAN addresses the previous GUARD.*)

THE WOMAN:

Yesterday you stood

Up against the wall.

Now you stand

Up against the wall again.

You are he

Who today

Stands up against the wall.

Man,

You are he.

Know yourself:

You are he.

A GUARD:

Only the Masses count.

THE WOMAN:

Only Man counts.

ALL THE GUARDS:

Only the Masses count.

THE WOMAN:

I give

Myself...

To all...

(*Lewd laughter from THE GUARDS.
Stands beside THE HUSBAND.*)

Then shoot!

I give up!...

I am so tired...

The stage darkens.

FIFTH PICTURE

Indicated: The Hall.
Grey dawn creeps through the window. Platform lit by gloomy light.
At the long table THE WOMAN sits left, THE NAMELESS right.
At the doors of the Hall WORKER-GUARDS. In the Hall
MEN and WOMEN WORKERS huddle scattered at tables.

THE WOMAN:

    Has any news come through in this last hour?

    I fell asleep, forgive me, Comrade.

THE NAMELESS:

    Report comes upon report.

    Struggle is struggle,

    A bloody game of force demanding cool deliberation.

    By twelve we occupied the railway station.

    Near one o'clock we lost it.

    Our battalions now are mounting

    A new attack.

    The post office is in our hands.

    And at this very moment

    Telegrams proclaim our work to all the peoples.

THE WOMAN:

    Our work! What a holy word!

THE NAMELESS:

    A holy word, Comrade!

    It calls for mighty armour!

    It calls for more than passionate speech.

    It calls for ruthless struggle.

        (For seconds long, a flickering silence in the Hall.)

THE WOMAN:

    Comrade, in the end I cannot overcome it.

    Struggle with weapons of steel is brutal rape.

THE NAMELESS:

    Struggle with spiritual weapons too is brutal rape.

    Yes, every speech is brutal rape. –

    Don't be so startled, Comrade,

    I grasp the naked facts.

If I thought like you, I would become a monk
And join the monastery of eternal silence.
  (*Silence is about to descend heavily upon the Hall.*
  FIRST WORKER enters.)

FIRST WORKER:
  I bring the report.
  We advanced three times against the station.
  The square is writhing with the dead.
  They are well entrenched out there,
  Armed with every kind of weapon,
  With flame-throwers, mines and poison gas.

THE NAMELESS:
  You advanced three times.
  And on the fourth?

FIRST WORKER:
  There never was a fourth,
  They mounted an attack.

THE NAMELESS:
  You held your ground.
  Do you need some reinforcements?

FIRST WORKER:
  We've been routed.

THE NAMELESS:
  Setbacks are to be expected.
  Listen – go to the thirteenth district,
  There you'll find reserves.
  Go – hurry up!

                          (*WORKER goes.*)

THE WOMAN:
  He spoke of the dead.
  Many hundreds.
  I cried out against all war just yesterday!
  And yet today... I allow
  My brothers to be flung to death! –

THE NAMELESS:
  Your view is not clear,
  We were slaves in yesterday's war.

THE WOMAN:
  And today?

THE NAMELESS:

We are free in the war of today.

(*Silence is feverish.*)

THE WOMAN:

In...both these wars...human beings...

In...both these wars...human beings...

(*Silence staggers.*

SECOND WORKER bursts in.)

SECOND WORKER:

Post office lost!

Our men in retreat!

Enemy shows no mercy.

Prisoners' fate is death.

(*FIRST WORKER hurries in.*)

FIRST WORKER:

I come from the thirteenth district,

Efforts useless.

Streets blockaded.

The district has given up.

They're surrendering their weapons.

THIRD WORKER:

The city is lost!

Our work has failed!

THE WOMAN:

It had to fail...

THE NAMELESS:

Once more: Be silent, Comrade!

Our work, it has not failed.

Today our force was just too weak,

Tomorrow new battalions roar.

FOURTH WORKER: (*Screams into the Hall.*)

They're advancing!

Horrific slaughter. My wife was shot,

My father shot!

THE NAMELESS:

They died for the Masses.

Build the barricades!

Now we are defenders!

Our blood is pregnant with struggle!
Let them come!
(*WORKERS storm into the Hall.*)

FIFTH WORKER:

They're slaughtering everyone.
Men and women and children.
We must not surrender,
They will kill us like captive cattle.
They're slaughtering everyone, we must resist!
International law protects their foreign enemies,
But us they murder like savage beasts that escaped,
Setting bounties on our skins. –
But we have weapons in our hands.
And we have bourgeois prisoners too.
I ordered half to be shot,
And then the other half, if storm troops attack.

THE NAMELESS:

You revenge your brothers.
Masses are revenge for the injustice of centuries.
Masses are revenge.

THE WORKERS:

Are revenge!

THE WOMAN:

Halt, you're crazy from struggle!
I have to make you stop.
Masses should be a people bound by love.
Masses should be community.
Community is not revenge.
Community destroys the foundations of injustice.
Community plants the forests of justice.
Man revenging himself will smash himself. –
Half of them shot!
That action isn't self-defence.
Blind rage! not service to our work.
You kill human beings.
Do you kill with them the spirit of the State
You struggle against?
I will protect the men outside.

I was prepared
To cripple my conscience
For the sake of the Masses.
I cry:
Smash the system!
But you, you want to smash human beings.
I cannot be silent, not today.
Those outside are human beings,
Born in the blood of groaning mothers...
Human beings, forever brothers...

THE NAMELESS:

One last time: Be silent, Comrade!
Violence... Violence...
The men out there won't spare our flesh.
This bitter struggle can't be won
By pious looks.
Don't listen to this woman.
With her petticoat prattle.

THE WOMAN:

I cry: Halt!
And you...who...are...you?
Does unchained lust for power,
Caged for centuries, drive you on?
Who...are...you?
God...who...are...you?
Murderer...or... Saviour?
Murderer...or... Saviour...?
Oh Nameless One: What face?
You are...?

THE NAMELESS:

Masses!

THE WOMAN:

You... Masses!
I cannot bear you!
I will protect the men outside.
For many years I've been your fellow-traveller.
I know...you've suffered more than I...
I grew up in bright and happy rooms,

Never suffered hunger,
Never heard the lunatic laugh of rotting wallpaper.
Still – I feel with you
And know about you.
See, I come as a begging child.
In all humility.
Listen to me:
Smash the foundations of injustice,
Smash the chains of secret slavery,
But also destroy the weapons of a rotten age.
Destroy all hate! Destroy revenge!
Revenge is not the will to transformation,
Revenge is not the revolution,
Revenge is the axe which splits
The crystal, glowing,
Angry, iron will to revolution.

THE NAMELESS:

How dare you, woman of your class,
Poison the hour of decision?
I hear you sing a very different song:
You're protecting those who grew up with you.
That's your deeper motive,
You are betrayal.

MASSES IN THE HALL: (*Crowd threateningly around THE WOMAN.*)

Betrayal!

CRY:

Intellectual!

CRY:

Up against the wall with her!

THE NAMELESS:

Your protection is betrayal.
The hour calls for action,
Ruthless action.
Those not with us are against us.
Masses must live.

MASSES IN THE HALL:

Must live.

THE NAMELESS:

    You are under arrest.

THE WOMAN:

    I'm...protecting...those...who grew up with me?

    No, I'm protecting you!

    You yourselves are standing up against the wall!

    I protect our souls!

    I protect mankind, eternal mankind.

    Crazed accuser...

    Fear in my words...

    Never stooped so low...

    I chose...

    You lie...you lie...

             (*A WORKER enters the Hall.*)

WORKER:

    One of our prisoners yelps like a dog,

    Goes on and on with the same dumb yelp.

    He wants our leader!

THE NAMELESS:

    Proof.

THE WOMAN:

    Once more...you lie... –

    Who wants to speak to me...who?

    Perhaps my husband.

    I never could betray you for his sake...

    It's you now, you betray yourselves...

    I know no more...

     (*THE NAMELESS leaves the platform, plunges into the*

              MASSES IN THE HALL.

          From outside WORKERS press in.)

WORKERS:

    Lost.

CRIES:

    Escape! Struggle!

    (*Outside scattered shots. The WORKERS flock to the door.*)

CRIES:

    The door is barred.

    Trapped like hares!

(*Silence of awaiting death.*)

CRIES:

Death!

(*Someone begins to sing 'The Internationale'.
The others join in. Powerfully.*)

SONG:

Awake, ye wretched of the earth,
All ye enchained by bitter plight,
To our new rights the depths give birth.
The dawn is nigh, the torch is bright.
The way stands clear, come take the crown,
Arise, ye Masses, seize the hour:
The world needs turning upside down,
We slaves shall grasp the reins of power.
People, hear the call,
Join with us, the die is cast,
The Internationale
Fights to free the world at last.

(*Suddenly short bursts of machine-gun fire.
The song breaks up, main door and side doors are forced open.
SOLDIERS with weapons levelled stand at each door.*)

OFFICER:

Resistance is useless!
Hands up!
Hands up, I order you.
Where is your leader?
Why don't you put your hands up?
Put the shackles on her.

(*SOLDIERS shackle THE WOMAN.*)

The stage darkens.

SIXTH PICTURE

(Dream Picture)

Boundless space.
In its core, a cage, lit by a flickering shaft of light.
Inside crouching down, THE SHACKLED PRISONER (face of
THE WOMAN).
Next to the cage, THE COMPANION in the
figure of THE WARDER.

THE SHACKLED:
Where
Am I?
THE WARDER:
In
The morgue of mankind.
THE SHACKLED:
Drive away the shadows.
THE WARDER:
Drive them away yourself.
(*From somewhere, a grey shadow without a head.*)
FIRST SHADOW:
Recognise me? I was shot.
You murderer!
THE SHACKLED:
I am not
Guilty.
(*From somewhere, a second grey shadow without a head.*)
SECOND SHADOW:
You murderer
Of me, too.
THE SHACKLED:
You lie.
(*From somewhere, grey shadows without heads.*)
THIRD SHADOW:
Murderer
Of me.

FOURTH SHADOW:
>And me.

FIFTH SHADOW:
>And me.

SIXTH SHADOW:
>And me.

THE SHACKLED:
>Warder!
>Warder!

THE WARDER:
>Haha! Hahahaha!

THE SHACKLED:
>I did not want
>Bloodshed.

FIRST SHADOW:
>You were silent.

SECOND SHADOW:
>Silent at the storming
>Of the town hall.

THIRD SHADOW:
>Silent at the theft
>Of weapons.

FOURTH SHADOW:
>Silent throughout the struggle.

FIFTH SHADOW:
>Silent at the calling up
>Of reserves.

SIXTH SHADOW:
>You are guilty.

ALL SHADOWS:
>You are guilty.

THE SHACKLED:
>I wanted
>To save
>The others
>From shooting.

FIRST SHADOW:
>Don't deceive yourself.
>They had already
>Shot us down.

ALL SHADOWS:
>You murderer
>Of all of us.

THE SHACKLED:
>So I am...

THE SHADOWS:
>Guilty!
>Three times guilty!

THE SHACKLED:
>I...am...guilty...
>
>(*The shadows fade out. From somewhere BANKERS, in top hats.*)

FIRST BANKER:
>Shares in guilt,
>I offer
>At par.

SECOND BANKER:
>Shares in guilt
>No longer
>Authorised.

THIRD BANKER:
>Bad speculation!
>Shares in guilt,
>Scraps of paper.

THE THREE BANKERS:
>Shares in guilt
>To be entered as a loss.
>
>(*THE SHACKLED rises.*)

THE SHACKLED:
>I...am...guilty.
>
>(*The BANKERS fade out.*)

THE WARDER:
>You fool,
>With your sentimental
>Way of life.
>Were they alive,
>They would dance
>Around the golden altar,

Where thousands were sacrificed.
And also you.
THE SHACKLED:
I, as Man, am guilty.
THE WARDER:
Masses are guilt.
THE SHACKLED:
So then I am doubly
Guilty.
THE WARDER:
Life is guilt.
THE SHACKLED:
So then I had to
Become guilty?
THE WARDER:
Everyone lives his own life.
Everyone dies his own death.
Man,
Like plant and tree,
Is a pre-enstamped
And fate-bound form,
Which in its becoming unfolds itself
And in its becoming destroys itself.
Struggle to find the answer for yourself!
Life is all that is.
(*From somewhere, PRISONERS in convict clothes appear
at intervals of five paces.
Pointed caps on their heads, to which cloth rags with eye
slits are attached, covering their faces.
On the breast of each prisoner a number.
They move in a monotonous rhythm noiselessly around the
cage in a square.*)
THE SHACKLED:
Who are you?
Numbers!
Faceless!
Who are you?
Masses
Of the faceless?

MUFFLED ECHO FROM AFAR:
  Masses...
THE SHACKLED:
  God!!
RECEDING ECHO:
  Masses...

  (*Silence drips.*)

THE SHACKLED: (*Screaming out.*)
  Masses are Must!
  Masses are guiltless!
THE WARDER:
  Man is guiltless!
THE SHACKLED:
  God is guilty!
ECHO FROM AFAR:
  Guilty...
  Guilty...
  Guilty...
THE WARDER:
  God is in you.
THE SHACKLED:
  Then I will overcome this God.
THE WARDER:
  Maggot!
  You are desecrating God!
THE SHACKLED:
  Am I desecrating
  God?
  Or is God
  Desecrating
  Man?
  Oh monstrous
  Law of guilt,
  In which
  Man upon man
  Must be ensnared.
  Put God
  On trial!
  I accuse.

ECHO FROM AFAR:
> God on trial.
> To justice.
>> (*The pacing PRISONERS stand still. Their arms jerk*
>> *upwards.*)

THE PRISONERS:
> We accuse.
>> (*THE PRISONERS fade out.*)

THE WARDER:
> You are healed,
> Come out
> From the cage.

THE PRISONER:
> Am I free?

THE WARDER:
> Unfree!
> Free!

The stage darkens.

SEVENTH PICTURE

Indicated: Prison cell.
Small table, bench and iron bed fixed into the wall.
Small barred window with opaque milk-glass.
THE WOMAN sits at the table.

THE WOMAN:

Oh path through field of ripening wheat
In August days...
Wandering at dawn in wintry mountains...
Oh tiny beetles in the breath of noon...
Oh world...
> (*Silence spreads softly around THE WOMAN.*)

Did I desire a child?
> (*Silence pulses.*)

Oh schism of all life,
Forged to husband and forged to our work.
To husband...to foe...
To foe?
Forged to foe?
Forged to myself?
Please let him come... I need confirmation.
> (*The cell is unlocked. THE HUSBAND enters.*)

THE HUSBAND:

Wife... I come.
Come, because you call.

THE WOMAN:

Husband...!
Husband...

THE HUSBAND:

I bring good news for you,
No longer can the gutters void their filth
At will on your...on my good name.
The investigation of the murderers
Proved you guiltless of the crime of shooting.
Courage, your death sentence has not yet been confirmed.
In spite of your crime against the state, all right-thinking
People respect your noble and honourable motives.

THE WOMAN: (*Cries softly.*)

    I am guiltless...

    I am guiltless guilty...

THE HUSBAND:

    You are guiltless.

    To the right-thinking that is certain.

THE WOMAN:

    To the right-thinking...

    I am so hurt...

    And glad your name is not besmirched...

THE HUSBAND:

    I knew that you were guiltless.

THE WOMAN:

    Yes...you knew...

    Respect for motives...so respectable you are...

    I see you now so...clearly...

    And you are guilty... Husband,

    You... Guilty of murder!

THE HUSBAND:

    Wife, I came to you...

    Wife...your word is hate.

THE WOMAN:

    Hate? Not hate,

    I love you... I love you deeply in my blood.

THE HUSBAND:

    I warned you of the Masses

    To churn up Masses is to churn up hell.

THE WOMAN:

    Hell? Who made this hell?

    Who found the torture rack of your golden mills

    Which grind and grind out profit day by day?

    Who built the prisons...who spoke of "holy war"?

    Who sacrificed the millions of human bodies

    On the altar of a lying game of numbers?

    Who drove the Masses into rotten hovels

    So that today they're loaded with the filth of yesterday,

    Who robbed our brothers of a human face,

    Who forced them to be mechanisms,

Degraded them to cogs in your machines?
The State!... You!...

THE HUSBAND:

Duty is my life.

THE WOMAN:

Oh yes...duty...duty to the State.
You are...respectable...
As I said, I see you now so clearly:
You are respectable.
You go tell the right-thinking,
They were never right...
They are guilty...
All of us are guilty...
Yes, I am guilty...guilty for myself,
Guilty for Man.

THE HUSBAND:

I came to you.
Is there a tribunal here?

THE WOMAN:

Now there is a tribunal here.
I, the accused, am also the judge.
I accuse...and I find guilty,
And I acquit...
And the final guilt...?
Can you divine...who bears the final guilt?
All human beings must desire action,
And action must turn red with human blood.
All human beings must desire life,
And round them rises a sea of human blood.
Can you divine...who bears the final guilt?...
Come and give your hand to me,
Beloved of my blood.
I have overcome myself...
Myself and you.

(*THE HUSBAND trembles. A sudden gushing thought distorts
his face.*

He staggers out.)

Give your hand to me...
Give your hand to me, my brother,

You also are my brother. –
You have gone…you had to go…
The final journey leads across the snowfield.
The final journey knows no companion.
The final journey is without a mother.
The final journey is in loneliness.
  (*The door is opened. THE NAMELESS enters.*)
THE NAMELESS:
 Cured of all delusion? Illusion all dispersed?
 Has the pointed dagger of insight pierced your heart?
 Did the judge say "Man" and "I forgive you"?
 It was a healthy lesson for you.
 I applaud your conversion. Now you're ours again.
THE WOMAN:
 You? Who sends you?
THE NAMELESS:
 The Masses.
THE WOMAN:
 They haven't forgotten me?
 The message…the message…
THE NAMELESS:
 My order is to free you.
THE WOMAN:
 Free me!
 Life!
 We'll escape? Is all prepared?
THE NAMELESS:
 Two warders have been bribed.
 The third one I'll strike down at the gate.
THE WOMAN:
 Strike down… For my sake…?
THE NAMELESS:
 For the sake of the cause.
THE WOMAN:
 I have no right
 To gain my life by the warder's death.
THE NAMELESS:
 The Masses have a right to you.

THE WOMAN:

> And the right of the warder?
> The warder is Man.

THE NAMELESS:

> As yet there is no "Man".
> Only men of the Masses here!
> And men of the State over there!

THE WOMAN:

> Man is naked Man.

THE NAMELESS:

> Masses are holy.

THE WOMAN:

> Masses are not holy.
> Violence made the Masses.
> Dispossession made the Masses.
> Masses are instinct born from need,
> Devout submissiveness...
> Brutal revenge...
> Blinded slavery...
> Pious will...
> Masses are a trampled field,
> Masses are a trapped and buried people.

THE NAMELESS:

> And action?

THE WOMAN:

> Action! And more than action!
> Man in Masses must be freed,
> Community in Masses must be freed.

THE NAMELESS:

> The bitter wind outside the gate
> Will cure you.
> Hurry,
> Only minutes left.

THE WOMAN:

> You are not our freedom,
> You are not salvation.
> I know who you are.
> "Strike down!" Always you strike down!
> Your father's name is War.

You are his bastard son.
You are the wretched head of all the hangmen now
With only a single cure: "Death! Exterminate!"
Throw off your cloak of lofty words,
It's become a paper web of lies.

THE NAMELESS:

The murderer Generals fought for the State!

THE WOMAN:

They murdered, but not for pleasure.
They believed in their mission the same as you.

THE NAMELESS:

They struggled for the oppressor State,
We struggle for mankind.

THE WOMAN:

You murder for mankind,
As they, deluded, murdered for their State.
And there were even some who thought
That through their State, their Fatherland,
They could save the earth.
I see no difference:
Some will murder for a single land,
And others for all the lands.
Some will murder for thousands of men,
And others for millions of men.
Anyone who's murdered for the State,
You call a hangman.
Anyone who murders for mankind,
You crown with wreaths and call him kind,
Moral, noble, great.
Yes, you even speak of good and holy violence.

THE NAMELESS:

Accuse others, accuse life!
Should I let more millions be enslaved
Because their enslavers claim the best intentions?
And will you be less guilty
If you are silent.

THE WOMAN:

The torch of lurid violence will not show the way.
You lead us to a strange new land,

The land of ancient human slavery.
If fate has thrust you forward in these times,
And promised you the power
To terrorise the desperate souls
Who yearn for you to be their newest saviour,
Then I know: this fate hates Man.

THE NAMELESS:

Only the Masses count, not Man.
You are not our hero or our leader.
Each one bears the disease of his own origin,
You the birthmarks of the bourgeois class:
Self-deception and weakness.

THE WOMAN:

You have no love for Man.

THE NAMELESS:

Our teachings above all else!
I love the men of the future!

THE WOMAN:

Man above all else!
For the sake of your teachings
You sacrifice
The men of here and now.

THE NAMELESS:

For the sake of our teachings I must sacrifice them.
But you betray the Masses, you betray the cause.
Now is the time for decision.
Whoever wavers and takes no decision
Supports the bosses who oppress us all,
Supports the bosses who let us starve,
And is our foe.

THE WOMAN:

I would betray the Masses,
If I demanded the life of a Man.
He who acts may only sacrifice himself.
Hear: no Man may kill another Man
For the sake of a cause.
Unholy the cause which makes that demand.
Whoever demands human blood for the sake of a cause
Is Moloch:

God was Moloch.

State was Moloch.

Masses were Moloch.

THE NAMELESS:

And who is holy?

THE WOMAN:

Some day...

Community...

A free people united in work...

A free mankind united in work...

Work – People.

THE NAMELESS:

You lack the courage to undertake action,

Hard and ruthless action.

A free people only comes to be through ruthless action.

Atone through death.

Perhaps your death will be of use to us.

THE WOMAN:

I live forever.

THE NAMELESS:

You live too soon.

(THE NAMELESS leaves the cell.)

THE WOMAN:

Yesterday you lived.

Today you live.

And tomorrow you are dead.

But I shall be forever,

From cycle to cycle,

From change to change,

And some day

I shall be

A purer,

More guiltless

Mankind.

(THE PRIEST enters.)

THE PRIEST:

I come to ease your final hours.

Even a criminal is not denied the refuge of the church.

THE WOMAN:

On whose orders?

THE PRIEST:

The State authorities instructed me.

THE WOMAN:

Where were you on the day of the trial?

Go away!...

THE PRIEST:

God forgives even you. I know about you.

Man is good – or so you dreamed

And sowed so many nameless crimes

Against the holy order of the holy State.

Man is evil from his birth.

THE WOMAN:

Man *wants* to be good.

THE PRIEST:

That's the lie of collapsing times,

Born from decay, despair and flight,

Protected by the waxy shell

Of begged and borrowed faith,

Yet threatened by bad conscience.

Man, believe me, doesn't ever *want* to be good.

THE WOMAN:

He *wants* to be good. Even when he's doing evil

He wears the mask of doing good.

THE PRIEST:

Peoples arise, peoples decay,

Earth has never seen a paradise.

THE WOMAN:

I believe.

THE PRIEST:

Remember:

The earthly rhythm: Greed for power! Greed for lust!

THE WOMAN:

I believe!!

THE PRIEST:

All earthly life is eternal change of forms.

Mankind is always helpless. Salvation rests in God alone.

THE WOMAN:

I believe!!!

I'm freezing... Go away!

Go away!

(*THE PRIEST leaves the cell. THE OFFICER enters.*)

THE OFFICER:

Here's the verdict.

Mitigating circumstances recognised.

Nevertheless. Crime against the State demands atonement.

THE WOMAN:

You will have me shot?

THE OFFICER:

Orders are orders. Obedience, obedience.

State interests. Law. Order.

Duty of an officer.

THE WOMAN:

And of Man?

THE OFFICER:

All conversation is forbidden.

Orders are orders.

THE WOMAN:

I am ready.

(*THE OFFICER and THE WOMAN go out. For a few
seconds the cell is empty.
Two female PRISONERS in convict dress scurry in.
They stand by the door.*)

FIRST PRISONER:

Did you see the officer? Such a golden uniform!

SECOND PRISONER:

I saw the coffin. In the washroom. Yellow wooden box.

(*The FIRST PRISONER sees bread lying on the table,
pounces on it.*)

FIRST PRISONER:

There, bread! Hunger! Hunger! Hunger!

SECOND PRISONER:

Me bread! Me bread! Me bread!

FIRST PRISONER:

There, mirror! Oh, how pretty.

Hide it. At night. Cell.

SECOND PRISONER:
> There, silk scarf.
>
> Bare breast, silk scarf.
>
> Hide it. At night. Cell.
>
> (*The sharp crack of a gun volley from outside rips through the cell. The PRISONERS thrust out their hands spread wide in fright. The FIRST PRISONER searches for the mirror hidden in her skirt. Hurriedly puts it back on the table. Sobs, falls to her knees.*)

FIRST PRISONER:
> Sister, why do we do these things?
>
> (*Her arms flail in space with a great helplessness. The SECOND PRISONER searches for the silk scarf hidden in her skirt.*
>
> *Hurriedly puts it back on the bed.*)

SECOND PRISONER:
> Sister, why do we do these things?
>
> (*The SECOND PRISONER collapses.*
>
> *Hides her head in her lap.*)

> *The stage closes.*

The End.

Appendix i

Note On The Production Of *Masses and Man*
By Jürgen Fehling

Ernst Toller's drama *Masse-Mensch* was first produced in Berlin at the Volksbühne in September, 1921, under my direction. Two years earlier *Die Wandlung*, by the same author had attracted attention in Berlin. But the first performance of *Masse-Mensch* made a far more vivid and lasting impression. The fact that Volksbühne audiences are largely socialist may in part account for its continued success in two consecutive seasons, but undoubtedly the profound impression made by these performances is in the main due to the inherent dramatic power of the play itself.

At first sight, Toller's text seems difficult and ungrateful material for the stage. But it has proved one of the most conspicuous theatrical events of recent years, because its latent dramatic force and truth, revealed by an imaginative producer using the resources of modern stagecraft, gives concrete form to a passionately moved and moving spiritual experience. In order to model the poet's vision in the animate and inanimate elements of the stage and make adequate use of the technical history of the first production, it is necessary to take a brief survey of the author and his work.

Ernst Toller is a social writer. This does not mean that his play is political propaganda, for he is a poet. But his poem, his play, was conceived in the midst of a social upheaval and inspired by the wrath of a war against social injustice. Though his battle cries may at times sound grotesquely, the living breath of anger and sorrow informs his work and gives his politics their universal dramatic values. Toller attacks capitalism as being responsible for the miseries of humanity in war and peace. The *Woman*, creator and preserver of life, represents the human soul, urged on by dreams, swaying between desires and fears, strong in thought and weak in deed, stumbling through the troubles of our age, but groping through darkness and despair to the hills of vision.

This play of human motives, for all its anger, its yearning and its conflict, has an underlying harmony of hope and love; and demands a delicately vigorous restraint and unity of presentation. The scene and action are universal and free from local detail, so that, in my opinion, not only the second, fourth and sixth acts, which the author designates as "dream-pictures", but the whole play should be staged without realism.

In my production I attempted to suggest this twilight of the soul by an elusive blending of the limelight rays. Not forgetting, nevertheless, that unless the theatre is to become a laboratory for sensory stimuli, the spoken word must, as always, dominate all scenic effects.

The scenes were severely architectonic, composed of light and space. Platforms and flights of steps, draped uniformly in black, served as a scaffolding for the actors, individually disposed in geometric patterns, or massed in opposition to the protagonists. This provided a visual continuity of scene and allowed invaluable freedom of action. The stage, curtained and carpeted in black, only occasionally opening on a domed horizon with white or yellow lighting, and itself tinged with glowing light, gave the illusion of illimitable space and freedom for the imaginative visualization of scenes appropriate to the changing dramatic situation. The brief transitions from one scene to the next are bridged by veiled music which completes and introduces the mood of each in turn. The second picture closes on a bizarre fox-trot. In the fourth, the ghostly rhythms of the concertina develop into a shrill *danse macabre*. The orchestral interlude before the seventh picture dissolves into a violin solo sounding under Sonia's opening lines.

The original production was fortunate in having Mary Dietrich to interpret the character of Sonia, on which the whole play hinges. Her fine dignity of gesture and her beautiful heavy voice transcended the occasional harshness of the text and revealed, in their aesthetic completeness, the broad lines of the tragedy.

The whole cast was young, for only the young can adequately transmit the fiery outpouring of Toller's own enthusiasm. If this statement seems to hold a latent criticism, I would say that the author himself desires and need desire no better valuation of his play. It is a prelude to the poetry of world-revolution, a stormy morning which may, in happier hours of daylight, be surpassed in lasting poetic value, but never in the passionate humanity from which it springs.

(*Masses and Man*, 1923, pp. 57–58)

Appendix ii

From *Works*

In *Masses Man,* the form is already purer. It was very remarkable: after the performance of the piece some said it was counter-revolutionary because it rejects all violence. Others said it was Bolshevik because the supporter of non-violence perishes and the Masses, although defeated for the moment, are victorious in the long run. Only a few recognised that the struggle between Individual and Masses doesn't take place just in the external world, but that everyone in his inner depths is at the same time both Individual and Masses. As Individual he acts according to the moral ideas he recognises as right. He wants to live *them,* even if the world perishes by so doing. As Masses he is driven by social impulses and situations; he wants to achieve his *goal,* even if he must give up his moral ideas. Even now this contradiction is unresolvable for the politically active, and I wanted to show exactly this unresolvability.

The Nürnberg Municipal Theatre risked the première performance of *Masses Man.* Soon all public and even all private performance of the work were prohibited by Minister President Herr von Kahr, who instituted this unconstitutional measure in the State Parliament [*Landrat*]. In doing this, he supported himself with, amongst other things, a complaint from the Central Committee of German Citizens of the Jewish Faith who "took offence" at the Stock Exchange scene.

(*Gesammelte Werke 1* p. 139. Originally published in *Quer Durch,* 1930)

Appendix iii

Man and the Masses: The Problem of Peace

After taking part in the Bavarian revolution in 1919, I spent several years in prison.

The more I became used to prison life, the more it became a mere matter of routine, the more time I had for thinking, and was increasingly oppressed by my recollections of the revolution.

I felt at odds with myself. I had always believed that Socialists, despising force, should never employ it for their own ends. And now I myself had used force and appealed to force. I remember how in the prison of Stadelheim, near Munich, an opportunity for escape had presented itself and I had refused to take advantage of it lest my flight should cost a warder his life. A great deal happened since then. I meditated on the position of men who try to mould the destiny of this world, who enter politics and try to realise their ideals in face of the masses. Is the man with wisdom right when he says that the only logical way of life for those who were determined never to overcome evil by force was the way of St. Francis? Must the man of action always be dogged by guilt? Always? The masses, it seemed, were impelled by hunger and want, rather than by ideals. Would they still be able to conquer, if they renounced force for the sake of an ideal? Can a man not be an individual and a mass-man at one and the same time? Is not the struggle between the individual and the mass decided in a man's own mind as well as fought out in the community? As an individual a man will strive for his own ideals, even at the expense of the rest of the world. As a mass-man, social impulses sweep him towards his goal, even though his ideals have been abandoned. The problem seemed to me insoluble. I had come up against it in my own life, and I sought to solve it.

It was the conflict that inspired my play, *Man and the Masses*. I was so oppressed by the problem, it so harrassed and bewildered me, that I had to get it out of my system, to clarify the conflict by the dramatic presentation of all the issues involved. I wrote the play in a very few days. The lights were turned out every evening at 9 o'clock, and we were not allowed candles; so I lay on the floor under the table and hung a cloth over it so as to conceal my candle. All night until morning I wrote in that way. The play had a remarkable reception, when it was first put on by the Municipal Theater at Nürnberg. Some people held that it was counter-revolutionary in so far as it was an indictment of force; others insisted that it was pure Bolshevism, because the apostles of non-violence went under in the end.

It is a widely spread error to suppose that a dramatist selects one of the characters of his play as one which shall represent himself and express his judgment of the world, his Weltanshauung, his formula of life.

The level on which the author acts as a man and the level on which he creates as a poet are quite distinct...

The struggle in *Masses and Man* between the woman and the Nameless One refers, as I have already said, to a conflict thousands of years old: that is, have we the right to change with violence a situation in which injustice and violence rule, in order to bring in the reign of justice and non-violence?

Have we the right to sacrifice the living for the future?

Have we the right to believe that the end justifies the means, that the despotic accumulation of deeds of violence is good, if thereby we can attain an end considered good?

Or is not the moral command to live without violence an absolute one?

May the individual sacrifice only himself, but never another, whatever the aim?

When the welfare of the soul, the absoluteness of the moral law, the sanctification of life are at stake, must not then earthly, material aims stand back?...

What happens when people, who are absolute pacifists and not only abhor violence but even force, come in contact with this destructive will and permit it full reign? I was a convinced pacifist, but reality set me right.

The moral plane of the single individual is one thing, the political plane of masses and peoples another.

On the one, I determine the path, there I can act or not, create or destroy. But on the other every deed has consequences, which I may not ignore, for which I must take the responsibility.

Whoever today fights on the political plane, in the hand-to-hand conflict of economic and human interests, must recognise that the laws and consequences of his struggle are determined by other forces than his good intentions, that often the means of offence and defence are forced upon him, means which he cannot but feel as tragic, upon which in the deep sense of the words, he may bleed to death...

(*Gesammelte Werke 1*, pp. 78–83. The original in the Yale University Toller Collection is a typed manuscript in English, originating before 1937, with corrections in Toller's own hand. Neither a German version nor an English printed version is known. This speech was translated partly by Alexander Henderson and, it would seem, partly by Toller.)

Appendix iv

The Internationale, (p. 171) was translated from the German version given in the text. The standard English version is as follows:

Arise ye starvelings from your slumbers;
Arise ye criminals of want
For Reason in revolt now thunders,
And at last ends the age of cant.
Now away with all your superstitions,
Servile masses arise! Arise!
We'll change forthwith the old conditions.
And spurn the dust to win the prize.
Then comrades come rally.
And the last fight let us face.
The International
Unites the human race.

And the American version is different still:

Arise, ye prisoners of starvation!
Arise, ye wretched of the earth,
For justice thunders condemnation.
A better world's in birth.
No more tradition's chain shall bind us.
Arise, ye slaves; no more in thrall!
The earth shall rise on new foundations.
We have naught, we shall be all.
'Tis the final conflict,
Let each stand in his place.
The International Party
Shall be the human race.

Appendix v: Plates

Masses Man

Directed by Jürgen Fehling and designed by Hans Strohbach with
music by Heinz Thiessen (Volksbühne, 29 September 1921)

5. **Fourth Picture.** Design for the Dream Picture of the Prison yard, which captures
the Expressionistic chiaroscuro effect vividly with the threatening shadows
of the inward-leaning walls. Colour was used in the production, too. The
cyclorama behind the curtains glowed with a green night sky. The Nameless
stood centre in purple costume with a concertina on a black box containing a
lantern which emitted a phosphorescent, greenish-blue light. The Condemned
Man entered dressed all in red. Multi-coloured, rhythmically pulsing light
bathed the dance while the sky pulsed in crimson. The Woman was dressed
in glowing blue. Colour and the chiaroscuro effect reinforced the visual
intensity of each other.

6. **Fifth Picture.** Design for the moment when the Soldiers attack the Workers at which the two levels of reality established by the play coalesced. After the singing of 'The Internationale' and the loud sound of gunfire which mowed the Workers down, the curtains looped up and the Soldiers were revealed against the yellow cyclorama in a haze of gunsmoke.

A rare colour version of the same design can be seen on the cover of this book – it gives a much better indication of how powerfully colour and chiaroscuro effects interacted to realise this climactic moment. Note the beams of light and the striking groupings.

7. **Fifth Picture.** A production photograph of the same moment, which is less expressive because it had to be taken posed under full light. It does indicate the effectiveness of the groupings, the postures and the dynamic use of the steps.

8. **Sixth Picture.** Design for the Dream Picture of the Woman in Prison, a very
striking image of imprisonment with the cage's twisted bars painted crimson
and the cage itself so small that she could only kneel. The Warder in purple,
the Woman in blue. The cyclorama lit with a luminescent light was used for
towering shadows which accused the Woman. The rare colour version of the
above is also included on the back cover of this book and reveals how vividly
effective this Expressionist staging was.

9. **Sixth Picture.**
A production photograph
of the same scene with
Mary Dietrich as the Woman.
Note the entranced facial
expressions, the poses and
the theatrical effectiveness
of the cramped image.

HOPPLA, WE'RE ALIVE!

A PROLOGUE AND FIVE ACTS

Greetings to Erwin Piscator
and Walter Mehring

Characters in the prologue

KARL THOMAS
EVA BERG
WILHELM KILMAN
ALBERT KROLL

FRAU MELLER
SIXTH PRISONER
WARDER RAND
LIEUTENANT BARON
    FRIEDRICH

SOLDIERS

Time: 1919

Characters in the play

KARL THOMAS
EVA BERG
WILHELM KILMAN
FRAU KILMAN
LOTTE KILMAN
ALBERT KROLL
FRAU MELLER
RAND
PROFESSOR LÜDIN
BARON FRIEDRICH
COUNT LANDE
MINISTER OF WAR
BANKER
BANKER'S SON
PICKEL
MINISTRY OFFICIAL
MADHOUSE ORDERLY
STUDENT

FRITZ
GRETE
FIRST WORKER
SECOND WORKER
THIRD WORKER
FOURTH WORKER
FIFTH WORKER
EXAMINING MAGISTRATE
HEAD WAITER
PORTER
RADIO OPERATOR
BUSBOY
CLERK
BARKEEPER
POLICE CHIEF
FIRST POLICEMAN
SECOND POLICEMAN
THIRD POLICEMAN

CHAIRMAN OF THE UNION OF INTELLECTUAL
BRAIN WORKERS
PHILOSOPHER X
POET Y
CRITIC Z
ELECTION OFFICER
SECOND ELECTION OFFICER

FIRST ELECTIONEER
SECOND ELECTIONEER
THIRD ELECTIONEER
VOTER
OLD WOMAN
PRISONER N
JOURNALISTS
LADIES, GENTLEMEN, PEOPLE

The piece takes place in many countries.
Eight years after the crushing of a people's uprising.
Time: 1927

NOTE TO THE DIRECTOR

All the scenes of the piece can be played on a scaffolding which is built up in tiers and which can be changed without rebuilding. In theatres where it is completely impossible to use film equipment, the film segments may be omitted or replaced by simple slide projections.

In order not to break the tempo of the work, there should be, as far as possible, only one interval, namely after Act II.

The staging information contained in square brackets in italics is based on the running notes in Piscator's Prompt-book. In the case of the film sequences for which neither the films nor the shooting scripts still exist, these notes have been augmented by material from contemporary reviews reprinted in Knellessen and Rühle. Other stage directions are from the text as published.

[*Auditorium lights go down. Then up and down three times. Curtain up to reveal film screen almost covering scaffolding.*]

Film Prologue

NOISES: SIRENS

FLASHING SEARCHLIGHTS

SCENES OF A PEOPLE'S UPRISING

ITS CRUSHING

FIGURES
OF THE DRAMATIC PROLOGUE
APPEARING ON AND OFF

[*Film: brief shot of General's headless chest with medals. Then documentary German war footage of infantry attack, charging tanks, explosions, barrage of gunfire, wounded soldiers, vast military cemeteries, retreat of worn-out German Army, disposal of weapons in a growing heap. KARL THOMAS visible among the marching soldiers. General's chest again: a hand roughly rips off the medals. As film ends screen is raised and white and black gauzes lowered in its place. Centre compartment where prisoners will be begins to light up. Façade of prison windows projected on to gauze and remains to end of scene. Prison noises begin to build. As lights brighten prisoners can be seen. Back projections of prison walls on centre compartment rear screen and on middle and upper left and right compartment screens – from audience viewpoint as in the Promptbook and in all the following directions. Bottom left and right compartments closed. Prologue begins.*]

*

PROLOGUE

Large Prison Cell

KARL THOMAS: Damned silence!

ALBERT KROLL: Like to sing hymns?

EVA BERG: In the French Revolution the aristocrats danced the minuet to the guillotine.

ALBERT KROLL: Romantic con! You should have inspected their knickers. The odour wouldn't have smelled like lavender.

(*Silence.*)

[*Lights dim centre compartment and film of guard passing from left to right projected on the gauze. Then back projection on central compartment rear screen of RAND climbing stairs which turns into enlarged head of RAND appearing from right, hovering over prisoners and returning right. WILHELM KILMAN reacts in fear as if it is his hallucination.*]

WILHELM KILMAN: Mother Meller, you're an old woman. You're always silent or smiling. Don't you have any fear of...of...? Mother Meller (*Edges towards her.*) my legs are shaking from the heat and there's ice packed around my heart... Understand, I've got a wife and child... Mother Meller, I'm so scared...

FRAU MELLER: Calm down, my boy, calm down. It only seems so bad when you're young. Later on it fades away. Life and death, they flow together. You come out of one womb and you journey into another...

WILHELM KILMAN: Do you believe there's life there?

FRAU MELLER: No, drop it. My teachers beat that belief out of me.

WILHELM KILMAN: Nobody's visited you. Didn't you want them to?

FRAU MELLER: They stole my parents and my two children in the war. Caused me great pain, but I thought to myself: times will change. And they sure did. All is lost... But others will go on struggling...

(*Silence.*)

[*Film on gauze of resting prisoners like caged animals,
crammed together like corpses.*]

KARL THOMAS: Listen! I've seen something.

EVA BERG: What?

[*Back projected film on centre rear screen of warders
approaching, growing larger, looking at prisoners, turning
and going away.*]

KARL THOMAS: No, don't crowd around. Bug-eyes is at
the spy-hole... We'll escape.

ALBERT KROLL: Like the taste of lead?

KARL THOMAS: Look at the window. The plaster around
the iron bars has crumbled.

ALBERT KROLL: Yes, you're right.

KARL THOMAS: And isn't that big piece of plaster faked
to look firm?...

ALBERT KROLL: Right.

KARL THOMAS: Do you see?

EVA BERG: Yes. Yes. A kid's trick to drive you mad.

FRAU MELLER: Yes. How true.

WILHELM KILMAN: That's where they once tried to get
into the cell from outside... Almost did it... Well, I don't
know.

FRAU MELLER: (*To WILHELM KILMAN.*) What, scaredy-
pants?

WILHELM KILMAN: Yes, but...

KARL THOMAS: What's with the 'but'?

ALBERT KROLL: You know I'm not reckless. It's night.
How late?

KARL THOMAS: It's just struck four.

ALBERT KROLL: Then the guard has changed. We're on
the first floor. If we stay here, we'll say good morning in
a mass grave. If we try to escape, the odds are ten to one
against. And even if they were a hundred to one, we
must take the risk.

WILHELM KILMAN: If not...

KARL THOMAS: Dead either way... Albert, you do a
parade march, six steps back and forth, from the window

205

to the door without stopping. Then the spy-hole will be blocked for a few seconds and outside they won't notice anything. The fifth time I'll jump up to the window and with all my strength pull the iron bars out and then "Bye-bye, boss".

EVA BERG: I could scream! Karl, I could kiss you to death.

ALBERT KROLL: Later.

[*Back projected film on centre rear screen of two guards approaching, turning and leaving.*]

KARL THOMAS: Leave her alone. She's so young.

ALBERT KROLL: Karl, you jump out first, then Eva second; then, Wilhelm, you grab Mother Meller and push her up...

WILHELM KILMAN: Yes, yes...only I think...

FRAU MELLER: Let him go first... No one needs to help me. I can cope like all of you.

ALBERT KROLL: Shut up. You go first, then Wilhelm, then me last.

WILHELM KILMAN: What if the escape doesn't work? We'd better think it over.

ALBERT KROLL: If the escape doesn't work...

KARL THOMAS: How can you know if any escape will work? You've got to take the risk, comrade! A revolutionary who doesn't take risks! You should have stayed home drinking coffee with your mother, not gone to the barricades.

WILHELM KILMAN: We'd all be lost afterwards. There'd be no more hope.

KARL THOMAS: To hell with hope! Hope for what? The death sentence was passed. For ten days we've been waiting for the execution.

FRAU MELLER: Last night they asked for the addresses of our relatives.

KARL THOMAS: So hope for what? A volley of gunfire, and if it misses the bonus of a finishing shot. A good victory or a good death – the battle cry hasn't changed for a thousand years.

(*WILHELM KILMAN cowers.*)

Or...have you been begging for mercy? If so, at least swear you'll keep silent.

WILHELM KILMAN: Why do you let him insult me. Haven't I drudged day and night? For fifteen years I've slaved for the Party and now I must be allowed my say... I don't get breakfast in bed.

FRAU MELLER: Peace, both of you.

KARL THOMAS: Just think of the trial. Are they likely to quash the death sentence? Strike a concrete wall and do you think it's going to ring clear as a bell?

ALBERT KROLL: Let's go! Everybody ready? Eva, you count. Take care, Karl...the fifth time.

(*ALBERT KROLL begins to march back and forth, from the window to the door, from the door to the window. Everybody tense.*)

EVA BERG: One...two...three...

(*KARL THOMAS steals to the window.*)

Four...

(*Noise at the door. Door creaks open.*)

ALBERT KROLL: Damn it!

(*WARDER RAND enters.*)

WARDER RAND: Anyone want the priest?

FRAU MELLER: He really ought to be ashamed of himself.

RAND: Don't commit a sin, old woman. You'll be standing before your Maker soon enough.

FRAU MELLER: I've learned the worms know nothing about religious faiths. Tell your priest Jesus drove the money-changers and usurers out of the temple with lashes of the whip. Tell him to write that down in his Bible, on the first page.

RAND: (*To the SIXTH PRISONER who's lying on a plank bed.*) And you?

SIXTH PRISONER: (*Softly.*) Forgive me, comrades... I left the Church at sixteen...now...before death...terrifying... understand me, comrades... Yes, I want to go to the priest, Herr Warder.

WILHELM KILMAN: Revolutionary? You shit-pants! To the priest! Dear God, make me holy so I'll go to heaven.

FRAU MELLER: Why attack the poor devil?

ALBERT KROLL: Before death… Leave him alone.

WILHELM KILMAN: A man can say what he wants.

> (*WARDER and SIXTH PRISONER leave. Door is closed.*)
> [*Back projected centre rear screen film of RAND and SIXTH PRISONER going off, turns into laughing head of RAND with distorted grimace as shooting starts.*]

ALBERT KROLL: Won't he betray us?

KARL THOMAS: No.

ALBERT KROLL: Look! Now that he has to go with him, he can't spy on us. Get going Karl, I'll help you. Here, on my back…

> [*Film on gauze of guns shooting. GUARD laughs and goes right.*]
> (*ALBERT KROLL bends over. KARL THOMAS climbs on ALBERT KROLL's bent back.*
> *As he stretches both hands towards the windowsill to grab the iron bars,*
> *rifles rattle*
> *from below,*
> *plaster and other fragments come flying into the cell.*
> *KARL THOMAS jumps off ALBERT KROLL's back.*
> *They all stare at each other.*)

Are you wounded?

KARL THOMAS: No. What was that?

ALBERT KROLL: Nothing special. They're guarding our window. A small company.

EVA BERG: That…means…?

FRAU MELLER: Prepare yourself, my child.

EVA BERG: For…for death…?

> (*The others are silent.*)

No…no… (*Sobs, cries.*)

> (*FRAU MELLER goes to her, strokes her.*)

ALBERT KROLL: Don't cry, dear girl. We revolutionaries are all dead men on leave, as someone once said.

KARL THOMAS: Leave her alone, Albert. She's young. Barely seventeen. For her death means a cold, black hole which she has to lie in forever. And on top of her grave there's life – warm, exciting, gay and sweet.

(*KARL THOMAS goes to EVA BERG.*)

Your hands.

EVA BERG: Dear you.

KARL THOMAS: I love you very much, Eva.

EVA BERG: Will they bury us together, if we ask them?

KARL THOMAS: Maybe.

(*ALBERT KROLL jumps up.*)

ALBERT KROLL: Damn torture! Why don't they come?
I once read that cats torture mice so long because they
smell so good in their death throes... For us there must
be other refinements. Why don't they come? Why don't
the dirty dogs come?

KARL THOMAS: Yes, why do we struggle? What do we
know? For the Idea, for Justice – we say. No one's dug
deep enough into himself to bow down before the
ultimate, naked reason – if there are ultimate reasons.

ALBERT KROLL: I don't understand. I've known that
our society lives off the sweat of our hands ever since
I was sixteen and was dragged out of bed at five in the
morning to deliver rolls. And what has to be done to end
injustice, that I knew even before I could reckon how
much ten times ten is...

KARL THOMAS: Look around at how everyone pounces
upon the Idea in times of revolution and war. One is
running away from his wife because she makes his life
hell. Another can't cope with life and limps along until
he finds a crutch which makes him look wonderful and
gives him a little heroic sheen. A third believes he can
all of a sudden change his skin, which has become
repulsive to him. A fourth seeks adventure. There are
fewer and fewer who must do so out of inmost necessity.

[*All but first and last lines of this speech cut.*]

(*Noise. Door creaks open. SIXTH PRISONER enters.*
Silence.)

SIXTH PRISONER: Do you hold it against me, comrades?
I'm not converted, comrades... But...it makes me
calmer...

KARL THOMAS: Judas!

SIXTH PRISONER: But dear comrades...

ALBERT KROLL: Still no decision! Still waiting! I'd like to smoke, has anyone got a butt?

(*They search in their pockets.*)

ALL: No.

KARL THOMAS: Wait...sure... I've got a cigarette.

ALL: Bring it here! Bring it here!

ALBERT KROLL: Matches? No go.

WILHELM KILMAN: I have one.

ALBERT KROLL: We must share it, of course.

WILHELM KILMAN: Really?

EVA BERG: Yes, please.

KARL THOMAS: Eva can have my share.

FRAU MELLER: Mine too.

EVA BERG: No, one puff each.

ALBERT KROLL: Good. Who'll start?

EVA BERG: We'll draw lots.

ALBERT KROLL: (*Tears a handkerchief into strips.*) Whoever draws the smallest strip.

(*All draw.*)

Mother Meller starts.

FRAU MELLER: Here goes. (*Smokes.*) Now your turn. (*Gives WILHELM KILMAN the cigarette.*)

WILHELM KILMAN: I hope they won't catch us.

ALBERT KROLL: What could they do to us? Four weeks solitary confinement for punishment! Ha, ha, ha.

(*They all smoke, one puff each. They watch each other closely.*)

Karl, you mustn't take two puffs.

KARL THOMAS: Don't talk rubbish.

ALBERT KROLL: Think I'm lying?

KARL THOMAS: Yes.

WILHELM KILMAN: (*To ALBERT KROLL.*) You sucked much longer than we did.

ALBERT KROLL: Shut up, coward.

WILHELM KILMAN: He's calling me coward.

ALBERT KROLL: Where did you creep off to during the days of decision? Where did you rub your trouser seat shiny while we stormed the town hall – with the enemy at our backs and a mass grave in front of us? Where were you hiding?

WILHELM KILMAN: Didn't I address the masses from the balcony of the town hall?

ALBERT KROLL: Yes, when we had power. But before, neither for nor against. Then in a flash you're at the feeding trough.

KARL THOMAS: (*To ALBERT KROLL.*) You have no right to talk like that.

ALBERT KROLL: Bourgeois lackey!

FRAU MELLER: What scum, to row five minutes before you're put up against the wall...

WILHELM KILMAN: He's calling me coward! For fifteen years I have...

ALBERT KROLL: (*Aping him.*) Fifteen years... Big shot... No great honour to bite the dust together with you.

EVA BERG: Shame!

KARL THOMAS: Yes, shame.

ALBERT KROLL: What shame! Go lie with your whore in the corner and give her a kid. Then it can hatch in the grave and play with the worms.

(*EVA BERG screams.*
KARL THOMAS jumps on ALBERT KROLL.)

SIXTH PRISONER: (*Jumping up.*) Heavenly Father, is this Thy will?

(*As they hold each other by the throat, noise. Door creaks open. They let go.*)

RAND: The Lieutenant is coming now. You must get ready. (*Goes.*)

(*ALBERT KROLL goes up to KARL THOMAS, embraces him.*)

ALBERT KROLL: We don't know anything about ourselves, Karl. That wasn't me just now, that wasn't me. Give me your hand, dear Eva.

KARL THOMAS: For ten days we've been waiting for death. That has poisoned us.

(*Noise. Door creaks open.*
LIEUTENANT enters with SOLDIERS.)

LIEUTENANT BARON FRIEDRICH: (*To ALBERT KROLL.*) Stand up. In the name of the President. The death sentence was pronounced in accordance with the law. (*Pause.*) As a sign of his clemency and his wish for reconciliation the President has quashed the death sentence. The condemned are to be held in protective custody and are to be transported to the internment camp immediately. With the exception of Wilhelm Kilman.

(*KARL THOMAS bursts into howls of laughter.*)

EVA BERG: Your laughter is terrifying, Karl.

FRAU MELLER: For joy.

LIEUTENANT BARON FRIEDRICH: Stop laughing, man.

EVA BERG: Karl! Karl!

ALBERT KROLL: He's not laughing for fun.

FRAU MELLER: Just look at him. It's convulsed him.

LIEUTENANT BARON FRIEDRICH (*To the WARDER.*) Take him to the doctor.

(*KARL THOMAS is led out. EVA BERG goes with him.*)

ALBERT KROLL: (*To WILHELM KILMAN.*): You're the only one to stay. Forgive me, Wilhelm. We won't forget you.

FRAU MELLER: (*Leaving, to ALBERT KROLL.*) Clemency. Who would have thought that the authorities could feel so weak.

ALBERT KROLL: Bad sign. Who would have thought that the authorities could feel so strong.

(*All leave, except LIEUTENANT BARON FRIEDRICH and WILHELM KILMAN.*)

LIEUTENANT BARON FRIEDRICH: The President has granted your petition. He believes you, that you came to be in the ranks of the rebels against your will. You are free.

WILHELM KILMAN: Thank you most respectfully, Herr Lieutenant.

Curtain.

[*Gauze up. Projection of prison windows off. Screen lowered for film.*]

Film Interlude

Behind the Stage:

CHORUS: (*In rhythmical crescendo and diminuendo.*)
Happy New Year! Happy New Year!
Special Edition! Special Edition!
Great Sensation!
Special Edition! Special Edition!
Great Sensation!

On the Screen:

Scenes from the years 1919-1927.
(*Between them:*
KARL THOMAS in asylum dress pacing back and forth
in a lunatic cell.)
1919:
Treaty of Versailles

1920:
Stock Market Turmoil in New York
People go mad

1921:
Fascism in Italy

1922:
Hunger in Vienna
People go mad

1923:
Inflation in Germany
People go mad

1924:
Lenin's Death in Russia
Newspaper Notice: Tonight Frau Luise Thomas died...

1925:
Gandhi in India

1926:
Battles in China
Conference of European Leaders in Europe

213

1927:

Dial of a Clock

The hands advance. First slowly...then faster
and faster...

Noises: Clocks

[*Seven minutes of documentary film of key events probably intercut with KARL THOMAS pacing in Lunatic Asylum, and a collage of popular images of Weimar life contrasting, as the play does, frivolity and hardship. It followed the above scenario quite closely, including the clock, adding in events like the election of Hindenburg in 1925 and some self-filmed scenes. As the film ended, screen out and gauze in with projection of façade of Lunatic Asylum which remains through scene. Lights come up in the centre and right bottom compartments to reveal PROFESSOR LÜDIN's Office. Back projections of filling cabinet centre compartment screen and wardrobe bottom right compartment screen.*]

ACT ONE

Scene One

Office Of A Lunatic Asylum

(ORDERLY at cupboard.
PROFESSOR LÜDIN at barred window.)

ORDERLY: One pair grey trousers. One pair woollen socks. Didn't you bring any underclothes with you?

KARL THOMAS: I don't know.

ORDERLY: Oh! One black waistcoat. One black coat. One pair of low shoes. Hat missing.

PROFESSOR LÜDIN: And money?

ORDERLY: None, Herr Doctor.

PROFESSOR LÜDIN: Relations?

KARL THOMAS: Notified me yesterday, that my mother died, three years ago.

PROFESSOR LÜDIN: You're going to find things difficult. Life is hard today. You've got to elbow your way. Don't despair. All in good time.

ORDERLY: Release date: 8 May 1927.

[*This date was changed to that of the performance every night.*]

KARL THOMAS: No!

PROFESSOR LÜDIN: Yes, indeed.

KARL THOMAS: 1927

PROFESSOR LÜDIN: So, eight little years of room and board with us. Clothed, fed, cared for. Nothing was lacking. You can be proud of yourself: clinically you've been a noteworthy case.

KARL THOMAS: As if obliterated. Yes... I do remember something...

PROFESSOR LÜDIN: What?

KARL THOMAS: The edge of a wood. Trees stretched brown to the sky like pillars. Beech trees. The wood glittered green. With a thousand tiny suns. So delicate. I wanted to go in, so very badly. I couldn't do it. Evilly the tree trunks bent outwards and threw me back like a rubber ball.

PROFESSOR LÜDIN: Wait! Like a rubber ball. Interesting association. Look here, your nerves are consistent with the truth. The wood: the padded cell. The tree trunks: walls of best quality rubber. Yes, I remember: once every year you began to rave. We had to isolate you. Always on the same day. What a perfect clinical masterpiece!

KARL THOMAS: On which day?

PROFESSOR LÜDIN: On the day when... But you must know.

KARL THOMAS: On the day of the reprieve...

PROFESSOR LÜDIN: Do you remember everything?

KARL THOMAS: Yes.

PROFESSOR LÜDIN: Then you are cured.

KARL THOMAS: To wait even minutes for death... But ten days. Ten times twenty four hours. Each hour sixty minutes. Each minute sixty seconds. Each second a murder. Murdered fourteen hundred and forty times in one day. And the nights!... I hated the reprieve. I hated the President. Only a dirty scoundrel could act like that.

PROFESSOR LÜDIN: Take it easy. You have every reason to be thankful... In here we don't mind strong language. But outside... You'd be rewarded with another year in prison for insulting the Head of State. Be reasonable. You must have already had a noseful of that.

KARL THOMAS: You have to say that because you belong to the bosses.

PROFESSOR LÜDIN: We should conclude this interview. You needn't be depressed because you were in a mad-house. Actually most people ought to be in one. Were I to examine a thousand, I would have to keep nine hundred and ninety-nine in here.

KARL THOMAS: Why don't you do it?

PROFESSOR LÜDIN: The State has no interest in it. On the contrary. With a little drop of madness men become respectable husbands. With two drops of madness they become socially conscious... Don't do anything stupid. I only want what's good for you. Go to one of your friends.

KARL THOMAS: Where could they have got to?...

PROFESSOR LÜDIN: Weren't there others in your cell back then?

KARL THOMAS: Five. Only one wasn't reprieved. His name was Wilhelm Kilman.

PROFESSOR LÜDIN: Not reprieved? Ha, ha, ha. His career has galloped ahead! Smarter than you.

KARL THOMAS: I don't understand you.

PROFESSOR LÜDIN: You'll understand me soon enough. Just go to him. He could help you. If he wants to help you. If he wants to know you.

KARL THOMAS: He's still alive?

PROFESSOR LÜDIN: You're going to experience a miracle. An excellent prescription for you. I have cured you clinically. He might cure you of your crazy ideas. Go to the Ministry of the Interior and ask for Mr Kilman. Good luck.

KARL THOMAS: Good day, Herr Doctor. Good day, Herr Orderly... It smells so strongly of lilac here... Of course, spring. Isn't it true that there are real beeches growing outside the window...not rubber padded walls... (*KARL THOMAS leaves.*)

PROFESSOR LÜDIN: Bad breed.

Blackout.

[*Gauze out. Screen in.*]

Film Interlude

Big City 1927

STREETCARS

AUTOS

UNDERGROUND TRAINS

AEROPLANE

*

[*Film of KARL THOMAS in hostel for the homeless, helplessly seeking work from factory to factory, searching for lodgings, in the hustle and bustle of Potsdam Square etc. Screen out and gauze stays out. Back projection of Kaiser centre compartment screen and of wall paper in middle left and bottom right compartments for next scene.*]

Scene Two

Two rooms visible: Minister's Antechamber, Minister's Office.

When the curtain rises both rooms can be seen.
The room in which nothing is said goes dark.

Office

WILHELM KILMAN: I sent for you.
EVA BERG: Of course.

Antechamber

BANKER'S SON: Will he receive you? He hasn't sent for you.
BANKER: Not receive me! Just let him try it.
BANKER'S SON: We need credits up to the end of the month.
BANKER: Why are you doubtful?
BANKER'S SON: Because he's rejected the chance both times now.
BANKER: I operated too crudely.

Office

WILHELM KILMAN: You sit on the Committee of the Union of Female Employees?
EVA BERG: Yes.
WILHELM KILMAN: You work as a secretary in the Revenue Office?
EVA BERG: Yes.
WILHELM KILMAN: For two months now your name has featured prominently in the police reports.
EVA BERG: I don't understand.

WILHELM KILMAN: You've been inciting the women workers at the Chemical Works to refuse overtime?

EVA BERG: I'm only exercising the rights which our Constitution guarantees me.

WILHELM KILMAN: The Constitution is intended for peaceful times.

EVA BERG: Aren't we living in them now?

WILHELM KILMAN: The State rarely knows peaceful times.

Antechamber

BANKER: The matter must be settled before the tariff announcement. Two hours of overtime, take it or leave it.

BANKER'S SON: The trade unions have decided to hold out for an eight hour working day.

BANKER: Whatever is good for the State will be right for heavy industry.

BANKER'S SON: We'll have to lock out half a million workers.

BANKER: And so what? We'll kill two birds with one stone. Overtime and lower pay.

Office

EVA BERG: I am against war. If I had the power, the Works would come to a standstill. What do they make? Poison gas!

WILHELM KILMAN: Your personal opinion, which doesn't interest me. I don't like war either. Do you know this leaflet? Are you the author?

EVA BERG: Yes.

WILHELM KILMAN: You have violated your duties as a State Official.

EVA BERG: There was a time when you did the same.

WILHELM KILMAN: We're having an official conversation, Fräulein.

EVA BERG: In the past you have...

WILHELM KILMAN: Keep to the present. I have to maintain order... Dear Fräulein Berg, be reasonable now. Do you want to bash your stubborn head in? The State always has a harder skull. I don't mean you any harm.

We need the overtime at the moment. You lack practical knowledge. It would be damned painful for me to proceed against you. I know you well from before. But I would have to. Really. Be reasonable. Promise me that...

EVA BERG: I promise nothing.

Antechamber

PICKEL: (*Who from the beginning of the scene has been pacing restlessly back and forth, stops in front of the BANKER.*) Pardon me, sir... I come from Holzhausen, namely. Perhaps the gentleman knows Holzhausen? Indeed with the building of the railway, it won't be started until October. Nevertheless the mailcoach was really enough for me. There's a saying we have...

(*BANKER turns away.*)

I believe, indeed, that the railway...

(*As no one is listening to him, he breaks off, paces back and forth.*)

Office

WILHELM KILMAN: The State must protect itself. I was not obliged to send for you. I wanted to give you my advice. No one can say that...you alone bear the responsibility. I warn you. (*Gesture.*)

(*EVA BERG goes.*)

(*On the telephone.*) Chemical Works... Herr Director?... Kilman... Well? Works meeting at 12 o'clock... Phone me the result... Thank you... (*Hangs up.*)

The MINISTER OF WAR walks through the

Antechamber

MINISTER OF WAR: Ah, good day, Herr Director-General. You here too?

BANKER: Yes, unfortunately. This wretched waiting... Permit me, Herr Minister of War, to introduce my son... His Excellency von Wandsring.

MINISTER OF WAR: Pleased... A delicate situation.

PICKEL: (*Turns to the MINISTER OF WAR.*) I think, Herr General, indeed the enemy...

(*As the MINISTER OF WAR doesn't pay him any attention, he breaks off, goes to the corner, fumbles in his pocket for a medal, pins it on hurriedly and with great difficulty.*)

BANKER: You will see to it, Herr General.

MINISTER OF WAR: Certainly. Only...it gives me no pleasure to shoot people whom we first give drumsticks to eagerly and then stop from beating the drum. These liberal utopias of democracy and freedom of the people are getting us into trouble. We need authority. The condensed experience of thousands of years. You can't refute that with slogans.

BANKER: Yet democracy, in moderation of course, needn't necessarily lead to mob-rule on the one hand, and on the other hand it could be a safety valve...

MINISTER OF WAR: Democracy...stuff and nonsense. The people rule? Where on earth? Well then, better an honest dictatorship. Let's not whitewash anything, Herr Director-General... Will we see each other at the club tomorrow?

BANKER: With great pleasure.
> (*MINISTER OF WAR leaves.*
> *COUNT LANDE follows him to the door.*)

COUNT LANDE: Excellency...

MINISTER OF WAR: Ah, Count Lande. Arranged?

COUNT LANDE: Yes indeed, Excellency.

MINISTER OF WAR: Are things going well for you?

COUNT LANDE: The front groups are waiting.

MINISTER OF WAR: Don't act hot-headedly, Count. Nothing foolish. The time for violence is over. What we want to achieve for our Fatherland, we can achieve by legal means.

COUNT LANDE: Excellency, we are relying on you.

MINISTER OF WAR: Count, with all my sympathy... I caution you.
> (*MINISTER OF WAR goes.*)

PICKEL: (*In a military manner.*) At your command, Herr General.
> (*MINISTER OF WAR leaves without noticing him.*)

BANKER: How long will Kilman hold out?

BANKER'S SON: Why don't you do the business through Wandsring?

BANKER: Today Kilman governs. No harm being on the safe side.

BANKER'S SON: He's *passé*. You can throw your Kilman into the bankrupt estate of democracy. Just sniff the air of industry. I'd advise you to bet on a national dictatorship.

PICKEL (*Turns to COUNT LANDE.*) Can you tell me, sir, what time it is?

COUNT LANDE: Fourteen past twelve.

PICKEL: The clocks in the city are always fast. I imagined that an interview with the Minister would be at twelve sharp... Indeed the clocks in the country are always slow, consequently...

> (*As COUNT LANDE doesn't notice him, he breaks off, paces back and forth.*)

COUNT LANDE: How do you address Kilman?

BARON FRIEDRICH: As Excellency, naturally.

COUNT LANDE: Do the comrades enjoy the taste of 'Excellency'?

BARON FRIEDRICH: Same old business, my dear friend. Dress a man in a uniform and he'll pine for even a lance-corporal's stripes.

COUNT LANDE: And he keeps us waiting in the antechamber. Ten years ago I wouldn't have shaken hands with his kind unless I was wearing buckskin gloves.

BARON FRIEDRICH: Don't get excited. I can dish you up other delicacies. Eight years ago I almost had him put up against the wall.

COUNT LANDE: Fabulously interesting. Were you involved at that time?

BARON FRIEDRICH: Not half! Let's not talk about it.

COUNT LANDE: And still he appointed you to the Ministry. Always in his presence. You must get on his nerves.

BARON FRIEDRICH: That's exactly what I feared. When he first came into the Ministry, the Great Court of Chancellery, I took the liberty of raking up old stories.

One must play the game in order to be ready for when times change again. He gave me a sharp look. From that day on, one promotion after another, however disagreeably. But he never talks about it.

COUNT LANDE: A sort of hush money.

BARON FRIEDRICH: Don't know. Let's speak about the weather. I suspect the rascal has first class spies at his disposal.

COUNT LANDE: The comrades have learned all the old tricks from us.

PICKEL: (*Turning to BARON FRIEDRICH.*) Indeed my neighbour in Holzhausen asserted, namely... Pickel, he asserted, for an interview with the Minister you must buy yourself white gloves. That's how it was in the old government, and that's how it still remains in the new one. The ceremonial regulations demand it. However I... I thought if the Monarchy demanded white gloves, in the Republic we ought to put on black gloves... Namely that, exactly!... Because we are now free men...

(*As BARON FRIEDRICH doesn't notice him, he breaks off, paces back and forth.*)

BARON FRIEDRICH: A clever rascal, you have to give him that.

COUNT LANDE: Manners?

BARON FRIEDRICH: I don't know whether he took lessons from actors like Napoleon did. In any case, a gentleman from head to toe. Rides every morning in full dress, immaculate, I tell you.

COUNT LANDE: And through which cracks can you smell the stink of the prole?

BARON FRIEDRICH: Through all of them. You only have to see how he puts a little too much into every word, every gesture, every step. People think that if they have their dress coats cut by a first class tailor, that's enough. They don't realise that first class tailors are only worth something for first class customers.

COUNT LANDE: In any case I'd dine with the devil's grandmother, if she'd help me get out of the provinces into the capital.

BARON FRIEDRICH: The 'grandmother' with whom
you'll dine keeps a table that's not to be despised.

COUNT LANDE: She's certainly been a house servant long
enough for that.

Office

MINISTRY OFFICIAL: Her Excellency and your daughter
would like to speak with you, Excellency. They are
waiting in the drawing room

WILHELM KILMAN: Please ask them to be patient for ten
minutes.

(MINISTRY OFFICIAL leaves.
Telephone rings.)

Hello. It's you, Herr Privy Councillor. Yes, it's me…
Nothing doing… No, no, you're not disturbing me at
all… The collapse of the Chemical Works… A stage
trick… It's fixed, of course it's fixed… Very cunning
people are behind it. We agreed State credits yesterday…
How? Unanimously… Three per cent… Always at your
service… Goodbye, Herr Privy Councillor.

(MINISTRY OFFICIAL enters.)

MINISTRY OFFICIAL: The ladies say…

WILHELM KILMAN: They must wait, I have to work.

Antechamber

BARON FRIEDRICH: Please, said the little daughter and
bared her knee.

COUNT LANDE: And the mother?

BARON FRIEDRICH: Thought it was refined manners and
blushed silently.

COUNT LANDE: The capital is worth the strains of a
maidenhead. How long it's taking. Governing doesn't
seem to come easily to him.

(KARL THOMAS enters, sits in a corner.)

Office

(WILHELM KILMAN rings.
MINISTRY OFFICIAL enters.)

MINISTRY OFFICIAL: Excellency…?

WILHELM KILMAN: Baron Friedrich and Count Lande…
> (*MINISTRY OFFICIAL bows, goes out.*)

Antechamber

MINISTRY OFFICIAL: (*To COUNT LANDE and BARON FRIEDRICH.*) His Excellency will receive you now…

BANKER: Excuse me, gentlemen. Give His Excellency this card. Only one minute.
> (*MINISTRY OFFICIAL goes into the office.*
> *BANKER and SON follow him.*)

Office

WILHELM KILMAN: Good day, Herr Director-General. Good day, Herr Doctor. Today I'm not really in a position to…

BANKER: Then we'd do better to meet at your leisure.

WILHELM KILMAN: Please.

BANKER: This evening at the Grand Hotel.

WILHELM KILMAN: Agreed.
> (*BANKER and SON go.*)

MINISTRY OFFICIAL: (*To COUNT LANDE and BARON FRIEDRICH.*) His Excellency will receive you now.
> (*Opens the door to the office. COUNT LANDE and BARON*
> *FRIEDRICH enter. MINISTRY OFFICIAL starts to leave*
> *through the side door.*)

KARL THOMAS: Excuse me.

MINISTRY OFFICIAL: His Excellency is busy. I don't know if His Excellency will receive anyone else today.

KARL THOMAS: I don't want to speak to the Minister. I want to speak to Herr Kilman.

MINISTRY OFFICIAL: Play your stupid jokes on someone else.

KARL THOMAS: Jokes, comrade…

MINISTRY OFFICIAL: I'm not your comrade.

KARL THOMAS: Perhaps Herr Kilman works as the Minister's secretary? The porter directed me to the Minister's antechamber when I asked for Herr Kilman.

MINISTRY OFFICIAL: Do you come from the moon? Are you trying to make me believe that you didn't know

His Excellency's name is Kilman? On the whole you're making a very suspicious impression... I'm going to call the Chief Detective Inspector.

KARL THOMAS: Don't you mean another Kilman? There are so many Kilmans.

MINISTRY OFFICIAL: What do you want?

KARL THOMAS: I would like to speak to Herr Wilhelm Kilman. Kilman. K-I-L-M-A-N.

MINISTRY OFFICIAL: That's how His Excellency spells it... What a shady character.

(*MINISTRY OFFICIAL starts to go out.*)

KARL THOMAS: Kilman Minister?... No, wait. I know the Minister, you see. I am his friend. Yes, really, his friend. Eight years ago we were... Just wait now... Do you have a piece of paper?... Pencil? I'll write down my name for the Minister. He will receive me immediately.

(*MINISTRY OFFICIAL is unsure.*)

Go on then!

MINISTRY OFFICIAL: You should keep up with the times.

(*Gives KARL THOMAS paper and pen.*
Goes out. KARL THOMAS writes.)

PICKEL: Well, well...a friend of the Minister... Although I namely... Pickel is my name... Oh, this lout of an official... Indeed one ought to take a stricter line with these old court flunkies, but nevertheless we Republicans put up with anything... I on the other hand understood the joke about your friend, the Minister, immediately... One ought to be allowed one's little joke about the Minister... I think something must be done... In the upper levels of administration for example this official... Namely that is a shortcoming in the Republic...

Office

WILHELM KILMAN: One must know how to deal with nations, gentlemen.

BARON FRIEDRICH: Excellency, don't you think that America has no interest in war...

COUNT LANDE: Consider, Excellency, France's peaceful attitude...

WILHELM KILMAN: Because Ministers prattle on about world peace and make a show of humanitarian ideas? But gentlemen. Observe how often 'world peace' and 'humanitarian idea' are flaunted in any ministerial speech, and I guarantee you that just so many poison gas factories and aeroplane squadrons are marked down for secret action. Ministerial speeches...gentlemen...

BARON FRIEDRICH: It is said that Machiavelli is one of your Excellency's favourite authors.

WILHELM KILMAN: What do we need Machiavelli for... Simple common sense.

(MINISTRY OFFICIAL enters.)

MINISTRY OFFICIAL: May the ladies now...

WILHELM KILMAN: Show them in.

(FRAU KILMAN and her daughter LOTTE KILMAN enter.)

You know, I'm sure, Herr Baron...

BARON FRIEDRICH: Excellency... Fräulein.

FRAU KILMAN: But please don't always call me 'Excellency'. You know I don't like it.

WILHELM KILMAN: Count Lande. My wife. My daughter.

COUNT LANDE: Excellency... Fräulein.

BARON FRIEDRICH: No doubt we're disturbing you...

FRAU KILMAN: No, as it happens I just wrote to you. I invited you for Sunday.

COUNT LANDE: Enchanted to meet you.

FRAU KILMAN: Perhaps you'll bring your friend with you.

BARON FRIEDRICH: Only too honoured, Excellency.

LOTTE KILMAN: *(Softly to BARON FRIEDRICH.)* You stood me up yesterday.

BARON FRIEDRICH: *(Softly.)* But darling...

LOTTE KILMAN: Your friend pleases me.

BARON FRIEDRICH: I congratulate him.

LOTTE KILMAN: I read your personal file.

BARON FRIEDRICH: When can we meet?

WILHELM KILMAN: Yes, Count, we must simply deny it. Slanders from the Left – I don't even read. Slanders from the Right – they are blessed with one of my answers. I know the qualities of the men of the old regime. A man is only a man, has weaknesses, but the most extreme conservatives cannot charge me with a lack of justice.

COUNT LANDE: But Excellency... You are esteemed in Nationalist circles.

WILHELM KILMAN: I'll write to your District Head today. You start your Ministry employment in four weeks.

Antechamber

KARL THOMAS: (*Pacing back and forth rapidly.*) Minister... Minister...

Office

(*The MINISTER says goodbye to COUNT LANDE and BARON FRIEDRICH.*)

Antechamber

BARON FRIEDRICH: What did I tell you?

COUNT LANDE: Some comrades!... Some comrades!...
(*Both leave.*)

KARL THOMAS: I have seen that face. Where?
(*MINISTRY OFFICIAL enters.*)
Here's the note for the Minister.
(*MINISTRY OFFICIAL takes the note and carries it into the Office.*)

Office

[*All other compartments dark. Scaffolding revolves to left to give close-up effect.*]

MINISTRY OFFICIAL: A man, Excellency.

WILHELM KILMAN: I don't want...
(*KARL THOMAS knocks on the door, enters without waiting for an answer.*)

KARL THOMAS: Wilhelm! Wilhelm!

WILHELM KILMAN: Who are you?

KARL THOMAS: You don't know me any more. The years...eight years...

WILHELM KILMAN: (*To MINISTRY OFFICIAL.*) You may go.
(*MINISTRY OFFICIAL leaves.*)

KARL THOMAS: You're still alive. Explain it to me. We were reprieved. You the only one not...

WILHELM KILMAN: Chance...a lucky chance.

KARL THOMAS: Eight years...walled up like a grave. I told the doctor I remembered nothing. Oh Wilhelm, when fully conscious I often saw... Often... Saw you dead... I gouged my eyes until they spurted blood...the orderlies thought I was having fits.

WILHELM KILMAN: Yes...those days... I don't like to remember.

KARL THOMAS: Death always huddled with us. Inciting us against each other.

WILHELM KILMAN: What children we were.

KARL THOMAS: Those hours in prison bond us together in blood. That's why I came to you when I heard you were alive. You can count on me.

FRAU KILMAN: Wilhelm, we must go now.

KARL THOMAS: Frau Kilman. Good morning, Frau Kilman. I didn't even see you before. Are you their daughter? You're so grown up.

LOTTE KILMAN: Everyone grows up sometime; meanwhile my father has also become Minister.

KARL THOMAS: ...Do you remember how you were allowed to visit your husband for the last time in the condemned cell? How sorry I was for you. They had to carry you out. And your daughter stood next to the door with her hands over her face and just kept on repeating: No, no, no.

FRAU KILMAN: Yes, I remember. It was a hard time. Wasn't it, Wilhelm? Things are going well for you now? That's nice. Pay us a visit sometime.

KARL THOMAS: Thank you, Frau Kilman.
(FRAU KILMAN and LOTTE KILMAN go.)
Must it be like that? That your daughter pretends to be a fine lady?

WILHELM KILMAN: What?

KARL THOMAS: Your ministerial office is just a trick, isn't it? Still it's a risky trick. Before such tactics wouldn't have been permitted. Is the whole apparatus almost in our hands?

WILHELM KILMAN: You talk as if we were still in the middle of a revolution.

KARL THOMAS: What?

WILHELM KILMAN: Since then ten years have passed. Just when we began to see a straight way ahead, hard reality rose up and bent it crooked. Still, things go on.

KARL THOMAS: So you take your office seriously?

WILHELM KILMAN: Certainly.

KARL THOMAS: And the people?

WILHELM KILMAN: I serve the people.

KARL THOMAS: Didn't you once prove that whoever sits in a Minister's chair in such a State, with his worst enemies as colleagues, would fail, would have to fail, no matter whether he is driven by good intentions or not?

WILHELM KILMAN: Life doesn't unreel according to theories. You learn by experience.

KARL THOMAS: They should have put you up against the wall!

WILHELM KILMAN: Still the hot-headed dreamer. I won't take offence at your words. We want to govern democratically. But what is democracy after all? The will of all the people. As Minister I do not represent a party, but the State. When one has responsibility, my dear friend, things down below look different. Power confers responsibility.

KARL THOMAS: Power! What's the use of imagining you possess power, if the people have none? For five days I've been looking around. Has anything changed? You sit on top and legitimise the big con. Don't you understand that you've deserted the Idea, that you govern against the people?

WILHELM KILMAN: Sometimes it requires courage to govern against the people. More than going to the barricades.

(*Telephone rings.*)

Excuse me... Kilman... Unanimous decision to refuse overtime... Thank you, Herr Director... Does the leaflet

contain names? Aha... Make note: whoever leaves the
factory at five o'clock is dismissed without notice...
Good, the factories will close for a few days. Do a deal
with the private companies. The order for Turkey must
be filled... Goodbye, Herr Director... (*Hangs up.
Telephones again.*) Connect me with the police... Eva
Berg's file... Hurry up... Thank you. (*Hangs up.*)

KARL THOMAS: What courage! You have mastered the
methods.

WILHELM KILMAN: Whoever works on top here must
see to it that the complicated machinery doesn't come to
a standstill because of clumsy hands.

KARL THOMAS: Aren't those women fighting for your
old Ideas?

WILHELM KILMAN: Could I countenance the women
workers of any factory to obstruct the mechanism of the
State?

KARL THOMAS: Would your authority suffer so much?

WILHELM KILMAN: Should I make a fool of myself?
Should I show myself to be less capable than the old
Minister? A lot of the time it's not so easy... If one fails
only once, then... There are hours... You imagine it is
so... Oh, what do you know?...

KARL THOMAS: What do we know? You help the
reactionaries get into the saddle.

WILHELM KILMAN: Nonsense! In a democracy I have to
respect the rights of the employer just as much as the
rights of the employee. We don't have a utopia yet.

KARL THOMAS: But the other side has the Press, money,
weapons. And the workers? Empty fists.

WILHELM KILMAN: Oh, you only ever see armed
struggle, beating, stabbing, shooting. To the barricades!
To the barricades, all you workers! But we renounce the
struggle of brutal violence. Unceasingly we have
preached that we want to gain victory with moral and
spiritual weapons. Violence is always reactionary.

KARL THOMAS: Is that the opinion of the masses?
Haven't you even asked for their opinion?

WILHELM KILMAN: What are the masses? Were they able to accomplish any positive work in the old days? Nothing! Talk big and smash things up. We would have slid into chaos. Every adventurer got a command post. People who for the whole of their lives only knew about the workers from coffee house discussions. But let's be honest. We have saved the revolution… The masses are incompetent and they will remain incompetent for the time being. They lack all specialist knowledge. How could an untrained worker, in our epoch, take over the position of, let's say, the head of a syndicate? Or of the director of an electricity works? Later…in decades…in centuries…with education…with evolution…things will change. But today it is we who must govern.

KARL THOMAS: And to think I did time with you…

WILHELM KILMAN: Do you really think I'm a 'traitor'?

KARL THOMAS: Yes.

WILHELM KILMAN: Oh, my dear friend, I am used to that word. For you every bourgeois is a dirty scoundrel, a bloodsucker, a satan, or whatever. If you only grasped what the bourgeois world has achieved and is still achieving.

KARL THOMAS: Stop! You're twisting my words. I have never denied that the bourgeois world has achieved great things. I have never maintained that the bourgeoisie are raven black and the people snow white. But what has become of the world? Our Idea is the greater. If we succeed with it, we will achieve more.

WILHELM KILMAN: It comes down to tactics, dear fellow. With your tactics the darkest reaction would soon govern.

KARL THOMAS: I see no difference.

WILHELM KILMAN: Have you completely forgotten the whip marks lashed on your backs? What children you are. To want the whole tree when you can have an apple.

KARL THOMAS: What props you up? The old bureaucracy? And even if I believed your intentions were honourable, what are you in reality? A powerless scarecrow, a ping pong ball!

WILHELM KILMAN: What do you really want? Have a look at the inner workings here. How everything fits. How everything runs like clockwork. Everyone has expertise.

KARL THOMAS: And are you proud of that?

WILHELM KILMAN: Yes, of course, I am proud of my civil servants.

KARL THOMAS: We are speaking different languages…you mentioned a name a little while ago on the telephone.

WILHELM KILMAN: I was speaking about official matters.

KARL THOMAS: Eva Berg.

WILHELM KILMAN: Oh, her. She works in the Revenue Office. She's giving me a great deal of trouble. To think what's become of the little darling.

KARL THOMAS: She must be twenty-five years old now.

WILHELM KILMAN: I wanted to spare her. But she is rushing to her own ruin… I must say goodbye to you. Here, take this. (*Tries to give KARL THOMAS money; he refuses it.*) Unfortunately I cannot employ you. Go to the Trade Union. Perhaps you'll find some old friends there. I suppose so. One is so busy. One loses contact. May all go well with you. Don't do anything stupid. We are surely united in our goals. Only the means…

(Pushes KARL THOMAS gradually into the Antechamber. WILHELM KILMAN remains standing for a few seconds. Gesture.)

Antechamber

(KARL THOMAS stares, dumbstruck.)

PICKEL: (*To MINISTRY OFFICIAL.*) Is it my turn now, Herr Secretary?

MINISTRY OFFICIAL: Do you have an appointment?

PICKEL: I travelled two and a half days on the railway, Herr Secretary. Indeed one gets the shock of one's life on it. Are you familiar with Holzhausen?

MINISTRY OFFICIAL: Does the Minister know?

PICKEL: It's just with regard to the railway in Holzhausen.

MINISTRY OFFICIAL: I will inquire.
　　　　(*MINISTRY OFFICIAL goes into the Office.*)
PICKEL: Is the Minister, I wonder, a very stern man?
　　　　(*KARL THOMAS doesn't answer.*)
PICKEL: If the good Lord has made someone a Minister, as
　　far as I am concerned, I imagine he is…
　　　　(*As KARL THOMAS doesn't answer, PICKEL breaks off,
　　　　　　paces back and forth.*)

Office

WILHELM KILMAN: No, I don't mind. Show him in.
　　　　(*MINISTRY OFFICIAL opens the door to the Antechamber.*)
MINISTRY OFFICIAL: Herr Pickel.
　　　　(*PICKEL enters.*)
PICKEL: Your servant, Herr Minister. I have so much on
　　my mind, Herr Minister. Indeed you are surely very
　　busy. But nevertheless I don't want to steal your time
　　from you, Herr Minister. Pickel is my name. Born in
　　Holzhausen, Waldwinkel District. It is only with regard
　　to the railway which you want to build through
　　Holzhausen, Herr Minister. You know, I'm sure, in
　　October… Indeed, there is a saying with us: Hannes
　　would grease the pope's nose of a fatted goose… But
　　nevertheless just such a fatted goose was Holzhausen.
　　Steamers call three times a week; the mailcoach stops
　　every day the good Lord sends. As far as I am concerned
　　I would have… Indeed I certainly don't want to bring
　　myself into it… The Minister will know better… But
　　nevertheless this is certain, the Minister didn't know
　　that if the railway should pass over my property then…
　　I hope I'm not detaining you, Herr Minister.
WILHELM KILMAN: Well, my dear man, what's all this
　　about the railway?
PICKEL: I told my neighbour straightaway that when
　　I stand *vis à vis* the Minister then he will… Indeed he said
　　something about white gloves, and such matters… But
　　nevertheless I have always thought to myself: a Minister,
　　what a lot he must know! Almost as much as our Lord
　　God. Whether the harvest will be good, whether there will

be war, whether the railway will run over one's own property or another's... Yes, such is a Minister... Oh, I haven't come only with regard to the railway... Indeed the railway has its importance... But nevertheless the other matter also has its importance. When I was sitting back in Holzhausen...the newspapers, you don't get wise from them... I said to myself, when you are first standing *vis à vis* the Minister...if it is not asking too much, where do you imagine, where is all this leading to?... If now the railway runs through Holzhausen and one can travel straight to India?... And if in China the Yellows are rising up... And if there are machines with which one can shoot as far as America... and the niggers in Africa are talking big and want to throw the Mission out... And they say the Government wants to abolish money... Indeed Herr Minister is sitting here on top and he has to deal with all of it... Nevertheless I said to myself you will ask him for once himself: Herr Minister, what will become of the world?

WILHELM KILMAN: What will become of the world?

PICKEL: I mean what do you want to make out of it, Herr Minister?

WILHELM KILMAN: No, let's first drink a cognac. Do you smoke?

PICKEL: Too kind, Herr Minister. Indeed I said to myself straightaway, you only have to stand *vis à vis* the Minister...

WILHELM KILMAN: The world...the world... Hm...it is not very easy to answer that. Go on, drink.

PICKEL: That's just what I've always said to my neighbour. Indeed my neighbour, I mean the one who has rented the village common, at first it ought to have cost two hundred marks, but nevertheless he is related to the Mayor, and if one is related...

(*There is a knock.*)

MINISTRY OFFICIAL: I would like to remind you, Excellency, that at two o'clock Your Excellency must...

WILHELM KILMAN: Yes, I know... So, my dear Herr Pickel, have a peaceful journey back to Holzhausen. Give my greetings to Holzhausen... Go on, drink your cognac.

PICKEL: Yes, Herr Minister. And the railway… Indeed if after all it should run over my property, then…

WILHELM KILMAN: (*Pushing PICKEL gradually into the Antechamber before PICKEL can finish his cognac.*) No one will suffer an injustice.

Antechamber

PICKEL: (*Going out.*) I will take care of things for you in Holzhausen.

MINISTRY OFFICIAL: (*To KARL THOMAS who stands as if paralysed.*) You must go, we are closing.

Curtain.

[*Scaffolding revolves two metres to right.*]

Film Interlude

WOMEN AT WORK:

WOMEN AS TYPISTS

WOMEN AS CHAUFFEURS

WOMEN AS TRAIN DRIVERS

WOMEN AS POLICE

*

[*This film sequence was unfortunately cut.*]

ACT TWO

Scene One

[*Back projections of a slum alley on centre compartment screen. Factories on upper and middle left compartment screens. Roof with hanging clothes on upper right compartment screen. Other rooms on middle and bottom right compartment screens. Bottom left compartment open for scene with white wall back projected on its screen. Alarm rings in the dark before lights come up.*]

Eva Berg's Room

(*EVA BERG jumps out of bed, starts to dress hurriedly.*)

KARL THOMAS: (*In bed.*) Where are you going?

EVA BERG: To work, dear boy.

KARL THOMAS: What time is it?

EVA BERG: Half six.

KARL THOMAS: Stay here in bed until eight. Your office job doesn't start until nine.

EVA BERG: I must go to the Trade Union first. The election is in one week. The leaflets they printed for the women are dreadful. Last night when you were asleep I drafted the text for a new one.

KARL THOMAS: This life without work makes me lazier day by day.

EVA BERG: Yes, it's time you found work.

KARL THOMAS: Sometimes I think... Do you call that cut 'bobbed hair'?

EVA BERG: Do you like it?... How stupid, we don't have any representatives in the Sixth District. Just where have I left the papers?... Oh, here. (*Reads, corrects, writes.*)

KARL THOMAS: That cut suits you because you have a face. Women without faces have to watch out. That cut makes them naked. How many can get away with nakedness?

EVA BERG: Is that what you think?

KARL THOMAS: The faces in the street, on the underground, awful. Before I never saw how few people have faces. Most are lumps of flesh bloated by fear and conceit.

EVA BERG: Not a bad conclusion... Do you have burning desires for women inside?

KARL THOMAS: For the first seven years it was like I was buried... In the last year I suffered terribly.

EVA BERG: What do you do then?

KARL THOMAS: Some carry on like boys; others fantasise that sheets, a piece of bread or a coloured cloth are lovers.

EVA BERG: That last, conscious year must have been desperate for you.

KARL THOMAS: How often I hugged my pillow like a woman, greedy to get warm.

EVA BERG: Inside everyone the ice hounds bark... You must find work, Karl.

KARL THOMAS: But why... Eva, come with me... We'll travel to Greece. To India. To Africa. There must be places where men still live, childlike, who simply are, are. In whose eyes sky and sun and stars spin, brightly. Who know nothing of politics, who live without always having to struggle.

EVA BERG: Do politics make you sick? Do you think you could break their hold? Do you think southern sun, palm trees, elephants, colourful garments could make you forget the real life of men? This paradise you dream about does not exist.

KARL THOMAS: Since I saw Wilhelm Kilman I can't bear it any more. For what? So that our own comrades can smirk at the world like distorted mirror images of the old gang? No thanks. You must be my tomorrow and my dream of the future. You, I want you and nothing more.

EVA BERG: Escape, is it?

KARL THOMAS: Call it escape. What's in a word?

EVA BERG: You deceive yourself. By tomorrow impatience will be gnawing away at you, and a burning desire for your...destiny.

KARL THOMAS: Destiny?

EVA BERG: Because we cannot breathe in this air of factories and slums. Because otherwise we'll die like caged animals.

KARL THOMAS: Yes, you are right.

(*KARL THOMAS starts to dress.*)

EVA BERG: You must look around for another place to live, Karl.

KARL THOMAS: Can't I live with you any more, Eva?

EVA BERG: Honestly, no.

KARL THOMAS: Is the landlady grumbling?

EVA BERG: I would get her to stop it.

KARL THOMAS: Why not then?

EVA BERG: I must be able to be alone. Understand me.

KARL THOMAS: Don't you belong to me?

EVA BERG: Belong? That word is dead. Nobody belongs to anybody.

KARL THOMAS: Sorry, I used the wrong word. Aren't I your lover?

EVA BERG: Do you mean because I slept with you?

KARL THOMAS: Doesn't that bind us?

EVA BERG: One glance exchanged with a stranger on a run-down street can bind me to him more deeply than some night of love. Which need be nothing but very beautiful play.

KARL THOMAS: Then what do you take seriously?

EVA BERG: The here and now I take seriously. I also take play seriously... I am a living human being. Have I renounced the world because I'm in the struggle? The idea that a revolutionary has to forego the thousand little joys of life is absurd. All of us should take part in exactly what we want to.

KARL THOMAS: What is sacred...to you?

EVA BERG: Why mystical words for human things?... Why are you looking at me like that?... When I talk to you I feel that the last eight years, during which you were 'buried', have changed us more drastically than a century normally would have done.

KARL THOMAS: Yes, sometimes I feel I come from a lost generation.

EVA BERG: To think what the world has experienced since that episode.

KARL THOMAS: Just listen to how you speak of the revolution!

EVA BERG: That revolution was an episode. It is past.

KARL THOMAS: What remains?

EVA BERG: Us. With our will to honesty. With our strength for new work.

KARL THOMAS: And what if you got pregnant during these nights?

EVA BERG: I wouldn't give birth.

KARL THOMAS: Because you don't love me?

EVA BERG: How you miss the point. Because it would be an accident. Because it wouldn't seem necessary to me.

KARL THOMAS: If I use stupid words now, wrong words, don't listen; listen to the inexpressible things which you too cannot doubt. I need you. I found you in days when we heard the very heartbeat of life because the heartbeat of death pounded so loudly and unstoppably. I cannot find my way now. Help me, help me! The glowing flame has gone out.

EVA BERG: You are wrong. It glows in a different way. Less sentimentally.

KARL THOMAS: I don't feel it anywhere.

EVA BERG: What do you see? You are scared of broad daylight.

KARL THOMAS: Don't speak like that.

EVA BERG: Yes, let me speak. All talking things out is over. Irrevocably. Either you will gain strength for a new beginning or you will be destroyed. To support your false dreams out of pity would be criminal.

KARL THOMAS: So you did have pity?

EVA BERG: Probably. I am not clear myself. There is never only one reason.

KARL THOMAS: What kind of experience has hardened you over these years?

EVA BERG: Again you are using concepts which don't apply any more. I was a child, granted. We cannot afford to be children any more. We can't throw away the lucidity and knowledge we've gained like toys which don't please us any more. Experience – sure, I have experienced a lot. Men and situations. For eight years I've worked like only men worked before. For eight years I've made the decisions about every hour of my life. That's why I am how I am... Do you think it was easy for me? Often, when I sat in one of those ugly furnished rooms, I threw myself on the bed...and howled, like having a breakdown...and I thought, I can't go on any more... Then came work. The Party needed me. I clenched my teeth and... Be reasonable, Karl. I must go to the office.

(*FRITZ and GRETE peer round the door. Disappear again.*)

Stay here this morning. Do you need money? Don't say no out of stupid pride. I'll help you as a comrade, that's all. Farewell.

(*EVA BERG goes.*

KARL THOMAS remains alone for a few seconds.

FRITZ and GRETE, the landlady's children, open the door, look in curiously.)

FRITZ: Can we come in now?

GRETE: We'd like to have a look at you, you see.

KARL THOMAS: Yes, come in.

(*FRITZ and GRETE come in, both look at KARL THOMAS.*)

FRITZ: We have to go soon, you see.

GRETE: We have tickets for the movies.

FRITZ: And this evening we're going to the boxing match. Want to box now?

KARL THOMAS: No, I can't box.

FRITZ: Oh, I see.

GRETE: But you can dance, can't you? Do you know the Charleston or the Black Bottom?

KARL THOMAS: No, not that either.

GRETE: Pity... Were you really in the madhouse for eight years?

FRITZ: She can't believe it.

KARL THOMAS: Yes. For sure.

GRETE: And before that were you sentenced to death?

FRITZ: Mother told her. She read it in the newspaper.

KARL THOMAS: Your mother rents rooms?

GRETE: Of course.

KARL THOMAS: Is your mother poor?

FRITZ: Only the black marketeers are rich today, mother always says.

KARL THOMAS: Do you also know why I was sentenced to death?

GRETE: Because you were in the war.

FRITZ: Goose! Because he was in the Revolution.

KARL THOMAS: What do you know about the war then? Has your mother told you about it?

GRETE: No, not mother.

FRITZ: We have to learn the battles in school.

GRETE: What day they were on.

FRITZ: Stupid that the World War had to come. As if we didn't have enough to learn already in our History lesson. The Thirty Years' War lasted from 1618 to 1648.

GRETE: Thirty years.

FRITZ: We have to learn only half as many battles for that one as for the World War.

GRETE: And it only lasted four years.

FRITZ: The battle of Lüttich, the battle of the Marne, the battle of Verdun, the battle of Tannenberg…

GRETE: And the battle of Ypres.

KARL THOMAS: Don't you know anything else about the war?

FRITZ: That's enough for us.

GRETE: And how! The last time I got 'unsatisfactory' because I mixed up 1916 and 1917.

KARL THOMAS: And…what do you know about the Revolution?

FRITZ: We don't need to learn so many dates about that, which is easier.

KARL THOMAS: What can the suffering and the knowledge of millions mean if the next generation is already deaf to it all? All experience rushes into a bottomless pit.

FRITZ: What are you saying?

KARL THOMAS: How old are you?

GRETE: Thirteen.

FRITZ: Fifteen.

KARL THOMAS: And what are your names?

FRITZ: Fritz.

GRETE: Grete.

KARL THOMAS: What you have learned about the war is meaningless. You know nothing about the war.

FRITZ: Oh, no!

KARL THOMAS: How to describe it to you?... Mothers were...no. What's standing there at the end of the street?

FRITZ: A big factory.

KARL THOMAS: What is made in it?

FRITZ/GRETE: Acids...gas.

KARL THOMAS: What kind of gas?

GRETE: I don't know.

FRITZ: But I do. Poison gas.

KARL THOMAS: What is poison gas used for?

FRITZ: For when enemies attack us.

GRETE: Yes, against enemies if they try to destroy our country.

KARL THOMAS: Who are your enemies then?
    (*FRITZ and GRETE are silent.*)
    Give me your hand, Fritz... What could happen to this hand if a bullet shot through it?

FRITZ: Thanks a lot. Kaput.

KARL THOMAS: What would happen to your face if it got caught in just a tiny cloud of poison gas? Did you learn that at school?

GRETE: Sure did! Be eaten all away. To the bone.

KARL THOMAS: Would you like to die?

GRETE: That's a funny question. Of course not.

KARL THOMAS: And now I want to tell you a story. Not a fairy tale. A true story which happened near where I was. During the war I was stationed somewhere in France in a trench. Suddenly, at night, we heard screams, like a man in his death agony. Then it went still. Somebody had been killed, we thought. An hour later we heard screams again, and then they never stopped. The whole night long a man screamed. The whole day long a man screamed. More and more painfully, more and more helplessly. When it grew dark, two soldiers climbed out of the trench and tried to rescue the man who lay wounded between the trenches. Bullets whizzed by, and both soldiers were shot dead. Two others tried again. They didn't come back. Then the order came: nobody else allowed out of the trench. We had to obey. But the man kept on screaming. We didn't know whether he was French or German or English. He screamed like a baby screams, naked, without words. He screamed for four days and four nights. To us, it was four years. We stuffed our ears up with paper. It didn't help at all. Then it went still. Oh, children, I wish I had the power to plant a vision in your hearts like seed in ploughed earth. Can you picture to yourselves what happened then.

FRITZ: Of course.

GRETE: The poor man.

KARL THOMAS: Yes, dear girl, the poor man! Not: the enemy. The man. The man screamed. In France and in Germany and in Russia and in Japan and in America and in England. At such times, when you, how should I say it, get down to the ground water, you ask yourself: why all this? What is all this for? Would you ask the same thing too?

FRITZ/GRETE: Yes.

KARL THOMAS: In all countries men brooded over the same question. In all countries men gave the same answer. For gold, for land, for coal, for nothing but dead things, men die and starve and despair – that is the answer. And in some places the most courageous of the people rose up and rallied the blind to their strong cry of no, and demanded that this war should cease, and all wars; and they struggled for a world in which all children could thrive... Here among us they lost, here they were defeated.

(Long pause.)

FRITZ: Were there many of you?

KARL THOMAS: No, the people didn't understand what we were struggling for; didn't see that we were rising up for the sake of their own lives.

FRITZ: Were there many on the other side?

KARL THOMAS: Very many. They had weapons and money and soldiers who were paid.

(*Pause.*)

FRITZ: And were you so dumb to believe you could win?

GRETE: Yes, you were real dumb.

KARL THOMAS: (*Stares at them.*) What did you say?

FRITZ: You were dumb.

GRETE: Very dumb.

FRITZ: We must go now. Hurry up, Grete.

GRETE: Yes.

FRITZ/GRETE: Goodbye. See you.

(*Pause.*

EVA BERG comes back.)

EVA BERG: Now I could go travelling with you.

KARL THOMAS: What's up?

EVA BERG: Quick answer.

KARL THOMAS: Say it!

EVA BERG: I didn't get into the office. The porter gave me my dismissal notice. Got the sack.

KARL THOMAS: Kilman!

EVA BERG: Because I addressed the locked-out women workers yesterday afternoon.

KARL THOMAS: That swine!

EVA BERG: Are you surprised? Anyone who does a botched job with clay has to keep working it.

KARL THOMAS: Are you satisfied now, Eva? Come. Here's a time-table. We'll travel this very night. Away! Let's get away, let's get away!

EVA BERG: Are you speaking for both of us? Nothing has changed. Do you seriously believe I'd leave my comrades in the lurch?

KARL THOMAS: Sorry.

EVA BERG: Maybe you'd like to work with us?… Think it over.

(*EVA BERG goes out.*

KARL THOMAS stares after her.)

Blackout.

[*Black gauze and screen in. During film scaffolding moves back one metre to make room for next scene which was played in front of scaffolding.*]

Film Interlude

East End of a Big City.

FACTORIES

CHIMNEYS

CLOSING TIME

WORKERS LEAVE FACTORIES

CROWDS IN THE STREETS

*

[*Instead of the above, an election film was projected from front. Film and screen out. For the scene, posters and slogans back projected on right and left compartment screens. Film of ballot papers falling into box, lasting until nine o'clock strikes, back projected on centre compartment screen.*]

Scene Two

Worker's Bar

(*The raised space at the back is fitted out as a polling station. ELECTION OFFICER at a table, next to him SECOND ELECTION OFFICER. On the right, the voting booth. Entrance turned towards the auditorium. In the front, customers at tables. When there is dialogue at a table, it is brightly lit and the rest of the space is darker.*
THIRD WORKER enters.)

THIRD WORKER: Well, it's all go here. The great con flourishes.

SECOND WORKER: Man, shut up. We wouldn't get very far with your bloody anarchism.

THIRD WORKER: Sure, I know, if you vote you get far.

FIRST WORKER: Everything's all right in it's own way. Even the election. Otherwise it wouldn't happen. If you're so dumb not to grasp that...

SECOND WORKER: Only the stupidest sheep of all elect their own butchers...

FIRST WORKER: Do you mean us?

SECOND WORKER: Like a punch in the face?

(From the back.)

ELECTION OFFICER: Quiet in front. We can't hear our own voices... What is your name?

OLD WOMAN: Barbara Stilzer.

ELECTION OFFICER: Where do you live?

OLD WOMAN: From 1st October I shall live at 7 Schulstrasse.

ELECTION OFFICER: I would like to know where you live now.

OLD WOMAN: If the landlord thinks he can bully me because I complained at the Rent Office... 11 Margaretenstrasse, Fourth Floor.

ELECTION OFFICER: Right.

(OLD WOMAN remains standing.)

You can go cast your ballot.

OLD WOMAN: I only came because it's said they will punish you, if you don't vote.

ELECTION OFFICER: Well then, my dear woman, take a pencil, mark a cross next to the name of your candidate and put it in the ballot box in there.

OLD WOMAN: I don't have a ballot, Herr Detective Inspector... I didn't know I had to bring a ballot with me... How can you know where you are with all those paragraphs...

ELECTION OFFICER: I am not a Detective Inspector. I am the Election Officer. The Electioneers are over there. Go get one and then come back.

(The OLD WOMAN goes to the front.)

FIRST ELECTIONEER: Here, young woman, you must make a cross next to Number One. Then you will be voting for the right President. The Minister of War is concerned about Peace and Order and about Women.

(*The OLD WOMAN turns the ballot to and fro indecisively.*)

SECOND ELECTIONEER: No, little mother, just put your cross next to Number Two. Don't you want coal and bread to be cheaper?

OLD WOMAN: Shameful, how prices have gone up again.

SECOND ELECTIONEER: All because of the big landowners, little mother. They're raking in the bacon. Put your cross here, then you're voting for National Reconciliation.

(*The OLD WOMAN turns the ballot to and fro indecisively.*)

THIRD ELECTIONEER: As a class conscious proletarian vote for Number Three. A clear decision, comrade. Peace and Order – rubbish. Peace and Order for the Capitalists, not for you. National Reconciliation – rubbish. If you bow and scrape, then you'll get to lick the hand of brotherhood – otherwise you'll get a kick in the teeth. Your cross next to Number Three, or else you twist the noose around your own neck.

(*The OLD WOMAN turns the ballot to and fro indecisively.*)

FIRST ELECTIONEER: Next to Number One, young woman! Don't forget!

SECOND ELECTIONEER: Next to Number Two, little mother!

THIRD ELECTIONEER: Only Number Three will help you break your chains, comrade!

(*OLD WOMAN goes to the back.*)

[*Film of ALBERT KROLL's lorry arriving projected from front on to gauze.*]

ELECTION OFFICER: Do you have your ballot now?

OLD WOMAN: Here, three of them.

ELECTION OFFICER: Only put one in. Otherwise your vote is invalid.

(*The OLD WOMAN goes into the booth.*)

OLD WOMAN: May I come out again?

(*Comes out.*)

A very good evening to you, Herr Detective Inspector.

(To the ELECTIONEERS while going out.) It's all right, it's all right, don't get excited, don't get excited. I've made a cross next to all three.

(At the table left.)

FIRST WORKER: Giving women the right to vote! Only the dog collars profit from that.

SECOND WORKER: Before, when I had work, I didn't sit in the bar in one month as much as I do now in one day.

FIRST WORKER: And your wife? I wouldn't like to hear the smacks. You got enough scratches.

SECOND WORKER: The aid we get lets us guzzle herring and jam for four days and sniff wind for the next three. It comes down to the same thing.

FIRST WORKER: Went out the door yesterday and a bourgeois lady was standing outside the bar, you know, in high class lace, larded up from head to toe. She said out loud: "One must take pity on these people". I answered: "Frau Chamber of Commerce", I said, "perhaps the time will come round when you'll be only too happy if I take pity on you", I said.

SECOND WORKER: They ought to hang, nothing else but hang. The whole lot of them.

FIRST WORKER: We'll show them with this election.

(KARL THOMAS enters.)

KARL THOMAS: *(To the BARKEEPER.)* Does Albert Kroll come here?

BARKEEPER: He was just here. He should be right back.

KARL THOMAS: I'll wait.

(Sits at the table right.
In front of the ELECTION OFFICER's table:)

VOTER: I won't put up with this.

ELECTION OFFICER: A mistake, sir...

VOTER: Which cost me my right to vote. I'll lodge a protest against the election! The election must be declared invalid. I won't drop it! I'll go to the highest authorities!

ELECTION OFFICER: I fully admit that your entry was wrongly left off the voting register...

VOTER: That doesn't help me at all! I want my rights! My rights!

ELECTION OFFICER: According to the law I cannot...

VOTER: But take away my rights, that you can do. I'll sort things out here! I'll denounce this pigsty!

ELECTION OFFICER: Be reasonable, sir. Just consider what unrest you'll cause among the people...

VOTER: Doesn't matter to me. Rights are rights...

SECOND ELECTION OFFICER: Please, sir...

ELECTION OFFICER: As a good citizen you would not wish to...

VOTER: It must get into the papers, in black and white. There's more to this than meets the eye. Of all people it has to happen to me, it always has to happen to me, always, always, always! But that's enough now!

> (*Runs off, collides in the doorway with ALBERT KROLL who is coming in.*
>
> *ALBERT KROLL stops short, recognises KARL THOMAS.*)

ALBERT KROLL: Incredible!

KARL THOMAS: At last I've found you.

ALBERT KROLL: Poor devil. Been hard times. For us, too. Found work?

KARL THOMAS: I've been at the Employment Office six times. I learned typesetting when they threw me out of university. Old workmates act like a bunch of clerks towards you! Like section managers in a department store. Cold shoulder, worse than the proper ones. They could work just as perfectly in any department store.

ALBERT KROLL: Everyday life.

KARL THOMAS: You say it as if it has to be like that.

ALBERT KROLL: No. Only it doesn't upset me any more. Wait a minute, I'm going up there. I'm on the Election Committee. You got to keep a close eye on the devils.

> (*Up at the election table:*)

SECOND ELECTION OFFICER: What a turn out! What a turn out! The election is over in one hour and already eighty per cent. Eighty per cent!

ALBERT KROLL: Three hundred workers have protested because they were not included on the voting register.

ELECTION OFFICER: Not my fault. The ones from the housing block at the Chemical Works had to be crossed off. They haven't lived here for four months yet.

ALBERT KROLL: But the students have the right to vote. And how long have they been here? Only three weeks!

ELECTION OFFICER: The Ministry of the Interior has made that decision, not I.

ALBERT KROLL: We will lodge a protest against the election.

SECOND ELECTION OFFICER: (*On telephone.*) Is that the Sixth District? How many have voted? Sixty-five per cent? Here it's eighty! (*Hangs up telephone.*) Gentlemen, we're in the lead, and you want to lodge a protest...

(*ALBERT KROLL goes to KARL THOMAS.*)

ALBERT KROLL: Kilman has stolen the right to vote from the workers at the Chemical Works!

KARL THOMAS: I don't care. What does it matter? Albert, comrade, look at what has become of our struggle. A department store I said before. Everyone's sitting pretty at his own little job. Cash register One... Cash register Ten... Cash register Twelve... No breath of fresh air. The very air is rotting with order. Because some little bit was missing I had to submit all my papers all over again to the proper authorities. It's all gone mouldy with bureaucracy.

ALBERT KROLL: We know. We know even more. Those who failed at the decisive moment are talking big again today.

KARL THOMAS: And you just take it?

ALBERT KROLL: We struggle on. We are too few. Most have forgotten, want their peace and quiet. We must win over new comrades.

KARL THOMAS: Hundreds of thousands are unemployed.

ALBERT KROLL: When hunger sneaks in the front door, understanding sneaks out the back.

KARL THOMAS: You sound like an old man.

ALBERT KROLL: Years like these count ten times as long. We are learning.

KARL THOMAS: Herr Minister Kilman said the same thing.

ALBERT KROLL: Possible. Because he had something to hide. I want to show you the truth.

FOURTH WORKER: (*Coming in.*) Albert, the police have seized our van.

ALBERT KROLL: Why?

FOURTH WORKER: On account of the pictures! We made fun of the Minister of War.

ALBERT KROLL: Choose a delegation at once to make complaints at the Ministry.

FOURTH WORKER: We already tried that earlier today because a leaflet distributor got arrested. Kilman admits no one.

ALBERT KROLL: He supplied the Minister of War with a military band for free... Go on, go to the Ministry. Telephone me at once, if he refuses you.

(*FOURTH WORKER goes.*)

Did you hear, Karl?

KARL THOMAS: What's the election got to do with me? Show me your faith, your old faith, that was going to make a clean sweep of heaven and earth and the stars.

ALBERT KROLL: You mean I don't have it any more? Do I have to count up for you how many times we tried to throw off the damned yoke? Do I have to name you the names of all the old comrades who were hounded, locked up and murdered?

KARL THOMAS: Only faith counts.

ALBERT KROLL: We don't want eternal bliss in heaven. One must learn to see clearly and still keep from getting discouraged.

KARL THOMAS: Great leaders have never spoken like that.

ALBERT KROLL: Do you think? I imagine it differently. They just marched straight for it. On top of glass. And when they looked down through it, they saw the abyss formed from the hatred of the enemy and the stupidity of their own troops. And they probably saw much more.

KARL THOMAS: They wouldn't have moved a hand's breadth if they'd ever measured the depths beneath them.

ALBERT KROLL: Never measured. But always saw.

KARL THOMAS: All wrong, what you're doing. You even take part in the election con.

ALBERT KROLL: And what are you doing? What do you want to do?

KARL THOMAS: Something must happen. Someone must set an example.

ALBERT KROLL: Someone? Everyone. Every day.

KARL THOMAS: I mean something different. Someone must sacrifice himself. Then the lame will walk. Night and day I've pounded my brains. Now I know what I have to do.

ALBERT KROLL: I'm listening.

KARL THOMAS: Come here. Be discreet.
> (*Speaks softly with ALBERT KROLL.*)
> [*Piscator added the line "Kilman must go" for KARL THOMAS.*]

ALBERT KROLL: You're no use to us.

KARL THOMAS: It's the only way I can help myself. Disgust chokes me.
> (*ALBERT KROLL goes to the ELECTION OFFICER's table again.*)

ALBERT KROLL: The police have seized our van. That's sabotage of the workers' candidate.

A VOTER: Your candidate's been bribed by foreigners.

ALBERT KROLL: Lies! Election propaganda!

ELECTION OFFICER (*To ALBERT KROLL.*) You must not electioneer. (*To VOTER.*) This isn't an information office, Herr Master Butcher.

ALBERT KROLL: I don't want to electioneer. But I'm still allowed to tell the truth.

SECOND ELECTION OFFICER: (*On the telephone.*) What time do you make it? Eight-fifty?... Yes, yes, it's all go here. Huge turnout. They're even bringing in the sick on stretchers. (*Hangs up.*) The clock in the Fifteenth District is eight minutes fast. Eight minutes! I didn't tell them. Because we'll get to know the results eight minutes sooner.

(ALBERT KROLL goes to KARL THOMAS' table.)

ALBERT KROLL: They shut me up when I tell the truth. I won't bow and scrape.

KARL THOMAS: What great courage! In truth you are all cowards. All, all, all! Wish I'd stayed in the madhouse! Now even my own plan disgusts me. What for? For a bunch of petit bourgeois cowards who believe in elections?

ALBERT KROLL: You'd like the world to be an eternal firework display set off just for you, with rockets and flares and the roar of battle. You're the coward, not me.

(At the table left.)

FIRST WORKER: Did'ya vote yet?

SECOND WORKER: No, I'm going now. Why shouldn't I vote for National Reconciliation when the ladyship my Lina works for is voting that way too. There must be something wrong with Kilman, I tell you; Lina's ladyship has brains in her head. She's really classy. On Sunday when Lina has a day off, her ladyship always comes into the kitchen. "Lina", she says, "I wish you a good Sunday". And then she shakes hands with her. Every time.

FIRST WORKER: How about that!

(SECOND WORKER goes to the election table. PICKEL comes in.)

PICKEL: Excuse me, can one vote here?

(The ELECTIONEERS surround PICKEL.)

FIRST ELECTIONEER: Law and Order in the land, with God for our dear Fatherland! Vote for Number One.

SECOND ELECTIONER: Awake, you people, it's not too late. Don't support the right or left, support the State. Vote for Number Two.

THIRD ELECTIONEER: The President of Number Three sets the workers and the peasants free! Vote for Number Three!

PICKEL: Thank you, thank you.

(PICKEL goes to the ELECTION OFFICER's table.)

ELECTION OFFICER: What is your name?

PICKEL: Pickel.

ELECTION OFFICER: Where do you live?

PICKEL: Indeed I live in Holzhausen, but nevertheless...

ELECTION OFFICER: You are not entered on the voting register... Do you spell your name with a B?

PICKEL: Where will I... Pickel... Pickel with a P... P... Not two Ps... Indeed I would like to explain that...

ELECTION OFFICER: Your explanation is of no use. You are not allowed to vote here. You are in the wrong polling place.

PICKEL: I must explain to you... Indeed I live in Holzhausen...

ELECTION OFFICER: What do you want here? Don't hold the election up. Next...

(*The voting continues.*)

PICKEL: (*Going to KARL THOMAS.*) Indeed it's all the same to me personally whether I vote or not, but nevertheless I don't want to be ungrateful to the Minister... I'd like to give him my vote.

KARL THOMAS: Leave me alone.

(*PICKEL goes to the THIRD WORKER.*)

PICKEL: Indeed I would have travelled home a long time ago. I only wanted to stay one day, but nevertheless it never stopped raining.

THIRD WORKER: Wish it was pissing down in here. Oughta flood out the whole show. All a fraud. They oughta wipe their bums with the ballots.

PICKEL: That's not what I meant. Namely I don't travel in rainy weather. I waited six weeks before I travelled to see the Minister, because there was always a thunderstorm in the sky.

(*BANKER comes in.*
ELECTIONEERS surround him.)

BANKER: Thanks.

(*Goes to the ELECTION OFFICER.*)

ELECTION OFFICER: At your service, Herr Director General. Herr Director General, do you still live in Opernplatz?

BANKER: Yes, I've come a little late.

ELECTION OFFICER: Early enough, Herr Director General. Over there, if you please.

   (*BANKER goes into the voting booth.*)

PICKEL: I had an uncle who was struck by lightning on the railway. Indeed the railways attract the lightning, but nevertheless it's men who bear the guilt for it with their new-fangled commotions.

ELECTION OFFICER: (*To BANKER who has left the voting booth.*) Your most obedient servant, Herr Director General, sir.

   (*BANKER goes.*)

THIRD WORKER: He comes first, no one else, and the stupid workers guzzle his dust.

PICKEL: The radio and the electric waves, they mess up the atmosphere. Indeed…

ELECTION OFFICER: The poll is closed.

   [*Film of falling ballots stops. Back projection of heap of ballots in its place on centre compartment screen.*]

FIRST WORKER: Now I'm really curious.

SECOND WORKER: Want to bet that the Minister of War is defeated?

THIRD WORKER: He'll be elected! And it serves you right!

SECOND WORKER: Don't talk such stupid rubbish, you old anarchist!

   RADIO:

Attention! Attention! First election results. Twelfth District. 714 votes for the Minister of War, His Excellency von Wandsring. 414 votes for Minister Kilman. 67 for Bricklayer Bandke.

SECOND WORKER: Ouch!

FIRST WORKER: Rigged!

THIRD WORKER: Bravo!

   (*FIRST and THIRD WORKERS go.*)

PICKEL: Herr Election Officer, you must not close. I insist… Indeed I am only…but nevertheless those in the big city always want us… Namely, I know Herr Minister Kilman, I've become friends with him…

ELECTION OFFICER: Make a complaint then.

PICKEL: If Minister Kilman now polls one vote too little.
   Just think if it's because of my vote...

RADIO:

Attention! Attention! Report from Osthafen. 6,000 for Bricklayer
Bandke. 4,000 for Minister Kilman. 2,000 for His Excellency von
Wandsring.

CROWD IN STREET: Hurrah! Hurrah!

ALBERT KROLL: The dock workers! Our pioneers! Bravo!

KARL THOMAS: Why bravo? How can you be pleased
   about votes? Are they a deed?

ALBERT KROLL: Deed – no. But a springboard to deeds.

RADIO:

Attention! Attention! According to the latest reports Minister
Kilman has the majority in the capital.

CROWD IN STREET: Three cheers for Kilman! Three
   cheers for Kilman!

SECOND WORKER: Didn't I tell you? Come on, my
   three glasses of beer! Pay up! Pay up!

FIRST WORKER: Who said anything about three glasses
   of beer? We agreed one round.

SECOND WORKER: Now you're wriggling out of it!

FIRST WORKER: Just shut up, or else...

PICKEL: As far as I'm concerned I will not be quiet... The
   Minister would have had, if my vote... He would have
   had another vote... Indeed his election...

SECOND ELECTION OFFICER: Gentlemen, we have
   broken the record. Ninety-seven per cent election turnout!
   Ninety-seven per cent!

KARL THOMAS: If I could only understand! If I could
   only understand! Have I got caught in a crazy house?

RADIO:

Attention! Attention! At nine-thirty we shall announce the results.

SECOND WORKER: I'll bet on Kilman. Ten rounds? Who
   takes it?

PICKEL: I would straightaway...if my vote...

SECOND ELECTION OFFICER: We must put it in the
   papers. Ninety-seven per cent election turnout. That's
   never happened before! That's never happened before.

PICKEL: If you had allowed me to vote, the percentage
would have…
(*Tumult outside the door. WORKERS come in.*)
THIRD WORKER: They've killed Mother Meller.
FOURTH WORKER: What gangsters! An old woman!
ALBERT KROLL: What's going on?
FIFTH WORKER: She tried to paste up an election leaflet
at the Chemical Works.
FOURTH WORKER: With a truncheon! An old woman.
THIRD WORKER: Smashed to the pavement and done
for!
FIFTH WORKER: Since when is it forbidden to paste up
leaflets?
THIRD WORKER: Good question! Since we have a free
election.
FOURTH WORKER: Smack on the head. An old woman.
KARL THOMAS: Did you hear?
ALBERT KROLL: Move, comrades.
(*ALBERT KROLL tries to go to the door.*
At this moment they bring in FRAU MELLER unconscious.
ALBERT KROLL makes a bed for her on the ground.)
A pillow… Water!… Unconscious. She's alive…
FOURTH WORKER: No warning. Smack with a truncheon.
An old woman.
ALBERT KROLL: Coffee!
FIFTH WORKER: What about the constitution! They're
going to have to answer for this.
THIRD WORKER: Who to? To their boss, the judge? Man,
you're naive.
ALBERT KROLL: Mother Meller, I… Breathe calmly…
Like that… Now you can lie back again. This is Karl
Thomas. Do you recognise him?
FRAU MELLER: You, Karl…
ALBERT KROLL: What happened? Can you tell us?
FRAU MELLER: Oh, we forgot to dot an i on the leaflet. So
some devil dotted the back of my head with a truncheon.
In bold type… They've arrested Eva.
(*Tumult at the door.*
FIRST and THIRD WORKERS come in with RAND.)

FIRST WORKER: Here's the little brother!

THIRD WORKER: I know him. Regular guest at our meetings. Always the most radical.

FIRST WORKER: Agent provocateur!

OTHER WORKERS: (*Closing in upon RAND.*) Smash him up! Smash him!

> (*ALBERT KROLL jumps in between them, grabs RAND's arm with his right hand.*)

ALBERT KROLL: Order!

KARL THOMAS: To hell with order! Should we swallow everything. That's your election victory for you!

> (*KARL THOMAS tries to knock RAND down.*
> *ALBERT KROLL grabs KARL THOMAS with his left hand.*)

You...you...let go!

ALBERT KROLL: You take him, Mother Meller.

FIFTH WORKER: Hadn't we better ask the Party?

ALBERT KROLL: The Party! Are we babies in nappies?

RAND: Thank you very much, Herr Kroll.

ALBERT KROLL: Where do we know each other from?

RAND: I was once your warder.

FRAU MELLER: Well I'll be damned. A great reunion! We ought to drink a little cup of coffee together.

RAND: Haven't I always treated you in a friendly way, Herr Kroll. You must grant me that.

ALBERT KROLL: So friendly that if they ordered you to bump us off, you would have fetched us one by one...with a voice sweet as honey and a face fit for kissing... "Please don't make it hard for me, I'm only doing my duty, it'll be over soon".

> (*WORKERS laugh.*)

RAND: What should a man do? I am only a worker like you. I have to live too. Got five children. And pay to make you puke. I'm only carrying out my orders.

FIRST WORKER: Here's the revolver we got off him.

> (*KARL THOMAS jumps up, grabs the revolver, aims it at RAND.*)

ALBERT KROLL: (*Hits his arm.*) Stop fooling about!

> (*FRAU MELLER has run over to KARL THOMAS, pulls him to her.*)

What have you stuffed up your belly? You don't care about the craze for being slim! (*Pulls leaflets about of RAND's waistcoat, reads.*) "Comrades, beware of the Jews"… "Foreign elements". "Don't allow the Elders of Zion…" So you've got principles too?

RAND: You bet! The Jews…

ALBERT KROLL: How much cash do your principles earn you?… Now get out! March! I've protected you once… I couldn't do it a second time – even if I wanted to.

(*RAND goes.*)

WORKERS: Just wait till you get caught again!

KARL THOMAS: No, Mother Meller, no, let me go. I want to speak to him… Why are you putting the breaks on me?

ALBERT KROLL: Because I want to go full steam ahead when it's time. It takes strength to have patience.

KARL THOMAS: Kilman says the same thing.

ALBERT KROLL: Fool.

KARL THOMAS: Then what should I do to understand you?

ALBERT KROLL: Work somewhere.

FRAU MELLER: I know what to do, boy. The hotel where I work needs an assistant waiter. I'll work on the head waiter. Got somewhere to stay? You can sleep at my place.

ALBERT KROLL: Do it, Karl. You must get involved in everyday life.

FRAU MELLER: I like you, Albert. Drinking my coffee like it was your own… Another cup, barkeeper…

FOURTH WORKER: With a truncheon. An old woman.

RADIO:

Attention! Attention! (*Radio fails… Buzzing noises.*)

PICKEL: The atmosphere…

RADIO:

[*Back projected on the centre compartment screen, the bottom of the WAR MINISTER appears out of the heap of ballots and then he turns to the front and climbs out of the pile.*]

The Minister of War, His Excellency Wandsring, has been elected as President of the Republic by a great majority.

(*While*
shouting and singing swirl up
in the street,
the picture
of the PRESIDENT
appears
on the cyclorama.)

[*Screen in and film of the WAR MINISTER projected on*
it from the front.]

Curtain.

[*The interval was here. During it, the scaffolding was pushed*
to the front again and revolved to the left so that it's back was
at an angle to the audience.]

ACT THREE

[*After the interval, Act Three began with Kate Kühl singing this song in the middle of the stage. She was lit by two follow-spots focused on her head and sang in a raucous cabaret style.*

Hoppla, We're Alive!

Intermezzo for the Hotel Scene in Toller's Play by Walter Mehring

The cream of society stay
    At Hotel Earth *à-la-mode* –
Blithely holding at bay
    Life's unbearable load!
    Partaking of good consummation –
    They proffer a war declaration
    Instead of a cheque for the till –
Here diplomats congregate,
Our plight to deliberate,
They say: We have need of a war
And much better times will arrive!
There's one politics and no more:
Hoppla, we're alive –
    We're alive and we'll settle the bill!

Sabre-rattling Chauvinisms – Ecstatical Populisms –
Which dance will you dance in the morn?
    Hoppla!
Poison Gas-isms – Humanity-isms –
Our cares forlorn!
    Hoppla!
    Our hearts do bleed in distress
    From the sensationalist press,
    Hoppla!
    Freedom – behind bars survive –
    Into trenches dive.
    Hoppla! We're alive!

The men of the military stay
    At Hotel Earth *à-la-mode* –

We fight their battles each day –
>> But hatred for us is their code!
>> Spending in blood at their whims,
>> They tip us in artificial limbs
>> And leave a mass grave to fill –
>> But when it's time to propose
>> They pay for all the death-throes:
The Commander-in-Chief comes along,
And with him the clergy connive –
To sing, so moved, this epic song:
Hoppla, we're alive –
>> We're alive! And we'll settle the bill!

The helmet-head – and the Red –
Will our enemies be come morn.
>> Hoppla!
And over three million dead –
Our cares forlorn!
>> Hoppla!
>> Our hearts do bleed all the more
>> Under the weight of iron ore!
>> Hoppla!
>> Freedom – behind bars survive –
>> Into trenches dive.
>> Hoppla! WE'RE alive!

Exposed to murder and war
>> At Hotel Earth *à-la-mode* –
In the cellar so mean and so sore
>> The proletarian herd makes abode –
>> They fork out an arm and a leg
>> For the little they're able to beg –
>> And the whole gang collapses drained of all will!
>> Then the managers come and they shout:
>> We have lost out!
>> We gave you emergency shelter, you see,
>> And also a crutch to revive,
>> You are half-dead! – But we,
>> Hoppla! We're alive –
>> We're alive and we'll settle the bill!

You have nothing to lose and you're choking!
Can't borrow from us we've sworn!
          Hoppla!
Starving, freezing – and croaking –
Our cares forlorn!
          Hoppla!
We're bleeding away our stash!
You proles, give us our cash!
          Freedom? Behind bars survive –
          Into trenches dive —
          Hoppla! We're alive!

The cream of society stay
          At Hotel Earth *à-la-mode* –
Blithely holding at bay
          Life's unbearable load!
          Our foes were thrashed with devotion –
          Do give that cripple a groschen!
          Our funds are almost at nil!
Ministers, Philosophers and Poets of fame:
They all once again look the same!
All is just like it was before the last war –
And before the next war to arrive —
For battlefield music, the Charleston's the score!
Hoppla! They're alive!
When we settle their bill!

If we bring it all down unawares –
Which dance will you dance in the morn
          Hoppla?
If it's our cares that reign, instead of theirs,
Our cares that were once so forlorn
          Hoppla!
Then pray for your God's absolution
From death by electric execution
Hoppla!
          With your generals we'll strive!
WE'LL command and WE'LL thrive:
Hoppla! We're alive!]

Scene One

[*Scaffolding revolved to the back to bring the STUDENT's room,
which had been set up and rolled in on the right, to the front. For
ten seconds, film of a busy city at night was projected directly on the
stage without the gauze and with appropriate night-life sounds,
probably including the Hoppla song. As film ends, lights up on
room in front of scaffolding.*]

Small Room

(*STUDENT is reading.
There's a knock.*)

STUDENT: Who's there?

(*COUNT LANDE enters.*)

COUNT LANDE: Well, what do you say about the new
President?

STUDENT: I'm sure he has the best intentions.

COUNT LANDE: What good is that for us... Kilman still
remains as Minister.

STUDENT: Really?

COUNT LANDE: Do you have a cigarette?... Our front
group ought to be disbanded.

STUDENT: What? What are you saying?

COUNT LANDE: Kilman...

STUDENT: Then something really must be done. We
always talk about the great deed...

COUNT LANDE: Can anyone eavesdrop at the door?

STUDENT: No... What's the matter?

COUNT LANDE: Here.

STUDENT: The decision?

COUNT LANDE: Read it.

(*COUNT LANDE gives STUDENT a piece of paper.*)

STUDENT: I and Lieutenant Frank?

COUNT LANDE: Both of you.

STUDENT: When?

COUNT LANDE: I can't say. You have to be ready at any
time.

STUDENT: How quick it's come.

COUNT LANDE: Are you hesitating? Haven't you volunteered twice? Can you forget that the same Kilman who should have been put up against the wall eight years ago now, as Minister, betrays the Fatherland?

STUDENT: Hesitating – no. It goes against the grain to have to wait for the deed.

COUNT LANDE: Hold your horses, *basta*! You took the oath of allegiance; Patriotism has sailed you into shore and now, quite rightly, you are ordered to drop anchor.

STUDENT: And what if we are hunted, hounded, and trapped...in front of closed frontiers?

COUNT LANDE: In the first place, that is not very likely... If you get stuck in a blind alley, you will be helped. If you reach the frontier, good. If you don't reach it... You must make the sacrifice... Besides you needn't doubt that the judges will be reasonable and show complete understanding for your motives.

STUDENT: May I leave a letter for my mother?

COUNT LANDE: Out of the question. Nationalism must not depend on chance. I know there are cowards ready to compromise in our ranks. They would readily sacrifice us for the sake of political tactics.

STUDENT: I understand so little about politics. I didn't even see service at the front. I joined up and one month later everything collapsed. I hate the Revolution like I've never hated anything. Ever since that one day. My uncle was a General. We boys worshipped him like a god. By the end he commanded an army corps. Three days after the Revolution I'm sitting beside him, the bell rings. A mere Private barges in. "I'm on the Soldiers' Council. It's been reported to us, Herr General, that you have provoked the people in the street by wearing your golden epaulettes. Today there are no more epaulettes. We all have bare shoulders." My uncle stood bolt

upright. "I should surrender my epaulettes, should I?"
"Yes." My uncle takes his sword, which is lying on the
table, and draws it out of its scabbard. I'm very
frightened. Move nearer so I can help him, when
I see the old man cough a hacking cough with tears in
his eyes. "Herr Soldiers' Council, for forty years I have
worn the uniform of my Emperor with honour. Once
I witnessed how a sergeant was disgraced by having his
stripes ripped off. What you demand of me today is the
lowest thing anyone can demand of me. If I can no
longer wear my uniform with honour, here..." And at
that moment the old man bent his sword, broke it in two
and threw it at the feet of the soldier. That soldier was
Herr Kilman...

COUNT LANDE: That dog!

STUDENT: The next day my uncle shot himself. On
a piece of paper he left behind there were these
words: "I cannot survive the shame of our beloved
Fatherland. May my death open the eyes of the
inflamed people."

COUNT LANDE: My career went bust too. What are we
today compared to the rabble? Stooges. And in society
always miles behind the moneybags... We will avenge
your uncle. The goods have got to be delivered.

Blackout.

[*As the same film is again projected directly on to the
stage, the scaffolding revolves to the right until its front is
again facing the audience. When it reaches halfway point,
a film of hotel scenes is projected from the back and when
the revolve stops this film continues on the centre
compartment screen. Throughout the revolve, all the characters run around the scaffolding with as much movement
as possible, particularly on the stairs, to their places in
frenzied cacophony.*]

Scene Two

The façade of the Grand Hotel can be seen.
The front wall opens.
Rooms of the Grand Hotel can be seen.

Diagram:

						Grand Hotel						
						Radio Station						
87	88	89	W C	90	91	92	93	94	95	96 open	97	98
26	27	28	29	30	31	32	33	34	W C	35	36	37
Private Room				Lobby					Club Room			
Hotel Staff Room and Servery									Writing Room			

Blackout.

Lights up:

The Lobby

(*Dancing couple.*)

Blackout.

(*Between the separate scenes the Lobby can be seen for a few moments and a jazz band heard.*)

Lights up:

Staff Room

[*This section was cut.*]
(*KARL THOMAS in waiter's uniform sits at a table. FRAU MELLER looks in through the door.*)

FRAU MELLER: Here, boy, a beef steak. It came back from a room. I warmed it up quick.

KARL THOMAS: Thanks a lot, Mother Meller. I have exactly five more minutes. My employment begins at eight o'clock.

FRAU MELLER: I must go to the kitchen again to wash up… What a sight you are! I really wouldn't have recognised you. Ten years younger. But Karl, Karl, why are you always laughing?

KARL THOMAS: Don't be frightened, Mother Meller. You needn't fear that I'll go crazy again. Everywhere I applied for a job, the bosses asked me: "Man, what's that undertaker's face for? You'll scare the customers away. Nowadays you have to laugh, always laugh." Then, because rejuvenation is only a sport for rich people, I went to a beautician. And here's the new façade. Aren't I sweet enough to eat?

FRAU MELLER: Yes, Karl. You'll go down a treat with the girls. But it was weird to me at first… What demands they make. Next we'll have to sign contracts to laugh the whole ten hours we slave away… Well, eat now, boy. I must go back to the kitchen.

Blackout.

Lights up:

Private Room

[*Scaffolding revolved one and a half metres right for close-up effect. Back projection of wallpaper in middle left compartment. Lobby back projection always on in centre compartment.*]
(*Enter BANKER, BANKER'S SON, HEAD WAITER, BUSBOY.*)

BANKER: Everything ready?

HEAD WAITER: Here's the menu. Would you like any changes, Herr Director General?

BANKER: Good. For me personally bring something light; I can't eat anything heavy, my stomach… Perhaps broth, a little chicken meat, compote, but unsugared.

HEAD WAITER: At your service, Herr Director General.
(*The HEAD WAITER goes out.*)

BANKER'S SON: I'm still not sure.

BANKER: Why shouldn't we drive our coach on the route through his wife? An attempt, what does it matter?

BANKER'S SON: She must be simplicity in person. Recently at a government banquet she told stories about her days as a cook.

BANKER: I would have liked to see Kilman's face… My dear man, one doesn't hear 'Excellency' here and 'Excellency' there every day without being punished. Yes, if there were still titles and orders… But today money is the only foundation. As soon as one has his first hundred-thousand, he hangs his idealism up on the hatstand. Don't worry, he'll get a fat bank account and I'll get the cheap public credits.

BANKER'S SON: Just as you think.
(*WILHELM KILMAN and his WIFE enter, accompanied by HEAD WAITER and KARL THOMAS as Waiter, who helps both take off their outer garments.*)
Good evening, Herr Minister. Extremely delighted, Madam.

WILHELM KILMAN: Government devours you. People always imagine that we sit around in club chairs and

smoke thick cigars. Excuse me for being late. I had to
receive the Mexican Ambassador.

BANKER'S SON: Now we can begin.

(*All sit at the table.*

HEAD WAITER brings food, KARL THOMAS helps.)

FRAU KILMAN: What's this lying next to my plate?

BANKER: A *petit rien*, madam. I took the liberty of
bringing a rose for you.

FRAU KILMAN: A rose? But I see a case... In gold?... Set
with pearls?...

BANKER: It opens here... This catch... See, the rose... La
France... My special rose. I hope you too like this sort...

FRAU KILMAN: Really, Herr Director General, very kind,
but I cannot accept it. Whatever could I do with it?

WILHELM KILMAN: Come now, Herr Director General...

BANKER: Please, my dear Minister, don't make a fuss. Just
yesterday I bought three of these things at auction,
eighteenth century, Louis Quartorze, even though
I already possess two or three.

FRAU KILMAN: You are so nice. We thank you for your
kindness, but please take the case back.

WILHELM KILMAN: You know malicious tongues. One
must avoid the least appearance...

BANKER: I am immensely sorry that I didn't think of it...

WILHELM KILMAN: So let's drink to a compromise.
Emma, please take the rose. What a scent it has, this La
France. Better than the real one, ha ha ha... And when
we visit you we'll be able to admire the case in your
display cabinet.

BANKER: To your health, Madam. Your good health, Herr
Minister... Waiter, bring a bottle of Mouton Rothschild
'21...

KARL THOMAS: Yes, indeed, sir.

Blackout.

Lights up:

Radio Station

[*This section was moved to after the second scene in Room 96. Piscator rewrote some of it to emphasise political and economic events affecting KARL THOMAS.*]

RADIO OPERATOR: You finally came? I rang all of three times.

KARL THOMAS: I was busy down below.

RADIO OPERATOR: Here's a telegram for Minister Kilman. It was transmitted here by order of the Ministry.

KARL THOMAS: Can you really listen to the whole earth here?

RADIO OPERATOR: Is that news to you?

KARL THOMAS: What are you listening to now?

RADIO OPERATOR: New York. A great flood on the Mississippi is being reported.

KARL THOMAS: When?

RADIO OPERATOR: Now, at this very moment.

KARL THOMAS: While we speak?

RADIO OPERATOR: Yes, while we speak, the Mississippi is breaking its banks, people are fleeing.

KARL THOMAS: And what are you listening to now?

RADIO OPERATOR: I've tuned in to the 1100 wavelength. I'm listening to Cairo. The jazz band at Mena House, the hotel near the pyramids. They're playing during dinner. Want to have a listen? I'll switch on the loudspeaker.

LOUDSPEAKER: Attention! Attention! All Radio Stations of the world! The latest hit is 'Hoppla, We're Alive!'!
(Jazz music can be heard.)

RADIO OPERATOR: You can see them too.
(Visible on the screen: restaurant at Mena House. Ladies and gentlemen are dining.)

KARL THOMAS: Can you also see the Mississippi?

RADIO OPERATOR: Of course. But where have you been that makes you act like such a babe in arms?

KARL THOMAS: Oh, I've lived only in a…little village for the last ten years.

RADIO OPERATOR: Here.

LOUDSPEAKER: Attention! Attention! New York.
Number of dead: 8,000. Chicago threatened. Further
report follows in three minutes.
(Visible on the screen: scenes from the flood.)
KARL THOMAS: Inconceivable! At this very second...
LOUDSPEAKER: Attention! Attention! New York. New
York. Royal Shell 104, Standard Oil 102, Rand Mines 116.
KARL THOMAS: What is that?
RADIO OPERATOR: The New York Stock Exchange.
Petroleum shares on offer... I'll turn the dial. Latest news
from around the world.
LOUDSPEAKER: Attention! Attention! Uprising in India...
Uprising in China... Uprising in Africa... Paris Paris:
Houbigant, the chic perfume... Bucharest Bucharest:
Famine in Roumania... Berlin Berlin: The lady of fashion
favours green wigs... New York New York: Largest
bomber in the world invented. Capable of demolishing
Europe's capital cities in a second... Attention! Attention!
Paris London Rome Berlin Calcutta Tokyo New York: The
complete gentleman drinks Mumm's Extra Dry...
KARL THOMAS: Enough, enough. Turn it off.
RADIO OPERATOR: I'll turn the dial.
LOUDSPEAKER: *(A clamour of cries is heard.)* Hey, hey,
hey! Give it to him hard!...he's dizzy... A fix! *(A bell.)*
he's saved!... MacNamara, Tonani! MacNamara!... Eviva,
eviva...
RADIO OPERATOR: Six-day bicycle race in Milan... Now
I'm getting something interesting. The first passenger
aeroplane from New York to Paris radios that a passenger
is having a heart attack. They are seeking contact with
heart specialists. They want medical advice. Right, now
you can hear the heartbeat of the patient.
(The heartbeats can be heard over the loudspeaker.
On the screen can be seen: The aeroplane over the ocean.
The patient.)
[*Piscator showed a beating heart.*]
KARL THOMAS: A human heartbeat over the middle of
the ocean...
RADIO OPERATOR: A great event.

KARL THOMAS: How wonderful it all is! And what does mankind do with it... They live like muttonheads a thousand years behind the times.

RADIO OPERATOR: We won't change things. I discovered a method to make petroleum out of coal. They bought up my patent for a handful of scraps of paper and then what did they do? Destroyed it! The high and mighty oil magnates... You have to go now. The telegram is urgent. Who knows what tomorrow brings. Perhaps there's war.

KARL THOMAS: War?

RADIO OPERATOR: These apparatuses lead the way there too, helping men kill each other with all the more sophistication. What's the star turn of electricity? The electric chair. There are machines with electric wavelengths such that if they're turned on in London, Berlin would be a heap of rubble by tomorrow. We won't change things. Off you go, hurry up.

KARL THOMAS: Yes, sir.

Blackout.

Lights up:

Club Room

[*This section was cut.*]
(*Discussion evening of the Union of Intellectual Brain Workers.*)

PHILOSOPHER X: I come to my conclusion: Where Quality is absent, there is nothing to counterpose Quantity. Therefore my precept runs: Let no one marry beneath his own level. Rather let everyone endeavour, by the appropriate choice of a mate, to raise his posterity to a higher level than he himself possesses. But what do we practice, gentlemen? Nothing but negative selective breeding. The very least, gentlemen, the very least condition of every marriage contract should be equality of birth. We trust instinct. But unfortunately instinct has been so thoroughly one-sided for centuries that it will not be so easy, for several generations, even in some two hundred years, to breed our way up to something better.

LYRIC POET Y: Where does that appear in Marx?

PHILOSOPHER X: I conclude: the instincts must be refined and spiritualised; they must strive ever more away from the Brutal-Vital and towards the Absolute-Superior.

LYRIC POET Y: Where does that appear in Marx?

PHILOSOPHER X: Only thus can the hopelessly degenerated white race be raised up again. Only thus can it nurture superior blooms as it once did. Yet, how can one, many will ask, recognise someone of good blood? Well, whoever cannot judge that in himself and in others, but in himself above all, cannot be helped to do so. He has become so lacking in instinct (*Directed to LYRIC POET Y.*) that I personally can only urgently recommend extinction. Indeed that is what is great in my Academy of Wisdom: it makes people wise by persuading those who formerly bred away blithely to become extinct of their own free will. Now when this is done logically, then in this domain, too, Evil will be conquered by Good once and for all.

SHOUTS: Bravo! Bravo! Point of order!

CHAIRMAN: Lyric Poet Y has the floor.

LYRIC POET Y: Gentlemen. We are gathered here together as intellectual brain workers. Indeed I would like to pose the question whether the theme about which Herr Philosopher X has spoken serves our task, which is the redemption of the proletariat. In Marx...

THE CRITIC: Stop showing off about having read Marx.

LYRIC POET Y: Herr Chairman, I beseech you to protect me. Yes, sir, I have read Marx, and I find that he is not at all so stupid. To be sure he lacks a sense of that new objectivity which we...

CHAIRMAN: You may not speak on a point of order: I'm taking the floor away from you.

LYRIC POET Y: Then I might as well go. Lick my arse! (*Goes.*)

SHOUTS: Outrageous! Outrageous!

THE CRITIC: He should be sent to a psychoanalyst. After analysis he'll stop writing poetry. All poetry is nothing but repressed complexes.

(*PICKEL comes in.*)

PICKEL: Indeed, I believe...but nevertheless, am I in the Green Tree Hotel?

CHAIRMAN: No. Private meeting.

PICKEL: Private?... Indeed I believed, the Green Tree...but nevertheless...

SHOUT: Don't disturb us.

PICKEL: Thank you kindly, gentlemen.

(*PICKEL goes.*)

CHAIRMAN: What do you want, Herr Philosopher X?

PHILOSOPHER X: A short postscript, gentlemen. To give an example. Herr Lyric Poet Y called into question the causal connection between my theme and the task which we have set ourselves: the intellectual redemption of the proletariat. Today unrepressed instincts are only to be found in the lower social classes. Let us ask a proletarian, let us ask a waiter, and it will prove my theory.

SHOUTS: Waiter! Waiter!

(*KARL THOMAS appears with a tray of bottles and glasses.*)

KARL THOMAS: The head waiter is coming right away.

SHOUTS: You must stay.

KARL THOMAS: I have work down below, gentlemen.

PHILOSOPHER X: Listen, Comrade Waiter, young proletarian. Would you perform coitus, sexual intercourse, with the first woman who comes your way or would you first consult your instincts?

(*KARL THOMAS bursts into laughter.*)

CHAIRMAN: That's nothing to laugh about. The question is serious. Besides we are guests and you are the waiter.

KARL THOMAS: Aha, first Comrade Waiter and now you play the boss. You... You want to redeem the proletariat? What, here in the Grand Hotel? Where were you when it started to happen? Where will you be? Always in the Grand Hotel! Eunuchs!

SHOUTS: Outrageous! Outrageous!

(*KARL THOMAS goes.*)

PHILOSOPHER X: Petit bourgeois ideologue!

CHAIRMAN: Now we come to the second item on the agenda. Proletarian communal love and the task of the intellectuals.

Blackout.

Lights up:

Private Room

[*Continued by Piscator directly from previous scene in Private Room.*]

BANKER: What took you so long with the liqueur, waiter?

KARL THOMAS: Excuse me, sir, I was held up.

BANKER: Pass the cigars. Do you smoke cigarettes, madam?

FRAU KILMAN: No, thank you.

[*RADIO OPERATOR brings telegram to WILHELM KILMAN in Piscator production.*]

WILHELM KILMAN: The telegram brings the conflict to a head. To deny us the oil concessions!

BANKER: Quite good I had a sharp enough nose to advise my clients to sell off their Turkish holdings... How do you actually invest your money, Herr Minister?

WILHELM KILMAN: Mortgage bonds, ha, ha, ha! I'm careful not to speculate.

BANKER: Who's talking about speculation? After all you have duties, you have to play the host. A man with your gifts ought to make himself independent.

WILHELM KILMAN: As a State Official, I ought...

BANKER: But you are also a private person. What does the State give you. A couple of coins. Why don't you make the most of your information? Don't refuse, even a Bismark, a Disraeli, a Gambetta, didn't disdain...

WILHELM KILMAN: Even so...

BANKER: I'll give you an example. The Council of Ministers had decided to reduce the contango funds. Then you opportunely sell your stocks. And who can reproach you, if you sell a few more. Of course, it mustn't be done in your own name.

WILHELM KILMAN: Enough of that…

BANKER: It would be an honour for me to advise you. You know that you can trust me.

WILHELM KILMAN: Waiter, where is the Press Conference taking place?

KARL THOMAS: In the Writing Room.

WILHELM KILMAN: Is Herr Baron Friedrich down there?

KARL THOMAS: Yes, sir.

WILHELM KILMAN: Tell Herr Baron that I shall expect him at the Ministry at midnight.

(PICKEL enters.)

PICKEL: If I am in the right place… Namely I would like… Indeed the prices…but nevertheless…

BANKER: Who is this man?

PICKEL: Ah, Herr Minister…

WILHELM KILMAN: I have no time. *(Turns away.)*

PICKEL: I didn't expect that from you, Herr Minister! Haven't we made you Minister?… Indeed, even if my vote in the Presidential election… But nevertheless, Minister, you have me to thank for your post…

(Goes.)

Blackout.

Lights up:

Writing Room

[*This section was cut.*]

(JOURNALISTS writing. KARL THOMAS at the door.)

BARON FRIEDRICH: Gentlemen, what was once the task of the historian – to depict the actions, which reason of State demands, as the only solution, as a moral necessity – is now yours. In these difficult times for our Fatherland, the Government has the right to expect that over and above all party differences every newspaper will do its duty. We don't seek war. Let us stress that over and over again, gentlemen. The so-called sanctions which they want to impose on us are better left unmentioned. We want peace.

But our patience will run out at once, gentlemen, if the prestige of our State is impugned.

KARL THOMAS: Excuse me, Herr Baron.

BARON FRIEDRICH: What is it?

KARL THOMAS: The Minister wishes to see you at midnight...

Blackout.

Lights up:

Hotel Room No. 96

[*Scaffolding revolves three metres to left for close-up effect. Back projection of red wallpaper on screen of middle right compartment.*]

COUNT LANDE: I clearly saw you make eyes at the blonde girl at the next table.

LOTTE KILMAN: Are you afraid that I'll betray you with her?

COUNT LANDE: That kind of business disgusts me.

LOTTE KILMAN: Maybe you men disgust me... Maybe you're beginning to bore me now.

COUNT LANDE: But my treasure...

LOTTE KILMAN: Only women can be tender in bed.
I don't deny I'd like to seduce the little darling.

COUNT LANDE: You are drunk.

LOTTE KILMAN: Maybe I would be, if you had been more generous.

COUNT LANDE: Let's order another bottle of Cordon Rouge.

LOTTE KILMAN: Please. But I'd like the little blonde better, or a snort of coke.

COUNT LANDE: Cover yourself up. I'll ring for the waiter.

Blackout.

Lights up:

Servery and Staff Room

[*Scaffolding revolves three metres right. Back projection of tiled wall lower left compartment. White light on centre compartment screen which is forward to show in silhouette cashier and cash register which rings throughout the scene.*]

(*HEAD WAITER, KARL THOMAS, PORTER, BUSBOY sit at supper.*)

HEAD WAITER: Mussolini won first prize at the Paris races. Thoroughbred. Three-year-old.

PORTER: Two hundred to win, eighty-four to place.

(*WAITER enters.*)

WAITER: Three *entrecôtes.*

HEAD WAITER: (*Calling through the hatch to the kitchen.*) Three *entrecôtes...* Did you bet anything?

PORTER: Of course, you can't get fat on the loot here.

WAITER: (*Enters.*) Six oxtail soups, double Madeira.

HEAD WAITER: Six oxtail soups, chef should put in double Madeira.

KARL THOMAS: I don't know what this soup tastes like.

PORTER: Do you want to eat *à la carte* instead?

WAITER (*Enters.*) Two dozen oysters.

HEAD WAITER: Two dozen oysters.

KARL THOMAS: I don't demand oysters, but this muck... Why doesn't the Works Council do anything?

PORTER: Because it's arm in arm with the hotel manager. I don't give a damn. I expect nothing from nobody. They're all the same. Before the inflation I saved one mark every week. Whenever I had ten, I went to the bank and got a gold piece. On Sunday I'd polish it bright and Monday I'd take it to the Savings Bank. I saved for six hundred weeks. Twelve years. And in the end what did I get? Damn all! Seven hundred million. Couldn't even buy myself a box of matches with it... The likes of us always get treated dirty.

HEAD WAITER: Posh spread in the Private Room tonight.

KARL THOMAS: For the posh People's Minister.

HEAD WAITER: You don't understand anything about it. If he's dining with a banker, he'll have his own good reasons. Otherwise he wouldn't be Minister.

BUSBOY: The gentleman up in 101 always pinches my bum-bum.

HEAD WAITER: Don't make a fuss, you. You know you can get something out of it.

(There's a ring.)

Which number?

BUSBOY: Ninety-six.

HEAD WAITER: Karl, you go up. The floor waiter is standing in for me.

Blackout.

Lights up:

Landing

[*This section cut.*]

PICKEL: (*On the stairs.*) Well there you are... Indeed one believes...one travels for two days on the railway...one is looking forward to it for his whole life...in Holzhausen I thought, up there...there one would certainly understand people, but up there it's exactly like it is with the railway, with one's own property...the atmosphere...

(KARL THOMAS goes by.)

Herr Waiter! Herr Waiter!

KARL THOMAS: No time.

PICKEL: No time...

Blackout.

Lights up:

Room No. 96

(There's a knock. KARL THOMAS enters.)

COUNT LANDE: What took you so long? Service. A bottle of Cordon Rouge. Well chilled.

Blackout.

[*Radio Station scene moved to here by Piscator.*]

Lights up:

Servant's Room

(*KARL THOMAS sits alone at the table, head buried in his hands. FRAU MELLER opens the door quietly.*)

FRAU MELLER: Tired, youngster?

(*KARL THOMAS doesn't stir.*)

It's a real strain the first day.

(*KARL THOMAS jumps up, tears the cravat from his neck, pulls off his tailcoat, throws it in the corner.*)

KARL THOMAS: There and there and there!...

FRAU MELLER: What are you doing?

KARL THOMAS: I'm awake, so awake that I'm afraid I'll never go to sleep again.

FRAU MELLER: Calm down, Karl, calm down.

KARL THOMAS: Calm down? Only a real rotter could calm down. Call me a fool now, like Albert called me. I resolved to be patient. I've been here half a day. I've seen everyday life, in tailcoat and nightshirt. You're all asleep! You're all asleep! You must be awakened. I don't give a damn about your common sense! If sensible people are like you, then I want to play the fool. All of you must be awakened.

(*There's a ring.*
Pause.)

FRAU MELLER: Karl...

KARL THOMAS: Let the devil go wait on them!

(*There's a ring.*)

FRAU MELLER: The Private Room.

KARL THOMAS: The Private Room?... Kilman?... Good, I'll go.

(*KARL THOMAS dresses hurriedly.*)

FRAU MELLER: I'll come right back. We'll have a talk, Karl.

(*FRAU MELLER goes.*)

KARL THOMAS: (*Looks at his revolver a few seconds.*) This shot will awaken them all!

Blackout.

Lights up:

Room No. 96

(*There's a soft knock.*)

COUNT LANDE: Coming.

Blackout.

Lights up:
Half-dark corridor.

STUDENT: Where?

COUNT LANDE: In the Private Room. Who is going in?

STUDENT: We drew lots. Me. Lieutenant Frank is waiting in the car.

COUNT LANDE: Are you wearing a waiter's tailcoat?

STUDENT: (*Opens his coat.*) Yes.

COUNT LANDE: Break a leg. Quick now. You must not be arrested. If you have bad luck, then... You mustn't make any statements... Take care of yourself.

STUDENT: I have given my word of honour.

Blackout.

Lights up:

Private Room

WILHELM KILMAN: Superb, that joke, superb. Just look at my wife. How red she's getting. She doesn't understand anything about that, ha, ha, ha.

BANKER: Do you know the one about Herr Meyer in the railway compartment?

WILHELM KILMAN: Tell it.

BANKER: The waiter at last! Another bottle of cognac... Why are you standing there? Why are you staring at me? Didn't you understand?

KARL THOMAS: Don't you recognise me?

WILHELM KILMAN: Who are you?

KARL THOMAS: Feel free to use my first name. When we waited together for the mass grave, we weren't so formal. Are you ashamed of knowing me?

WILHELM KILMAN: It's you... Don't talk crazy nonsense. Come to the Ministry tomorrow.

KARL THOMAS: You will answer for it today.

WILHELM KILMAN: (*To BANKER.*) Leave him be. A fantasiser whom I knew from before. Off the rails because of a romantic episode in his youth. Can't find a firm grip any more.

KARL THOMAS: I'm waiting for your answer.

WILHELM KILMAN: To what? What is going on in your head? What's going on in your head, Karl? Do I need to tell you again that times have changed? You'd rather damn the world than give up your insane demands; you'd rather damn the very men who are trying to make things progress a bit.

KARL THOMAS: Wilhelm…

WILHELM KILMAN: Please stop the hollow phrases. They don't work.

BANKER: Hadn't I better call the Hotel Manager?

WILHELM KILMAN: For God's sake, don't make a scene.

BANKER: Calm down, waiter. He's in a bad way isn't he? Here, take ten marks.

WILHELM KILMAN: May I add another ten?

(*KARL THOMAS, clutching the revolver in his pocket with one hand, looks at the money bewildered, shrugs his shoulders in disgust as if he had gone off doing the deed and starts to turn away.*)

KARL THOMAS: It's not worth it. I couldn't give a damn about you now.

(*Then the door opens quietly.*
STUDENT in waiter's tailcoat enters.
Raises his revolver over KARL THOMAS's shoulder.
Turns the electric light out.
Shot.
Scream.)

BANKER: Lights! Lights! The waiter has shot the Minister.

Curtain.

[*Scaffolding revolves right so stairs are visible. KARL THOMAS and STUDENT run down them followed by spotlights. Gauze in and park is projected on it from front as scaffolding revolves face-on to audience for next act.*]

ACT FOUR

Scene One

Left of Hotel. In a Park.

KARL THOMAS is running after the STUDENT.

KARL THOMAS: You! You!
> (*STUDENT turns his head, runs on.*)
You, I want to help you, comrade.

STUDENT: What, comrade! I'm not your comrade.

KARL THOMAS: But you shot Kilman...

STUDENT: Because he's a Bolshevik, because he's a revolutionary. Because he's selling our country out to the Jews.
> (*Bewildered, KARL THOMAS takes a step towards him.*)

KARL THOMAS: Has the world become a madhouse? Has the world become a madhouse!!!

STUDENT: Get back, or I'll shoot you down.
> (*STUDENT runs on, jumps into a car which speeds away.*
> *KARL THOMAS catches on, tears the revolver out of his pocket,*
> *shoots after it twice. Then he reflects, stands still*
> *in front of a tree.*)

KARL THOMAS: Are you a beech tree? Or are you a rubber-padded wall? (*Feels it.*) You feel like bark, rough and cracked, and you do smell of earth. But are you really a beech tree?
> (*Sits on a bench.*)
My poor head. Drumfire. Roll up, Ladies and Gentlemen. The bell is ringing. The ride is starting. Only one shot a go.
You see a house burning, grab a pail, try to put it out, and instead of water you pour buckets of oil on the flames...
You sound the alarm throughout the whole city to awaken all the people, but the sleepers just turn over on their bellies and snore on...
When night covers others in brown shadows, I see murderers crouching naked with brains exposed...

And I run through the streets like a night watchman,
with thoughts which wound themselves on the beam of a
spotlight…
Oh, why did they open the gate of the madhouse for me?
Wasn't it good in there in spite of the North Pole and the
flapping wings of grey birds?
I have lost my grip on the world
And the world has lost its grip on me
(*During the last phrases two POLICE DETECTIVES
have entered.*
Both go up to him, grab him by the wrists.)

FIRST POLICEMAN: Well, young man, no doubt you just
found that revolver somewhere?

KARL THOMAS: What do I know? What do you know?
Even the revolver turns against the gunman, and spurts
laughter out of its barrel.

SECOND POLICEMAN: Just speak respectfully, you got
that?

FIRST POLICEMAN: What is your name?

KARL THOMAS: Every name is a con… See, I once
believed that if I took the path straight through the park,
I'd reach a hotel. A cup of coffee. Fifty pfennigs. Do you
know where I landed? In the madhouse. And the police
make sure that no one gets sane.

FIRST POLICEMAN: I'd like to make sure of that for you.
You're under arrest.

SECOND POLICEMAN: Don't try to resist. You'll get shot
trying to escape.

KARL THOMAS: Let me go.

FIRST POLICEMAN: Just the opposite. Be glad that we're
protecting you. The people would lynch you.

SECOND POLICEMAN: Do you admit that you shot the
Minister?

KARL THOMAS: Me?

FIRST POLICEMAN: Yes, you.

SECOND POLICEMAN: Come on, to the police station.

Blackout.

(*Shouts from a crowd of people are heard.*)

Scene Two

[After sounds of many ringing telephones and alarm during blackout, the top left compartment and bottom right compartments were lit, probably in that order, to show COUNT LANDE, top left, telephoning the CHIEF OF POLICE, bottom right. This underlined the complicity between him and the police and echoed the secret telephone line between Chancellor Ebert and General Groener. Beginning of the scene was rewritten by Piscator, identifying that the conversation was with COUNT LANDE and underscoring their secret understanding as they spoke in a kind of shorthand code.]

Police Headquarters
Room of the Chief of Police

(*CHIEF OF POLICE at a table. Piercing ring.*)

CHIEF OF POLICE: (*On telephone.*) Hello? What's up?… What?… Assassination attempt on Minister Kilman at the Grand Hotel?… The Minister's dead?… Cordon off the Grand Hotel… Clear the streets… A suspect arrested?… Bring him here… I'll wait… (*Hangs up. To SECRETARY.*) Stay here. You must make a transcript. (*Telephones.*) All stations on alert… Thanks… Report any suspicious incidents… From the Left, of course… Crush any demonstrations… That's it…

(*Meanwhile a POLICEMAN has come in with PICKEL.*)

PICKEL: (*To the POLICEMAN.*) You don't have to hold me like that, sir… Who are you after all? Indeed you live in a big city where there's riff-raff, but nevertheless you should discriminate.

CHIEF OF POLICE: What's up?

POLICEMAN: This man was hanging about in the corridor of the Grand Hotel… Shortly before the assassination he was in the Minister's room. He isn't staying at the Hotel, behaves suspiciously, and cannot account for why…

CHIEF OF POLICE: Good. What is your name?

PICKEL: Indeed my name is Pickel, but nevertheless…

CHIEF OF POLICE: Just answer my questions.

PICKEL: Namely I would like to…

CHIEF OF POLICE: You were in the room of the murdered Minister shortly before the assassination. What did you want there?

PICKEL: I believed he... Indeed, Herr General, I believed the Minister was a man of honour... But nevertheless when I went up to him in the hotel room...

CHIEF OF POLICE: You admit you were involved in the deed? You had a personal grudge against the Minister?

PICKEL: Namely I wanted...

CHIEF OF POLICE: What did you want? Are you an anarchist? Do you belong to an illegal group?

PICKEL: Namely the veterans of the front have... Although I was only behind the lines...to the Soldiers' Union, Herr General.

CHIEF OF POLICE: To the Soldiers' Union?... Can you prove that?

PICKEL: Yes, sir. Here is my membership card.

CHIEF OF POLICE: Aha... Are you a Nationalist?... Therefore... Tell me, why did you murder the Minister?

PICKEL: I believed... I would have gone through fire for him...

CHIEF OF POLICE: Pay attention to my questions.

PICKEL: Namely... I came only on account of the railway... And there I am in the Ministry... And I haven't any more...

CHIEF OF POLICE: To the point.

PICKEL: Oh, Herr General, let me go home. The weather is changing... I could travel now... And my cows... My wife has always said...

(*Telephone rings.*)

CHIEF OF POLICE: (*On the telephone.*) Police Headquarters... You have interrogated the eye witnesses?... A man in a waiter's tail coat?... One moment... Pickel, take off your coat.

PICKEL: I'm wearing namely...

CHIEF OF POLICE: Frock-coat... Aha...

PICKEL: But nevertheless only because I...

CHIEF OF POLICE: Be quiet. (*On telephone.*) ...Thanks... Fräulein, take down Pickel's personal details...

SECRETARY: Your name? Surname and Christian name?

PICKEL: Trustgod Pickel is my name, Fräulein... As a boy my name was Godbeloved...nevertheless my name is really Trustgod... Namely the official at the Registry Office who with my father...as long as they were well, every evening they played...

(POLICE DETECTIVE enters.)

CHIEF OF POLICE: What's up?

FIRST POLICEMAN: We arrested a man in the park. He was holding a revolver in his hand. Two bullets are missing.

CHIEF OF POLICE: Bring him in.

(POLICE DETECTIVE enters with KARL THOMAS.)
What is your name?

KARL THOMAS: Karl Thomas.

CHIEF OF POLICE: What did you want with this revolver?...

KARL THOMAS: To shoot the Minister.

CHIEF OF POLICE: Things are going very fast... The second one... So, a confession... Do you belong to Herr Pickel's Soldiers' Union too?

KARL THOMAS: To the Soldiers' Union?...

PICKEL: Herr General, I must point out that our Soldiers' Union in Holzhausen... Indeed we don't after all accept any foreigners...not even anyone from the neighbouring villages...but nevertheless the President of the Reich is an Honorary Member...

CHIEF OF POLICE: Silence... *(To the POLICEMAN.)*
What did the man look like then?

SECOND POLICEMAN: The people wanted to lynch him. We could hardly hold the crowds back.

CHIEF OF POLICE: Sit down. Tell me, why did you shoot the Minister?

KARL THOMAS: Is he dead?

CHIEF OF POLICE: Yes.

KARL THOMAS: I didn't shoot.

CHIEF OF POLICE: But you must admit you just confessed...

PICKEL: No, Herr General, you are wrong there. I know him. He is namely a friend of the Minister...

CHIEF OF POLICE: Why are you always interrupting?

PICKEL: Because you don't believe me... I am namely the Treasurer of the Soldiers' Union. And our statutes...

CHIEF OF POLICE: I'll have you removed straight away. (*To KARL THOMAS.*) You saw the Minister as vermin, didn't you? A traitor to his country?

KARL THOMAS: The murderer thought he was.

CHIEF OF POLICE: The murderer?

KARL THOMAS: I chased him. I shot at him.

CHIEF OF POLICE: What kind of crazy nonsense are you talking?

PICKEL: If he says so, Herr General...

(*POLICE DETECTIVE goes over to the CHIEF OF POLICE, speaks softly with him.*)

CHIEF OF POLICE: He makes the same impression on me. Moreover the other one, Pickel, also... Hand them both over to Department One. I'll come over straight-away... (*On telephone.*) Connect me with the Public Prosecutor...

PICKEL: Herr General...namely I would like... I would like to ask...

CHIEF OF POLICE: What is it now?

PICKEL: Is it decided, Herr General? Will I be put in prison?

CHIEF OF POLICE: Yes.

PICKEL: Indeed... Then... Namely in Holzhausen... And if they hear... And if my wife... And if my neighbour... who is related to the Mayor... And if the Soldiers' Union... Do you know what you are doing?... Now that I am 'previously convicted'. Where can I go, when I come out of prison? Where? I definitely couldn't show my face in Holzhausen again...

CHIEF OF POLICE: If it turns out that you are not guilty, you can go home.

PICKEL: But nevertheless 'previously convicted'.

CHIEF OF POLICE: I have no time. (*On telephone.*) Connect me with the Public Prosecutor.

PICKEL: No time either... White gloves, black gloves... What can one believe in?...

Blackout.

Scene Three

[*This scene was cut.*]

Room of the Examining Magistrate

(*EXAMINING MAGISTRATE and CLERK at a table. In front of the table, KARL THOMAS in handcuffs.*)

EXAMINING MAGISTRATE: You are only making your situation more difficult. Witnesses have testified that in the bar, The Bear, you expressed the intention to murder the Minister.

KARL THOMAS: I don't deny that. But I didn't shoot.

EXAMINING MAGISTRATE: You admit the intention...

KARL THOMAS: The intention, yes.

EXAMINING MAGISTRATE: Have the witness, Rand, brought in.

(*RAND enters.*)

Herr Rand, do you know the suspect?

RAND: Very good, sir, yes.

EXAMINING MAGISTRATE: Is this the same man who pocketed your revolver during the attack in the polling station?

RAND: Very good, sir, yes.

EXAMINING MAGISTRATE: Thomas, what do you say to that?

KARL THOMAS: I don't dispute that. But...

RAND: If I might be allowed to express my opinion, the Jews are behind all this.

EXAMINING MAGISTRATE: Haven't you shot the revolver, Rand?

RAND: Very good, sir, no. All the bullets ought to be in the cylinder.

EXAMINING MAGISTRATE: Two are missing. Is this nevertheless your revolver?

RAND: My service revolver, Herr Examining Magistrate.

EXAMINING MAGISTRATE: Do you still want to deny the deed, Thomas? Don't you want to relieve your conscience with a confession?

KARL THOMAS: I have nothing to confess, I did not shoot.

EXAMINING MAGISTRATE: How do you explain the two missing bullets?

KARL THOMAS: I fired at the assassin.

EXAMINING MAGISTRATE: So, fired at the assassin. Now only the great unknown assassin is missing. Do you perhaps know the mysterious culprit who, as you declare, came into the room behind you and shot?

KARL THOMAS: No.

EXAMINING MAGISTRATE: Well then, the famous Herr X.

KARL THOMAS: He was someone on the Right. He said so himself. I chased after him. I thought he would be a comrade.

EXAMINING MAGISTRATE: Don't talk nonsense. Are you trying to cover the traces of your back-room cronies? We know them; this time there's no amnesty. Your closest comrades are behind bars... Have the Head Waiter of the Grand Hotel brought in.
    (*HEAD WAITER enters.*)
Do you know the suspect?

HEAD WAITER: Yes indeed, sir. He was an assistant waiter at the Grand Hotel. If I had known, sir, that...

EXAMINING MAGISTRATE: Did the suspect call Herr Minister Kilman abusive names?

HEAD WAITER: Yes indeed, sir; he said "a perfect People's Minister". No, "a posh People's Minister", he said.

EXAMINING MAGISTRATE: Thomas, did you say that?

KARL THOMAS: Yes, but I did not shoot.

EXAMINING MAGISTRATE: Have Frau Meller brought in.
    (*FRAU MELLER enters.*)
You know the suspect?

FRAU MELLER: Yes, he is my friend.

EXAMINING MAGISTRATE: So, your friend. Do you call yourself his...comrade?

FRAU MELLER: Yes.

EXAMINING MAGISTRATE: Did you recommend the suspect to the Head Waiter of the Grand Hotel?

FRAU MELLER: Yes.

EXAMINING MAGISTRATE: The suspect is supposed to have said to you: "You are all asleep. Someone must be done away with. Then you will awaken".

FRAU MELLER: No.

EXAMINING MAGISTRATE: Pull yourself together, witness. You are suspected of aiding and abetting. You procured a place for the suspect at the Grand Hotel. The prosecution assumes that this position was only a pretence so that the suspect should get the opportunity to be near the Minister.

FRAU MELLER: If you know better about everything, then, go on, arrest me.

EXAMINING MAGISTRATE: I'm asking you for the last time: did the accused say, Someone must be done away with?

FRAU MELLER: No.

EXAMINING MAGISTRATE: Have the busboy come in.
(*BUSBOY comes in.*)
Do you know the accused?

BUSBOY: Thank you, yes. When he had to carry the plates in, he broke one straight away and told me I should hide the pieces so no one could find them.

EXAMINING MAGISTRATE: That is very interesting. Did you do that?

KARL THOMAS: Yes.

EXAMINING MAGISTRATE: That throws a proper light on your character… Pay close attention, boy.
Did you hear the suspect say: "You are all asleep! Someone must be done away with. Then you will awaken"?

BUSBOY: Thank you, yes, and along with that he rolled his eyes and clenched his fists; he looked all bloodthirsty. I've only seen faces like that at the movies. I was shuddering.

EXAMINING MAGISTRATE: What did you do then?

BUSBOY: I… I… I…

EXAMINING MAGISTRATE: You must tell the truth.

BUSBOY: (*Begins to cry, turns away from the EXAMINING MAGISTRATE to the HEAD WAITER.*) Sir, I won't do it any more, I know I told you I needed to pee, I didn't go to pee at all, I was so tired I laid down under the table and tried to sleep a little... Sir, please don't report me to the boss.

EXAMINING MAGISTRATE: (*Laughing.*) That won't be so serious... Thomas, what do you say to these statements?

KARL THOMAS: That I'm gradually getting the impression that I'm in a madhouse.

EXAMINING MAGISTRATE: I see, in a madhouse. The witnesses may leave. Frau Meller, for the present you are under arrest. Take her away.

(*Witnesses go.*)

Bring in Eva Berg, who's under arrest.

(*EVA BERG is brought in.*)

Your name is Eva Berg?

EVA BERG: Hello, Karl... Yes.

EXAMINING MAGISTRATE: You are not allowed to speak to the suspect.

EVA BERG: I can't shake hands with him; you must take the handcuffs off first. Why is he handcuffed? Do you think he will escape? Outside there are a dozen warders. Or are you afraid of him? You don't seem to be very brave. Or are you only trying to intimidate him? They'll be disappointed, won't they Karl?

EXAMINING MAGISTRATE: I'll have you taken away at once, if you don't change your tone.

EVA BERG: I don't doubt you can summon up enough courage for that... I'm waiting for you to have enough to set me free.

EXAMINING MAGISTRATE: I am not authorised by the law to do so.

EVA BERG: When it suits you, you hide behind the law. For weeks I've been held in custody. I've only exercised the rights which the constitution grants to everyone. Because public rights are public duties, you would have to resign your judgeship before admitting the law was broken.

EXAMINING MAGISTRATE: I have two questions to put to you. Did the suspect live with you?

EVA BERG: Yes.

EXAMINING MAGISTRATE: Have you had relationships with him which are punishable by law?

EVA BERG: What kind of a ridiculous question is that? Do you come from the fifteenth century?

EXAMINING MAGISTRATE: I want to know whether you have had sexual relations with the suspect?

EVA BERG: Will you first explain to me what an unsexual union looks like?

EXAMINING MAGISTRATE: You come from a respectable family... Your father would...

EVA BERG: My family is none of your business. And I consider your question so unrespectable that I would be ashamed of myself if I answered it.

EXAMINING MAGISTRATE: So you refuse to answer the second question... During the time he lived with you, did the suspect express the intention of murdering Minister Kilman?

EVA BERG: Herr Examining Magistrate, I think we know each other from the old days... You chose to remember that... Wouldn't you class a fellow club member and friend who betrayed his comrades as the lowest of the low? Thus your third question is also unrespectable, because you believe in the probability that he said that. But I swear, on that honour which you can neither give nor ever take away from me, Karl Thomas never expressed the intention of murdering Kilman.

EXAMINING MAGISTRATE: Thank you. Take her away.

EVA BERG: Farewell, Karl. Don't give in.

KARL THOMAS: I love you, Eva.

EVA BERG: Even at a moment like this I must not lie to you. (*EVA BERG is taken away.*)

EXAMINING MAGISTRATE: I've learned from your files that you spent eight years in a madhouse. You shall be referred to the Psychiatric Department to ascertain whether you are of sound mind.

Blackout.

Scene Four

The façade transforms into the façade of the Madhouse.

Open:

Examination Room

[*This scene was played in the centre compartment of the scaffolding, revealed behind the projection of the façade. Back projection of filing cabinet as before.*]

PROFESSOR LÜDIN: You were referred to me by the Public Prosecutor for psychiatric treatment... Stand still. Pulse normal. Open your shirt. Breathe deeply. Hold it. Heart healthy... Tell me honestly, why did you commit this deed?

KARL THOMAS: I did not shoot.

PROFESSOR LÜDIN: (*Leafing through the files.*) The police first took you for a man who fired the shots for Nationalist motives. They believed a certain Pickel to be your accomplice. The Examining Magistrate came to the conclusion that this supposition was wrong. He takes the view that you belong to a radical left-wing terrorist group... Your like-minded comrades have been arrested... I, mind you, think... Confide in me with full assurance, only your motives interest me.

KARL THOMAS: I have nothing to confess because I am not the culprit.

PROFESSOR LÜDIN: You wanted to avenge yourself, didn't you? You probably believed that the Minister would give you a top position. You saw that your high and mighty comrades, once they sit on top, also only take care of themselves. You felt sold out, betrayed? The world looked different from the picture of it in your head.

KARL THOMAS: I don't need a psychiatrist.

PROFESSOR LÜDIN: You feel sane?

KARL THOMAS: Sound as a bell.

PROFESSOR LÜDIN: Hm. This notion still dominates you? I think I remember that your mother also suffered from this complex.

(*KARL THOMAS laughs.*)
Don't laugh. No one is sound as a bell.
(*Short pause.*)

KARL THOMAS: Herr Professor!

PROFESSOR LÜDIN: Do you want to confess to me now why you shot? Understand, only the Why interests me. The deed is no concern of mine. Deeds are of no importance. Only motives are important.

KARL THOMAS: I want to tell you everything exactly, Herr Professor. I've lost my bearings. What I experienced... May I tell you, Herr Professor.

PROFESSOR LÜDIN: Begin then.

KARL THOMAS: I must have clarity. The door slammed shut behind me, and when I opened it eight years had passed. A whole century. As you advised me, I first paid a visit to Wilhelm Kilman. Condemned to death like I was. I discovered he was Minister. Wedded to his former enemies.

PROFESSOR LÜDIN: Normal. He was just more cunning than you.

KARL THOMAS: I went to my closest comrade. A man who with just a revolver in his hand repulsed a whole company of Whites, all alone. I heard him say "One must be able to wait".

PROFESSOR LÜDIN: Normal.

KARL THOMAS: And at the same time he swore he remained true to the Revolution.

PROFESSOR LÜDIN: Abnormal. But not your fault. He ought to be examined. Probably a mild dementia praecox in a catatonic form.

KARL THOMAS: I was a waiter. For one whole evening. It stank of corruption. The people I worked with found it all in order and were proud of it.

PROFESSOR LÜDIN: Normal. Business is thriving again. Everybody makes money out of it in his own way.

KARL THOMAS: You call that normal? In the hotel I met a banker. They told me he harvests money like hay... What does he get from it? He can't even fill his belly up with delicacies. When the others feed on pheasants, he has to slurp soup, because his stomach is bad. He speculates day and night. What for? What for?

[*Distorted mask of BANKER projected middle left.*]
(*Behind the projection, the Private Room in the Hotel lights up.*)

BANKER: (*On the table telephone.*) Hello! Hello! Stock Exchange? Sell everything! Paints and Potash and Pipes... The assassination of Kilman... Chemical Works shares already fallen about a hundred per cent... What?... Operator!... Fräulein, why did you cut me off?... I'll hold you liable... Ruined by a telephone breakdown... God in heaven!

PROFESSOR LÜDIN: What for? Because he's smart and because he wants to achieve something. Dear friend, the banker whom you saw – I wish I had his fortune – was normal.

BANKER: (*Grinning in the Hotel Room.*) Normal... Normal...
(*Blackout in Hotel Room.*)

KARL THOMAS: And the porter at the Grand Hotel? For twelve years he saved a gold piece every week. Twelve years! Then the inflation came. They paid him six hundred million and he couldn't even buy a box of matches with all his savings. But he wasn't cured, he thinks the whole con is unchangeable, today he scrapes and stints on food and then gambles away his last groschen. Is that normal?

[*Distorted mask of PORTER projected bottom left.*]
(*Behind the projection, the Staff Room in the Hotel lights up.*)

PORTER: Who won the Paris race? The beautiful Galatea... A fix! A fix! I put all my savings on Idealist, and that damned jockey goes and breaks his neck...
I want to get my stake back! Or else...

PROFESSOR LÜDIN: Nothing venture, nothing gain. The porter at the Grand Hotel, and I lived there once, is absolutely normal.

PORTER: (*In Hotel Room, grinning as he stabs himself with his knife.*) Normal... Normal...
(*Blackout in Hotel Room.*)

KARL THOMAS: Perhaps you also call a world normal in which it is possible for the most important inventions,

inventions which could make the life of mankind easier, to be destroyed just because some people are frightened they won't make as much money any more?

[*Distorted mask of RADIO OPERATOR projected top of centre compartment.*]

(*Behind the projection, the Radio Station in the Hotel lights up.*)

RADIO OPERATOR: Attention! Attention! All radio stations of the world! Who will buy my invention? I don't want money. The invention will help everyone, everyone. Silence… No one responds.

PROFESSOR LÜDIN: What's abnormal about that? Life is no meadow in which people dance ring-a-ring-o'-roses and play on pipes of peace. Life is struggle. Might is right. That is absolutely normal!

RADIO OPERATOR: (*In Hotel Room, grinning as he causes a short circuit.*) Normal…

(*All the rooms of the Hotel light up.*)

CHORUS OF HOTEL OCCUPANTS: (*In a crouching position, leaning down towards the Examination Room, grinning and nodding.*) Normal!… Normal!…

(*Explosion in Hotel.*
Blackout.)

KARL THOMAS: How could I have borne this world any longer!… I formed a plan to shock mankind. I was going to shoot the Minister. At the very same moment some-one else shot him.

PROFESSOR LÜDIN: Hm.

KARL THOMAS: I called after the culprit. Believed he was a comrade. Wanted to help him. He rejected me. I saw his twisted lips. He screamed at me: "Because the Minister was a Bolshevik, a revolutionary".

PROFESSOR LÜDIN: Normal. Relatively so, if this unknown person existed.

KARL THOMAS: Then I shot at the murderer of the same man I myself wanted to murder.

PROFESSOR LÜDIN: Hm.

KARL THOMAS: The fog suddenly lifted. Perhaps the world is not crazy at all. Perhaps I am… Perhaps I am… Perhaps it was all only a crazy dream.

PROFESSOR LÜDIN: What do you want? That's simply the way the world is… Let's go back to your motives. Did you want to get rid of your past with this shot?

KARL THOMAS: Insanity! Insanity!

PROFESSOR LÜDIN: Don't play-act with me. You can't sway an old psychiatrist like that.

KARL THOMAS: Or is there no boundary between mad-house and world these days? Yes, yes …really… The same kind of people who are kept here as mad gallop around outside as normal and are permitted to trample others down.

PROFESSOR LÜDIN: I see…

KARL THOMAS: And you! Do you dare say that you too are normal? You are a madman among madmen.

PROFESSOR LÜDIN: Enough of this strong language now!… Or else I'll have you put in the padded cell. You're just trying to save yourself with the Section for the mentally ill, aren't you?

KARL THOMAS: Do you believe you're alive? You imagine that the world will always stay like it is now!

PROFESSOR LÜDIN: Well you've stayed the same… You still want to change the world, set fire to it, don't you? If nature had not wanted some to eat less than others, there wouldn't be any poverty at all. Whoever achieves what he's capable of needn't go hungry.

KARL THOMAS: Whoever goes hungry needn't eat.

PROFESSOR LÜDIN: With your ideas men would become scroungers and shirkers.

KARL THOMAS: Are you happy with your ideas?

PROFESSOR LÜDIN: What, happiness! You suffer from overestimating this idea. Chimera! Phobia! The happiness concept sits in your brain like a stagnant reservoir. If you would cherish it for your own sake, that's fair enough. You'd probably write lyric poems full of soul and love blue violets and beautiful maidens…or you'd become a harmless religious sectarian with a mild paraphrenia phantastica complex. But you want to make the world happy.

KARL THOMAS: I don't give a damn about your soul.

PROFESSOR LÜDIN: You undermine every society. Every one! What do you want? To turn the very foundations of life upside down, to create heaven on earth, the Absolute, isn't that it? Delusion! Like infectious poison you act on the weak in spirit, on the masses!

KARL THOMAS: What do you understand about the masses?

PROFESSOR LÜDIN: My collection of specimens opens even the blindest of eyes. The masses, a herd of swine. Cram to the trough when there's something to guzzle. Wallow in muck when their bellies are stuffed. And then every century psychopaths come and promise the herd paradise. The police ought to hand them over to us madhouse doctors at once, instead of watching them go berserk among mankind.

KARL THOMAS: You certainly aren't harmless.

PROFESSOR LÜDIN: It is our mission to protect society from dangerous criminals. You are the arch enemies of every civilisation! You are chaos! You must be neutralised, sterilised, eradicated!

KARL THOMAS: Orderlies! Orderlies!

(*ORDERLIES enter.*)

Lock this madman up in the padded cell.

(*PROFESSOR LÜDIN gives the ORDERLIES a sign.
ORDERLIES grab KARL THOMAS.*)

PROFESSOR LÜDIN: Tomorrow you will be sent back to prison.

Curtain.

[*At the end of this act, the Mary Wigman female dance group performed a frenzied Charleston across the stage. They were dressed in black with phosphorescent skeletons painted on their costumes which glowed under the ultraviolet light, eerily commenting on the skull beneath the skin of the Weimar Republic. Screen and gauze were lowered to human height so the Prison could be prepared behind. After the dance, white gauze remained in for projection of façade of prison windows from the front. Back projections of cells on the compartment screens. Captions for the knocking projected on the gauze running left and right and up and down. See the promptbook scene at end.*]

ACT FIVE

Scene One

Prison

(For a moment all cells visible.
Blackout.
Then lights up:
ALBERT KROLL's cell.)

ALBERT KROLL: *(Knocks on adjoining cell.)* Who is there?
(Lights up:
EVA BERG's cell.)

EVA BERG: *(Knocks.)* Eva Berg.

ALBERT KROLL *(Knocks.)* You too?...

EVA BERG: *(Knocks.)* Early today.

ALBERT KROLL: *(Knocks.)* And the others?

EVA BERG: *(Knocks.)* All arrested. Why did Karl do it?

ALBERT KROLL: *(Knocks.)* He says no, he didn't. Where is Karl?

EVA BERG: *(Knocks.)* Maybe Mother Meller knows.

ALBERT KROLL: *(Knocks.)* Mother Meller? Is she here too?

EVA BERG: *(Knocks.)* Yes. Above me. Wait, I'll knock.
(Noise at ALBERT KROLL's door.)

ALBERT KROLL: *(Knocks.)* Look out! Someone's coming.
(ALBERT KROLL's door creaks open.
RAND enters.)

RAND: Soup... Eat quick. Today is Sunday.

ALBERT KROLL: Oh, it's you.

RAND: Yes, I'm a prison officer again. You have something firm under your feet... Well, now I have you all together again. Except Kilman. They're dedicating a memorial to him today.

ALBERT KROLL: Really?

RAND: Kilman was the only one among you worth anything, you have to admit that. I always said so.

ALBERT KROLL: *(Eats.)* Muck.

RAND: Doesn't the soup taste good to you? There's roast pork at Christmas. Be patient until then.

ALBERT KROLL: Tell me, is Karl Thomas here too?

RAND: Since yesterday evening... What a life he's got behind him...

(*RAND leaves.*)

ALBERT KROLL: (*Knocks.*) Now, Eva.

EVA BERG: (*Knocks.*) Where is Karl?

KNOCKING EVERYWHERE: Where is Karl?

(*Blackout in cells.*
Lights up:
KARL THOMAS' cell.)

KARL THOMAS: Waiting again...waiting...waiting...

(*Lights up:*
FRAU MELLER's cell.)

FRAU MELLER: (*Knocks.*) Where is Karl?

KARL THOMAS: (*Knocks.*) Here... Who are you?

FRAU MELLER: (*Knocks.*) Mother Meller.

KARL THOMAS: (*Knocks.*) What? Old Mother Meller. (*Knocks.*) Who else is here?

FRAU MELLER: (*Knocks.*) All of us... Eva... Albert... And the others... On account of the assassination. We are with you, dear boy...

KARL THOMAS: (*Knocks.*) Do you still remember eight years ago?

FRAU MELLER: (*Knocks.*) I don't really understand what you have done... But I'll stick with you...

(*Blackout in FRAU MELLER's cell.*)

KARL THOMAS: (*Knocks.*) Listen now!...

(*Lights up:*
PRISONER N's cell.)

PRISONER N: (*Knocks.*) Not so loud... Think of the rules... You'll hurt us...

KARL THOMAS: (*Knocks.*) Who are you?

PRISONER N: (*Knocks.*) If you keep on like that, there's no hope left for us. I won't answer anymore...

(*Blackout in PRISONER N's cell.*)

KARL THOMAS: Ah, it's you... You're here again too?...
I thought you were dead!... Are you all here again?...
All here again... Is it really so?... The dance is
beginning again? Waiting again, waiting, waiting...
I can't... Don't you see?... What are you doing?... Go
on, resist!... No one hears, no one hears, no one... We
speak and hear each other not... We hate and see each
other not... We love and know each other not... We
murder and feel each other not... Must it always, always,
be like this?... You, will I never understand you?... You,
will you never comprehend me?... No! No! No!... Why
do you gas, burn and destroy the earth?... Is everything
forgotten?... Everything in vain?... Then keep on
spinning on your merry-go-round, dance, laugh, cry, and
copulate – good luck! I'm jumping off...
Oh madness of the world!...
Where to? Where to?... The stone walls press nearer and
nearer... I am freezing...and it is dark...and the glacier
of darkness clutches me mercilessly... Where to? Where
to?... To the highest mountain... To the highest tree...
The Deluge...

> [*Piscator cut and changed a lot of this speech.*]
> (*KARL THOMAS makes a rope out of the sheet,
> climbs on the stool, fastens the rope to the door hook.*)

Blackout.

Scene Two

[*This scene was cut.*]

A group before a covered memorial.

COUNT LANDE: ...and so I present to the people...this
memorial to this outstanding man ...who in dark times...

Blackout.

Scene Three

Prison

(Lights up:
ALBERT KROLL's cell.
Noise. Door creaks open.
RAND enters.)

RAND: Because you were kind to me once, I'll tell you something.

ALBERT KROLL: You don't need to.

RAND: We're not like that. The Ministry of Justice has just telephoned, Thomas is not the murderer. They caught the real one in Switzerland. A student. Just as he was about to be arrested, he shot himself.

ALBERT KROLL: Will we be released straightaway?

RAND: Not today. Today is Sunday... So I congratulate you, Herr Kroll.

(RAND goes.)

ALBERT KROLL: *(Knocks.)* Eva! Eva!

(Lights up:
EVA BERG's cell.)

EVA BERG: *(Knocks.)* Yes.

ALBERT KROLL: *(Knocks.)* We are free! Rand told me. The real murderer was found.

EVA BERG: Thank goodness! *(Knocks on the other wall of the cell.)* Mother Meller!

(Lights up:
FRAU MELLER's cell.)

FRAU MELLER: *(Knocks.)* Yes.

EVA BERG: *(Knocks.)* We are all free. Karl didn't shoot after all. They have the murderer.

FRAU MELLER: *(Knocks on the other wall.)* You, Karl!... You!... You!... You!... *(Knocks on the floor.)* Eva, Karl does not answer.

EVA BERG: *(Knocks.)* Knock louder.

FRAU MELLER: *(Knocks.)* Karl! Karl! Karl!

EVA BERG: *(Knocks.)* Albert, Karl doesn't reply.

ALBERT KROLL: *(Knocks.)* Let's all knock. Now it doesn't matter.

(They knock.
The other prisoners knock too.
Silence.
The whole prison knocks.
Silence.)
EVA BERG: He does not answer…
(WARDERS run through the gangways.
The cells go dark.
Blackout in the prison.)

The stage closes.

The End.

Appendix i

In Erwin Piscator's Promptbook, the last scene of the play is given as follows. See *Gesammelte Werke 3* (pp. 325–326).

Lights up:

ALBERT KROLL's cell.

*(Noise. Door creaks open.
RAND enters.)*

RAND: Kroll, Kroll, I congratulate you. The Ministry of Justice has just telephoned, Thomas is not the murderer. They caught the real one in Switzerland. A student. Just as he was about to be arrested, he shot himself.

ALBERT KROLL: Will we be released?

RAND: Not today. Today is Sunday… So I congratulate you, Herr Kroll.

(RAND goes.)

ALBERT KROLL: *(Knocks.)*

Film

*After Rand's exit, moving captions from the front:
From below right to below left:
"Thomas is not the murderer, they have another".*

*below left to first level left:
"Thomas is not the murderer"*

*First level left to first level right:
"We are all free. Karl, my boy,
you didn't shoot after all. They have
the murderer. You Karl, you."*

*"he does not answer"
"he does not answer"*

> *knocking*
> *knocking*
> *knocking*
> *knocking*
> (*over the whole area*)
>
> *Film out*
>
> *They knock*
> *The other prisoners knock too*
> *Silence*
> *Knocking in the whole prison*
> *Silence*

RAND: (*Screams.*) Hanged!!

FRAU MELLER: Is it true?

ALBERT KROLL: He shouldn't have done that; no revolutionary dies like that.

EVA BERG: Everyday life destroyed him.

FRAU MELLER: Damned world! – We have to change it.

Curtain.

Erwin Piscator reports in *Das Politische Theater* (Hamburg: Rowohlt, 1963, p. 154), first published in 1929, that the Berlin production ended with this speech:

FRAU MELLER: There is only one choice – hang yourself or change the world.

As the curtain fell, he relates, "the proletarian youth spontaneously burst into *The Internationale* which, standing, we all sang up to the end." The play then became the occasion for a stirring political demonstration.

Appendix ii

Toller's original, but never published, ending for the play was a different version of Act IV, scene 4, with no Act V to follow. Written before his collaboration with Piscator, it exists in printed manuscript form (presumably ready for publication.) with later handwritten corrections by Toller, in the possession of John M Spalek. See *Gesammelte Werke 3* (pp. 318–325).

ACT FOUR

Scene Four

The façade transforms into the façade of the Madhouse

Open below right to:

Examination Room

PROFESSOR LÜDIN: Stand still. Pulse normal. Open your shirt. Breathe deeply. Hold it. Heart healthy... Tell me honestly, why did you commit this deed?

KARL THOMAS: I did not shoot.

PROFESSOR LÜDIN: Confide in me.

KARL THOMAS: I have nothing to confess, because I am not the culprit.

PROFESSOR LÜDIN: You wanted to avenge yourself, didn't you? You believed the Minister would give you a top position in the Ministry. You felt betrayed.

KARL THOMAS: You'll torment me until I am really crazy.

PROFESSOR LÜDIN: Only your motives interest me.

KARL THOMAS: I don't need a psychiatrist.

PROFESSOR LÜDIN: You feel sane?

KARL THOMAS: Sound as a bell.

PROFESSOR LÜDIN: Very suspicious.

(KARL THOMAS laughs.)

PROFESSOR LÜDIN: Don't laugh. No one is sound as a bell.

KARL THOMAS: No one?

PROFESSOR LÜDIN: With the exception of madhouse doctors who make correct diagnoses.

(*Short pause.*)

KARL THOMAS: Professor!

PROFESSOR LÜDIN: Do you want to confess to me now why you shot? Understand, only the Why interests me. The deed is no concern of mine. Deeds are of no importance. Only motives are important.

KARL THOMAS: I want to tell you everything exactly, Herr Professor. I've lost my bearings. What I experienced... May I tell you, Herr Professor?

PROFESSOR LÜDIN: Begin then.

KARL THOMAS: I must have clarity. The door slammed shut behind me, and when I opened it eight years had passed. A whole century. I went out into the world. Life thundered in my head. Every flash of lightning struck me down. As you advised me, I first paid a visit to Wilhelm Kilman. Condemned to death like I was. I discovered he was Minister. Wedded to his former enemies. A profiteering potbelly.

PROFESSOR LÜDIN: Normal. He was just more cunning than you.

KARL THOMAS: I went to my closest comrade. A man who with just a revolver in his hand repulsed a whole company of Whites, all alone. I heard him say: "One must be able to wait".

PROFESSOR LÜDIN: Normal.

KARL THOMAS: And at the same time he swore he remained true to the Revolution.

PROFESSOR LÜDIN: Abnormal. But not your fault. He ought to be examined. Probably a mild dementia praecox.

KARL THOMAS: I was a waiter. For one whole evening. I was stewed in a witches' cauldron. It stank of corruption, of lechery, of arrogance, of muck. The people I worked with found it all in order and were proud of it.

PROFESSOR LÜDIN: Normal. Business is thriving again. Everybody makes money out of it in his own way.

KARL THOMAS: I formed a plan to shock mankind out of despicable lethargy. I bought myself a revolver. I wanted to shoot the Minister, the traitor. At the very same moment others shot him.

PROFESSOR LÜDIN: Hm.

KARL THOMAS: I asked one of them, one who didn't yell 'Hurrah', for the reason. I saw his twisted lips move. I heard his voice. Because the Minister was a Bolshevik, a revolutionary, he whispered.

PROFESSOR LÜDIN: Normal. Relatively so, if this unknown person existed.

KARL THOMAS: I wanted to put an end to myself. I wanted to shoot myself. The fog suddenly lifted. Perhaps the world is not crazy at all. Perhaps I am... Perhaps I am...

PROFESSOR LÜDIN: What do you want? Your logic is functioning perfectly. You must drink what you have brewed. Whoever goes over to the masses goes to rack and ruin there.

KARL THOMAS: What do you know about it?

PROFESSOR LÜDIN: You can tell me nothing about the psyche of the masses. My collection of specimens opens even the blindest of eyes. The masses: a herd of swine. Cram to the trough when there's something to guzzle. Wallow in muck when their bellies are stuffed.

KARL THOMAS: To sic a crazy man like you on the world, what a crime!...

PROFESSOR LÜDIN: If you really didn't want to avenge yourself – something I assume as I don't believe in abstract motives and perhaps the real reason is unknown to you – then if we assume you really wanted to 'awaken' mankind with your foolish deed, what did you expect to achieve by that? What should the awakened do? Change the world? My dear fellow, if nature had not wanted some to eat less than others, then there wouldn't be any poverty at all. Whoever achieves what he's capable of needn't go hungry. With your ideas men would become scroungers and shirkers. Nature has organised things most beneficently.

KARL THOMAS: Stop it! My head is splitting.

PROFESSOR LÜDIN: I wish I was as healthy as you. I suffer from gout.

KARL THOMAS: Insanity! Insanity! Insanity!

PROFESSOR LÜDIN: Don't play-act with me. You can't sway an old psychiatrist like that.

KARL THOMAS: You must be cured! You first and foremost!

PROFESSOR LÜDIN: When someone gets stuck in a trap, when it's a matter of life and death, then he finally gives up the heroic pose and tries to save himself with the Section for the mentally ill.

KARL THOMAS: Why did I doubt it? Yes, yes, I am really crazy. How else could I have seen what I saw!…

PROFESSOR LÜDIN: This institution is here for the mad, not for the sane.

KARL THOMAS: Charlatan! You are unmasked as a quack! Charlatan!

PROFESSOR LÜDIN: Right then, I'll show you what the crazy really look like. Then you'll have to stop fooling yourself… Orderly, set up the projector.

(*On the façade of the Madhouse in the place where the BANKER and his SON sat in the Hotel, a madman can be seen gesticulating.*

Mask of the BANKER distorted into madness.)

Look at the screen. That man up there, formerly a banker imagines he can command a great boom with one word to all the Stock Exchanges of the world and thus become the richest man in the world.

(*Behind the projected image, the Private Room of the Hotel lights up.*

In the Hotel Room:)

BANKER: (*On the table telephone.*) Hello! Hello! Stock Exchange! Sell everything! The assassination of Kilman… Paints and Potash and Pipes… Chemical Works shares already fallen about a hundred per cent… What?… Operator!… Fraülein, why did you cut me off?... I'll hold you liable... Ruined by a telephone breakdown... God in Heaven!

KARL THOMAS: But he is very normal! I saw him in person. Just yesterday evening at the Hotel. A speculator like the dozens and dozens who buy and sell the world for profit.

PROFESSOR LÜDIN: My dear friend, the banker whom you saw – I wish I had his fortune –was normal.

KARL THOMAS: Ha ha ha, normal!

BANKER: (*Grinning in Hotel Room.*) Normal... Normal...
(*Blackout in Hotel Room.*)

PROFESSOR LÜDIN (*To ORDERLY.*) Proceed.
(*On the façade of the Madhouse in the place where the Staff Room of the Hotel was, a madman can be seen gesticulating. Mask of the PORTER distorted into madness.*)

Type Two. This man went mad in the inflation. He lost his assets. In place of the ten thousand marks he had saved he got fifty million. Because of that he went mad. He is forever scribbling numbers on paper and counting. He wants to get his assets back at any price and imagines that he won first prize in the lottery.

(*Behind the projected image, the Staff Room of the Hotel lights up.*)

PORTER: Who won the Paris race? The beautiful Galatea... A fix! A fix! I put all my savings on Idealist, and that damned jockey goes and breaks his neck...
I want to get my stake back! My stake, I want to get it back!

KARL THOMAS: He is also very normal! I am sure that's the porter of the Grand Hotel!

PROFESSOR LÜDIN: Type Two suffers from mental fixation. The porter of the Grand Hotel, and I lived there once, is absolutely normal.

PORTER: (*Grinning in the Hotel Room.*) Normal... Normal...
(*Blackout in Hotel Room.*)

PROFESSOR LÜDIN: Proceed.
(*On the façade of the Madhouse in the place where the Radio Station of the Hotel was, a madman can be seen gesticulating. Mask of the RADIO OPERATOR distorted into madness.*)

Type Three. He suffers from persecution mania. An inventor. He imagines he has invented an apparatus which can distil sugar from wood and is capable, just like Jehovah once was, of feeding all the hungry with wood. The apparatus, he thinks, was destroyed by a sugar beet farmer.

(Behind the projected image, the Radio Station in the Hotel lights up.)

RADIO OPERATOR: Attention! Attention! All radio stations of the world! Who will buy my invention? I don't want money. The invention will help everyone, everyone. Silence… No one responds.

KARL THOMAS: He too is normal! He too is normal! That's the Radio Operator from the Grand Hotel! Nobody wanted to buy his invention from him because it serves peace, not war.

PROFESSOR LÜDIN: The Radio Operator at the Grand Hotel is a competent, hard-working official. A little fanciful, because he operates the radio, but otherwise normal!

RADIO OPERATOR: *(Grinning in Hotel Room.)* Normal… Normal…

(Blackout in Hotel Room.)

PROFESSOR LÜDIN: Proceed!

(On the façade of the Madhouse in the place where the EXAMINING MAGISTRATE was in the Prison, a madman can be seen gesticulating.
Mask of the EXAMINING MAGISTRATE distorted into madness.)

Type Four. A former Public Prosecutor who imagines he is on the trail of all the criminals who have ever committed murder and not been found out. He thinks his nose, unusually developed, can sniff out the very smell of murder.

(Behind the projected image, the Examination Room in the Prison lights up.)

EXAMINING MAGISTRATE: The circumstantial evidence is perfectly conclusive. Put it on file. Next case…

KARL THOMAS: The Examining Magistrate! I would have recognised his craziness without you.

PROFESSOR LÜDIN: I can well believe that you'd wish the Examining Magistrate not to be normal.

EXAMINING MAGISTRATE: (*Grinning in the Examination Room.*) Normal... Normal...

(*Blackout in the Examination Room.*)

PROFESSOR LÜDIN: Proceed!

(*On the façade of the Madhouse in the place where the Private Room in the Hotel was, a madman can be seen gesticulating. Mask of WILHELM KILMAN distorted into madness.*)

In conclusion the Innocent Type. Formerly a chauffeur. He's fixated on the idea that it's not the motor which drives his car, but that he drives it...with the horn.

(*Behind the projected image, the Private Room in the Hotel lights up.*)

WILHELM KILMAN: The text of my decree will prevent any back-pedalling. Let it be printed. I am proud of it. A milestone of progress.

KARL THOMAS: Yes, I saw him like that at the end, Herr Minister Kilman. But innocent – no!

PROFESSOR LÜDIN: You should not mock your victim, Thomas. I wish we had many men like him. Level-headed, normal.

WILHELM KILMAN: (*Grinning in Hotel Room.*) Normal... Normal...

(*Blackout in Hotel Room.
On the façade a Face laughs.
Mask of PROFESSOR LÜDIN distorted into madness.*)

KARL THOMAS: (*Speaking to the Face up above.*) And you, are you going crazy too? How do you dare lock up normal men?

PROFESSOR LÜDIN: To whom are you speaking?

KARL THOMAS: (*Speaking to the Face above.*) Just dare say that you too are normal – go on, I'm waiting for your response! Normal... Normal...

(*The Face disappears.*)

PROFESSOR LÜDIN: No funny business, Thomas. Every psychiatrist knows that trick of speaking to thin air. You would have a happier and more dignified look if you, with free and full repentance, confessed to your crime.

KARL THOMAS: I'm a fool! Now I see the world clearly again. You have turned it into a madhouse. There is no dividing wall between inside here and outside there. The world's become an animal pen in which the sane are trampled down by a small herd of galloping crazies. And that is normal! Ha, ha, ha...

(*All the rooms of the Hotel light up.*)

CHORUS OF HOTEL OCCUPANTS: (*In a crouching position, leaning down towards the Examination Room, nodding.*) Ha, ha, ha!... Normal!...

(*Blackout in Hotel.*)

PROFESSOR LÜDIN: Nothing can help you. Tomorrow you will be sent to prison. You've caused enough mischief. Now you must take your punishment.

KARL THOMAS: I see everything clearly. In former times we marched under the flag of paradise. Today we have to wear out our boots on earthly roads. You believe you're alive. You're headed for the abyss if you imagine that the world will always stay like it is now.

(*From outside, a distant song which gradually stops.
Noise of marching men.*)

PROFESSOR LÜDIN: (*To ORDERLY.*) What is it?

ORDERLY: (*At window.*) A demonstration. The people are demonstrating for the prisoner.

CHORUS FROM OUTSIDE: Support Karl Thomas! Support Karl Thomas!

(*Then in the street, shown on film, a vast silent crowd of demonstrators.*)

PROFESSOR LÜDIN: They're starting up again... You've caused this with your lunatic deed!

KARL THOMAS: Me?

PROFESSOR LÜDIN: Yes, you! Don't play so innocent!

KARL THOMAS: But I have done nothing at all!

(*Short pause.*)

But I have done nothing at all!!

(*Suddenly KARL THOMAS roars with laughter.*)

PROFESSOR LÜDIN: Don't laugh so cynically. Even they can't save your neck.

(*KARL THOMAS laughs.*)

If you want to see a mass of crazy men, look out the window.

(*KARL THOMAS laughs.*)

Incurable crazies.

(*KARL THOMAS laughs.*)

ORDERLY: (*Pointing at KARL THOMAS.*) Professor, I think…

PROFESSOR LÜDIN: (*Stands still in front of KARL THOMAS, observes him for a little while.*) A fit. Take him to the padded cell. To his…beech wood.
[*In German "beech wood" is Buchenwald which gives a horrific, if unintended, resonance to this ending for the play.*]

(*KARL THOMAS is led away by the ORDERLY.*)

Unfit for life.

While the People march past silently, the stage closes.

Appendix iii

In addition to some criticism of Toller's writing style, Piscator gives a table of three endings he claims were considered for *Hoppla, We're Alive!* in *Das Politische Theater* (Hamburg: Rowholt, 1963, p. 148):

The Three Endings for "Hoppla"

Arrest	Escape	Arrest
Police Station		Police Station
	Voluntary	
Transfer to Madhouse	return to Prison	Madhouse
	From conical masks filmic	
Lüdin scene up to:	dissolve to officer's chest,	Prison
Masses march past	crucibles, war pictures,	(Dialogue by
	run backwards.	knocking)
	In place of Kilman-mask –	Thomas hangs
	Kilman-monument. During	himself
	Thomas' laughter and the last words	
	a giant cannon appears on film	
	and aims at the audience	

It may be that Piscator misremembered here and that what was considered was a voluntary return to the Madhouse. This would make sense of Toller's denial (p. 320) and also of the filmic sequence described here which could have been used for Toller's original final scene (p. 309).

Appendix iv

Reviewing his works in 1930, Toller wrote as follows about his collaboration with Piscator on *Hoppla, We're Alive!*, a response to Piscator's criticism of him in *The Political Theatre*. See "Arbeiten", *Gesammelte Werke 1* (pp. 145–147).

From *Works*

Hoppla, We're Alive! is the name of the first play I wrote "in freedom". Once again I was concerned with the collision of a man who is determined to realise the absolute in the here and now with the forces of the time and his contemporaries who either abandon this work of realization from weakness, betrayal and cowardice or prepare for it to come in later days with strength, faith and courage. Karl Thomas doesn't understand either of them, equates their motives and actions and is destroyed. Alienated from true art by that childish American fashion for the "happy end", many critics and spectators today demand from the playwright something which is not his task at all – that he ought to dismiss them at the end with those silly household sayings which our parents used to have written on sofa cushions, plates and posters for practical guidance, like: "Always be faithful and honest", "Ask not what others do, but attend to your own affairs", "Have a sunny disposition", or as Durus wrote in No. 134 of the *Red Flag*, 1930: "Let the fresh air of class struggle into the fresh air of nature". Proletcult officials and arts-section critics on capitalist newspapers, who, from a guilty conscience and an obsession to roam like birds of passage through the newspaper columns, are more preachers of revolution than revolutionary activists, called the end of the drama "not revolutionary" – and this was repeated many times and will continue to be repeated – because it didn't dismiss them with a little moral tract and the cry: "Long live political line No. 73". –

Today I regret that I, swayed by a trend of the times, broke up the architectonics of the original work for the benefit of the architectonics of the direction. The form that I strived for was stronger than that which appeared on the stage. I alone am responsible for that, but I have learned, and today I prefer a director to get too little out of a work than to put too much into it. Moreover, Piscator in Gasbarra's book *The Political Theatre*, really has no reason to complain about me and my style.*

At the time of revising the script I considered three endings as possible, but never the "voluntary return to prison" which was falsely and unscrupulously attributed to me in the book. In my first version Thomas, who didn't understand the world of 1927, ran to the psychiatrist in the madhouse, discovers in his discussion with the doctor that there are two kinds of dangerous fools: the ones who are held in padded cells and the ones who, as politicians and military men, go berserk against mankind. At that moment he understands his old comrades who carry on with the Idea in the tougher work of everyday life. He wants to leave the madhouse, but because he has understood, because he has connected to reality like a mature man, the psychiatric official will never release him. Now for the first time – and not before when he was a troublesome dreamer – he becomes "dangerous to the State"!

*

* Or are these sentences, which Piscator proposed in place of those written by me, "functional, advancing the dramatic action, building the mental tension", in short, do they provide "the realistic substructure" and "replace the poetic lyricism" of the author? (p. 147). I quote from Piscator's manuscript:

Scene after the murder of Wilhelm Kilman. Monologue of Karl Thomas:

KARL THOMAS: "They shot him because he was a
    revolutionary; I wanted to shoot him because he was a
    nobody and ended up shooting at his murderer, as if
    I defended Kilman's henchmen and in so doing had
    become his friend, brother and comrade again... Only
    one shift was needed, only one small step, and the
    liberation of the world from nationalist hatred, degrading

class oppression, and rough justice would have been helped to victory. (*In a somewhat raised voice.*) If only, Wilhelm, I weren't unbearably guilty. Albert Kroll, Mother Meller, Eva, guilty, guilty. You there, you down there in the park, guilty, guilty, we and they (*He tries to go on speaking.*)…"

Or:

Last prison scene. Monologue of Karl Thomas:

KARL THOMAS: "… I am awake, so awake that I can see right through you and still would have experienced nothing new…
Oh, the merry-go-round spins and everything begins all over again. Yes, my dear friends, and my enemies, can't you see how the ground is cracking under your feet? Kilman, dead man, celebrated perhaps because of your murder…if you were living, comrade, you could not begin all over again. You, undo it, undo it: tactics, betrayal. Volcanoes, fiery eyes of the earth open, crack open before you. You stand on the edge of a crater. What madness has seized you, to crouch there and stare into the white-hot glow! Save yourselves! Save yourselves! It's rising! In the boiling depths the lava is forming into a dreadful instrument of destruction! It's rising up unstoppably! Its hissing is scornful laughter at your stupidity not to see your solution: divide and rule…"
Nothing at all to be said about the scene which was rehearsed one day and which, as I to my horror was forced to learn from [hearing] the character names, was "written in" overnight without even asking me.

Appendix V

Herrn
Ernst Toller
Berlin – Grunewald
König Allee 45

10 August 1927

Dear Toller!

After very serious reflection, I sat down yesterday evening and made the attempt to work out the end scenes, just as we presented them to you in rough outlines several times before. After I went through it with Gasbarra this morning, we are both convinced that now the end, from the two shots up to the big Prison scene, has an ongoing dramatic build and that there is no longer any retardation in the dramatic action. The driving forces of each scene are nevertheless so distinct that every possibility is given to bring out at all points again the overall tendency in its full sharpness and forcefulness, without taking anything away from the climax in the Prison.

It strikes me as a main point that Thomas achieves a certain clarity from his last experiences, so that, in the midst of the confusion all around him, he now takes a pause. It must be like a last flash of spiritual strength, before the collapse in Prison takes place. Thus the monologue after the two shots must be written very calmly and clearly and also spoken in the same way. The monologue in the Prison scene picks up from this one. The full inner life of Thomas once again, without phrase-mongering, becomes transparent. It is the last attempt of a man to understand the world and to come to terms with himself.

When Thomas is arrested, his particular kind of madness can be indicated. One must have the feeling that he is already somewhat removed from the situation and also faces his arrest with indifference.

The most controversial point in our debates has probably been the scene before the Examining Magistrate. We have examined the meaning and content of this scene from every point of view and have come to the conclusion that this scene contributes nothing to the onward drive of the action. The characters who appear in it neither undergo a change nor does their legal confrontation possess any dramatic tension. The only reason it mattered to you was to get Thomas back into the Madhouse, in order to symbolically contrast the normal and the abnormal there. It would be a complete mistake to open up a test case about circumstantial evidence here. Only to show that circumstantial evidence doesn't hold up. The scene before the Examining Magistrate would perhaps be better than the scene in Police Headquarters, if the Examining Magistrate was some low down type and the case from the beginning on was handled in such a way that it seemed to the spectator, exactly at this place in the piece, especially abnormal and strange. That is to say, if the scene showed Thomas' environment as such or his character as such in a completely new light. But then, in turn, Lüdin standing face to face with an unchanged Thomas would be eliminated. And consequently the Lüdin scene would be ineffective. But ultimately both, according to the latest version, are not very important before the Prison scene. Above all we must achieve a dramatically effective and unstoppable forward development up to the end.

In the Police Headquarters scene in the dialogue between Count Lande and the Chief, the first assassin must be depicted as explicitly as possible. It is not enough for example to say: "Young man, speaks literary German, closes his eyes when thinking!" [details almost exactly like those on Toller's "Wanted Poster" from 1919!] or something similar. But some distinguishing mark must be given by which the Police Chief can be in no doubt whatsoever that he has the assassin described by Count Lande in front of him. Hence we are of the opinion that the student worms his way into the hotel as a waiter, for which Lande gives him the appropriate instructions in the preparation scene. Lande can report that he wears a waiter's tailcoat as a special, external mark, whereby the confusion with Thomas, who is also arrested in a tailcoat, then seems immediately believable.

Furthermore, I've come to think that it is better to have Lande appear in person at Police Headquarters than to have him telephone the Chief of Police, which in such a situation and given the importance of the matter perhaps seems unbelievable. The conversation between Lande and the Chief drafted by me is intentionally allusive and unclearly worded, and in my opinion no longer needs to be translated into Tolleresque literary German. On the other hand, the end of the scene could be even more fully worked out in formal respects.

Your version of the Lüdin scene, my draft aside, suffers from two defects: In his first conversation with Thomas, Lüdin cannot say that no one is sane because later he declares all those people Thomas regards as mad to be normal.

That is in itself a small change. On the other hand, in my opinion the moment of "normal-normal" still needs to be thought through thoroughly, so that the types in the Hotel really seem mad to the spectator. For the different characters, for example the Porter, both true and false elements of madness are jumbled together. For the Porter, the passion for betting which devours him is mad, if that's the way you want to look at it. On the other hand one can't forget that the Porter has been a victim of the inflation. If you want to bring in the inflation, then it must be depicted very differently.

For the Banker, as well, you must intensify his mad hunt for money by showing that he (perhaps) can personally make no use whatsoever of the money for himself, possibly hampered by stomach problems. In this way, the absolute emptiness of such a character would be brought out.

Finally, it still hampers the flow of this "Normal-normal" scene that Thomas states substantially the same thing about the madness of the Hotel occupants that they act out a few seconds later. Thomas must depict much earlier which functions these people could perform normally, for example the Banker as an administrative functionary of the commodities owned by society, as a purposefully and systematically active element. So with this in mind! All the best

Erwin Piscator

(*Der Fall Toller,* pp. 182–185)

Appendix vi: Plates

Hoppla, We're Alive!

Directed by Erwin Piscator, designed by Traugott Müller, music by Kurt Meisel, film by Kurt Oertel, projections by John Heartfield, choreography by Mary Wigman (Piscator-Bühne Nollendorfplatz, 3 September 1927).

10. A photographic collage of the production showing, in the back, Ernst Toller and the scaffolding set for the last prison scene. In the front there are, from left: a moment from the Voting scene (Act III, scene 2) and two from the Prologue – the last cigarette and the attempted escape.

11. The bare scaffolding structure which stood on the revolving stage. It shows the playing compartments with stairs and the screens which could be moved backwards and forwards for the back and front projections.

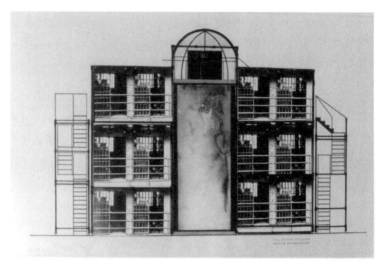

12. **Prologue/Act V.** Traugott Müller's design for the Prison scene, a version of which was used for the Prologue and Act V. This, together with the other three designs, shows how effectively the scaffolding could be transformed and façades projected upon it.

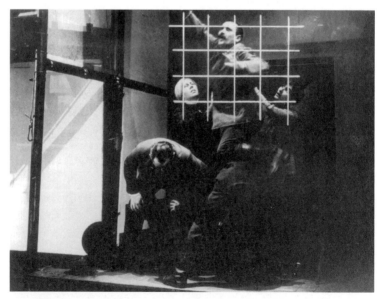

13. **Prologue.** The moment of attempted escape in the centre bottom compartment. The bars give an indication of how the front gauze could be used for projections.

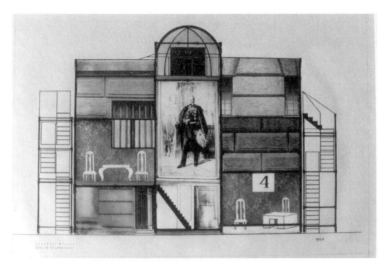

14. **Act I, scene 2.** Design for the Ministry with projection of the Kaiser on the centre screen and two compartments, middle left and lower right, in use, with monumental stone architectural features projected on the other screens.

15. **Act I, scene 2.** Production photograph, showing Antechamber upper left and Minister's Office lower right, with projection of the Kaiser above and behind the staircase which links them.

16. **Act II, scene 1.** Design for a collage of the slum where Eva Berg lives, just prior to the beginning of Act II, scene 1. The lower left compartment opened for the scene in her bedroom. The rest of the collage remained through scene.

17. **Act II, scene 1.** Production photograph. Lower left is Eva's room where the scene was played. The collage remained and placed the scene in its socio-political surround.

18. **Act II, scene 2.** Production photograph of voting in the Workers' Bar. The centre screen showed ballot papers falling into a ballot box and later the elected Minister of War. The voters changed costume and rejoined the line as the scene progressed. The scene was played in front of the scaffolding with posters and slogans projected on the other screens.

19. **Act III, scene 1.** Production photograph. The Student's Room was on a wagon set up to the right of the scaffolding which was revolved to the back so that the room was brought to the front.

20. **Act III, scene 2 / Act IV, scene 4.** Production photograph for the Hotel with all its rooms lit. Each had back-projected wallpaper. This was probably meant to depict the moment in the latter scene when all the Hotel rooms light up behind the projected façade of the Madhouse, with the explosion at the top.

21. **Act III, scene 2.** Production photograph of the Hotel. It shows the Private Room (left) and Room No. 96 (right) where Lotte Kilman and Count Lande have their tryst.

22. **Act III, scene 2**. Another production photograph of the Hotel. It depicts the section when the cash register rings as Karl complains about the food given to the staff. The cash register and cashier are shown in silhouette by means of the backlight on the centre screen. Staff Room and Private Room also in use.

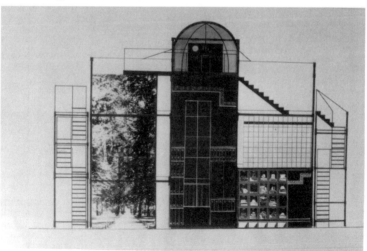

23. **Act IV, scene 1**. Design showing on the left a projection of the Park where Karl chases the student.

24. **Act IV, scene 2**. Production photograph. Count Lande, upper left, conspiratorially telephones Chief of Police, bottom right. This photograph shows the effectiveness of simultaneous staging and underscores the parallel with the secret telephone line between Chancellor Ebert and General Groener which did so much to undermine the Weimar Republic.

25. **Act IV, scene 4**. Production photograph. Professor Lüdin (Leonhard Steckel, left) re-examining Karl Thomas (Alexander Granach), before sending him to Prison. Note the "Dr. Strangelove" pose.

Further Reading List

Works by Toller in German

Der Fall Toller, ed. Wolfgang Frühwald u. John M. Spalek. München/Wien: Carl Hanser, 1979.

Gesammelte Werke, ed. John M. Spalek u. Wolfgang Frühwald, 5 vols. München: Carl Hanser, 1978.

Hoppla, wir leben!: Ein Vorspiel und fünf Akten. Potsdam: Gustav Kiepenheuer, 1927.

Masse Mensch: Ein Stück aus der sozialen Revolution des 20. Jahrhunderts. Potsdam: Gustav Kiepenheuer, 1921. The second edition of 1922 contains Toller's Foreword.

Die Wandlung: Das Ringen eines Mensch. Postdam: Gustav Kiepenheuer, 1919.

Other Useful German Sources

Droop, Fritz. *Toller und seine Bühenwerke*. Berlin: Schneider, 1922. The first ever critical study of Toller which also contains a short autobiographical statement.

Knellessen, Friedrich Wolfgang. *Agitation auf der Bühne: Das politische Theater der Weimarer Republik*. Emsdetten: Lechte, 1970.

Rühle, Gunther, ed. *Theater für die Republik: Im Spiegel der Kritik*, 2 vols. Frankfurt am Main: S. Fischer, 1988.

Works by Toller in English

Hoppla!: A Play in a Prologue and Five Acts, trans. Hermon Ould. London: Ernest Benn, 1928. Appears as *Hoppla! Such is Life!* in *Seven Plays*.

I Was a German, trans. Edward Crankshaw. London: John Lane The Bodley Head, 1934.

Letters from Prison, trans. R. Ellis Roberts. London: John Lane The Bodley Head, 1936. Also published in New York the following year by Farrar & Rinehart as *Look Through the Bars*.

Man and the Masses: A Play of the Social Revolution in Seven Scenes, trans. Louis Untermeyer. Garden City: Doubleday, Page, 1924. This is the text used for The Theatre Guild Production in New York (April 14, 1924) and also for the first English production about a month later (May 18) by The Stage Society at the New Theatre. The book contains six photographs from The Theatre Guild production.

Masses and Man: A Fragment of the Social Revolution of the Twentieth Century, trans. Vera Mendel. London: Nonesuch, 1923. This translation is reprinted in *Seven Plays.*

Seven Plays. London: John Lane The Bodley Head, 1935. Published a year later in New York by Liveright.

Selected Secondary Literature

Barron, Stephanie, and Wolf-Dieter Dube, eds. *German Expressionism: Art and Society.* New York: Rizzoli, 1997

Benson, Renate. *German Expressionist Drama: Ernst Toller and Georg Kaiser.* London: Macmillan, 1984.

Davies, Cecil. *The Plays of Ernst Toller: A Revaluation.* Amsterdam: Harwood, 1996.

Dove, Richard. *He was a German: A Biography of Ernst Toller.* London: Libris, 1990.

Dove, Richard. *Revolutionary Socialism in the Work of Ernst Toller.* New York etc.: Peter Lang, 1986.

Dukes, Ashley. *The Scene Is Changed.* London: Macmillan, 1942.

Gay, Peter. *Weimar Culture: The Outsider as Insider.* New York: Harper and Row, 1968.

Gordon, Donald E. *Expressionism: Art and Idea.* New Haven and London: Yale UP, 1987.

Kuhns, David F. *German Expressionist Theatre: The Actor and The Stage.* Cambridge: Cambridge UP, 1997.

Leviné-Meyer, Rosa. *Leviné: The Life of a Revolutionary.* Farnborough: Saxon House, 1973.

Macgowan, Kenneth, and Robert Edmond Jones. *Continental Stagecraft.* New York: Harcourt, Brace, 1922.

Moussinac, Léon. *The New Movement in the Theatre*. London: Batsford, 1931.

Ossar, Michael. *Anarchism in the Drama of Ernst Toller: The Realm of Necessity and the Realm of Freedom*. Albany: State University of New York, 1980.

Patterson, Michael. *The Revolution in German Theatre 1900 – 1933*. London: Routledge, 1981.

Piscator, Erwin. *The Political Theatre*, trans. Hugh Rorrison. London: Methuen, 1980.

Pittock, Malcolm. *Ernst Toller*. Boston: Twayne, 1979.

Roters, Eberhard, ed. *Berlin 1910 – 1933*, trans. Marguerite Mounier. Secaucus: Wellfleet, 1982.

Samuel, Richard, and R. Hinton Thomas. *Expressionism in German Life, Literature and the Theatre (1910-1924)*. Cambridge: Heffer, 1939.

Scheffauer, Herman G. *The New Vision in the German Arts*. New York: Huebsch, 1924.

Schräder, Bärbel, and Jürgen Schebera. *The "Golden Twenties": Art and literature in the Weimar Republic*. New Haven and London: Yale UP, 1990.

Sokel, Walter H. *The Writer in Extremis: Expressionism in Twentieth-Century Literature*. New York etc.: McGraw Hill, 1964.

Spalek, John M. *Ernst Toller and his Critics: A Bibliography*. Charlottesville: University Press of Virginia, 1968.

Watt, Richard M. *The Kings Depart: The Tragedy of Germany: Versailles and the German Revolution*. London: Weidenfeld & Nicolson, 1969.

Willet, John. *The Theatre of Erwin Piscator: Half a Century of Politics in the Theatre*. London: Methuen, 1978.

Willet, John. *The Theatre of the Weimar Republic*. New York and London: Holmes & Meier, 1988.

Williams, Raymond. *Drama from Ibsen to Brecht*. New York: Oxford UP, 1969.

Willibrand, William Anthony. *Ernst Toller and his Ideology*. Iowa City: University of Iowa, 1945.

An Ernst Toller Society (*Ernst Toller Gesellschaft*) has been established in Neuberg-an-der-Donau, close to where Toller was imprisoned in Neiderschönenfeld. This possesses a research archive based on John Spalek's important collection of Toller editions and other material which he has donated to the Society. It is dedicated to further research on Ernst Toller and to regaining for his works the full attention that they deserve. It also possesses a web site which can be found on: <http://www.neusob.de/toller/de/de/_soc.htm>